Squeaky Wheels

Scott Hippe

Copyright © 2012 Scott Hippe

www.createspace.com/4106612

All rights reserved.

ISBN: 1481816314
ISBN-13: 978-1481816311

To all the beautiful people who made this story possible. Mom and Dad too, ultimately for the same reason.

Acknowledgements

Thanks to my family for encouraging me to pursue my dreams. I am forever indebted to Zach, Liz, Joe, Courtney, Charlie, and the rest who read my drafts, listened to me talk about writing, and then had the patience to read more drafts. A thousand thanks to all of you who provided assistance and inspiration along every step of the way. I would have loved to leave your real names unchanged in this story so people would know how truly incredible you are, but would hate to jeopardize your safety or privacy. Lastly, thanks to Joe and Oliver. We made a good run of it, boys.

Table of Contents

Prologue..11

Chapter 1..17

Chapter 2..27

Chapter 3..41

Chapter 4..51

Chapter 5..65

Chapter 6..79

Chapter 7..91

Chapter 8..101

Chapter 9..117

Chapter 10..127

Chapter 11..141

Chapter 12..159

Chapter 13..171

Chapter 14..183

Chapter 15..199

Chapter 16..211

Chapter 17..227

Chapter 18..235

Chapter 19..245

Chapter 20..259

Chapter 21..273

Epilogue...289

PROLOGUE

THERE IS A FIRST TIME for everyone. Mine came in a dingy motel room on a cold Montana evening. The town was West Yellowstone and the season was early May. Tourists were months away from overrunning the city and the streets were silent. A fire danced and cackled, albeit on the television screen, as I lay still on the squeaky queen bed exhausted from effort.

This story actually starts some hours before in the Moose Droppings Bar and Grill with a person named Butch. Butch would not leave us alone.

"You know, you're really offending me by not making an offer. I am serious as a starving grizzly bear. No price is low enough to piss me off."

The ordeal stretched over an hour. I was with two friends named Joe and Oliver, and each of us was tired of this man named Butch. But there was no escape, because buffalo nachos had just arrived at our table and we were desperately hungry.

Butch owns the motel in West Yellowstone. After learning the three of us were pedaling our bicycles across the country, he insisted we stay a night at his establishment. No price we could name would be too low for these services. I tried to explain why we were not interested in his generous proposition.

"Listen Butch, we are grateful that you are trying to look out for us. But we have been at this trip for a while and have yet to spend a single dime on lodging."

He did not listen, and repeated his argument for the fifth time.

"You do know that it is supposed to snow a foot tonight, right? And the bears are just starting to wake up from a five-month nap and they are *hungry*. I would hate to be caught outside having anything to do with one of them sons of bitches."

Finally we made an offer, although it was not because of the grizzly bears or the threat of snow. We were not particularly keen on staying at his motel; I knew we would be able to find an inconspicuous place to pitch our tent, already having survived almost two weeks in such fashion. I just wanted Butch to quit bothering us.

"Alright Butch, how does thirty bucks sound?"

"What?! No way! That's too much. Room is yours for twenty-five. No—I'm comin' down on my own offer. Tell you what: you give me fifteen in cash right now—that's five a person—and the room is yours."

The three of us looked at each other. The opportunity for a fifteen dollar motel room does not come around very often. We agreed to take the room and forked over three five-dollar bills. There is a first time for everyone. In our case, this meant the first time paying for a place to sleep on our bicycle adventure across the country. To this day, the hot shower that night was the best ever in my life.

Not only was this the first time we paid for lodging, it was the only time in nearly two months of cycling. Some call me crazy. Some say we were freeloaders. Some just shake their heads in disbelief. Even for cash-strapped touring cyclists it is uncommon to spend so little on sleeping arrangements.

How did we manage to cross the country by bicycle on a lodging budget dwarfed by a *vente* mocha frappuccino? You will have to continue reading to find out. What I can say right now is that navigating on such a tight budget led us into many spontaneous, dicey, and serendipitous situations. The individuals of this story are equally as colorful.

The roots of the adventure reach two years into the past. It all began with Ralph, a friend of mine in college who returned from one summer break with an intriguing idea. He made a college career out of coming up with creative, humorous, and at times dubious ideas. Ralph is a dreamer.

"*What if?...*" he mused to a small group of us seated with legs crossed apple-sauce in a semicircle. The best dreams start with the best "*what if?*" questions. "*What if* we rode our bikes across the country..." It was less a question and more an impetus to consider the delicious intrigue and enormous possibility held in those simple words. The lights in the room were dim and all was hush-puppy quiet while the idea marinated.

Dreamers are the people who incite the world to move forward. At times they are also the ones who fall asleep in class, get distracted when you talk to them, and do not seem to have any connection to the physical world. Life would be dull if it were not for dreams and their respective dreamers.

Next time you are about to scold a daydreaming pupil or spacey spouse, hold back your judgment—you never know what untold goodness could be brewing in that noggin.

Many people are immune to dreams, as if they wore Teflon jackets denying access to any notion even slightly out of the ordinary. Not me; if dreams were fireflies, I fancy wearing a flypaper suit. The cogs in my head were already spinning. *A bike ride across the country...*

My friend Joe, always open to ideas with rock-the-boat potential, was also around to hear Ralph's pitch. (Aside: Oliver, the third character in West Yellowstone, would not come into the picture until much later). The conversation went something like this:

"What if, guys? But I mean seriously, *what if?*" Joe.

"It would be incredible," Ralph.

"An adventure," I added.

"Original."

"Risky."

"Liberating." That last word hung in the air for a few sauce-dripping seconds. I cannot remember who said it, but the silence was broken by the words "let's make it happen."

That was two years ago, and a lot can happen in two years. Ralph took a job immediately after graduating college and could not ride. But the ride never dropped out of the minds of Joe and me. While responsible graduating students at my school were landing respectable jobs in accounting firms, engineering companies, and even volunteer organizations, I steadfastly maintained that I was going to ride my bicycle across the country. After that, I had absolutely no plan.

Before the embarking on the trip people asked me many varieties of the basic question "Why would anyone in their right mind ride their bicycle all the way across the country?!" Before long I had formulated a neatly packaged, preprogrammed response.

"Funny you should inquire," I would say. "The thought of spending two months sleeping on the ground without a pillow sounds extremely appealing to me. I heard the weather is unpredictable in about 95% of the country and I am excited to get caught riding in a thunder storm. And I really have been pampered with all the Ramen I've eaten in college—not knowing when my next hot meal will come is the perfect thing to rectify my entitled soul."

Sounds convincing enough, right? Obviously that was a humorous response I would give to people who thought I was crazy, but I also had real reasons.

I spent twenty-two years seeing my country from a television screen. I watched Katrina and Columbine happen from the safety of my living room. I see the Statue of Liberty every time Seattle plays a New York sports team. When I think of the South, the first images that come to mind are supplied by the movie *Oh, Brother*. In short, I did not know my own country.

I did not just want to see more of my homeland—I wanted to experience it firsthand. I wanted to see if the waves of grain are really colored amber. I wanted to know if my country is really as dangerous a place as the headline news makes it out to be. I wanted to meet my people.

To all of that I would confess an obsession: I am fascinated by the unknown. After twenty-two years of relative predictability, I was craving the uncertainty of the open road. I wanted to jump straight into something way over my head, just to see how I would come out on the other end. I had no idea what would happen the second we started riding. That is what had me hooked even before the trip started.

It was time to insert myself into the diverse American experience and learn what it is like to live from sea to shining sea. I wanted to see the big sky of Montana, cross the continental divide, and retrace the footsteps of Lewis and Clark. I was hankerin' to see the endless corn fields of the Midwest, ogle the mighty Mississippi, and experience that good ol' Southern hospitality. I dreamed of seeing our nation's capital and saying "hello" to the Big Apple. I was ready to become a genuine citizen of this country.

Chapter ONE

Seattle, WA to Ellensburg, WA

"SCOTT, I'VE GOT SOME GOOD news and some bad news. Which do you want to hear first?" It was Joe. My heart instantly started beating faster. This was not what I wanted to hear.

"Shoot, I don't care. Just hit me with it," I replied, bracing for any number of excuses, complications, or alterations to our trip plan.

"Hmm, ok… I'll go with the good news first: I got the job at Regis University!" There was hesitation behind his enthusiasm for what was very good news for him. "The bad news—" the pause was killing me, "—is that I have to report early to mid-June."

There was the dagger I was waiting for. It was the dull Gong of Rationality tolling for Joe, telling him it was time to grow up. Life is a balancing act between the practical and the ideal, a boxing match between rationality and dreams. Sometimes rationality wins.

The plan had originally been to start sometime around the first of June, allowing me time to move back home after graduating college and Joe time to get himself and his bicycle to Seattle at a leisurely pace. But there I was in my apartment on the Friday of graduation weekend in early May, my extended family recently arrived and eager to congratulate me, listening to my friend effectively sabotage the trip of a lifetime.

"Right now you're probably disappointed and even a bit frustrated at me," Joe continued, diplomatic and quite prophetic, "but don't worry because I've got a plan." *A plan, he says...* "We're getting on the road next Thursday."

I choked on my tongue. *Next Thursday?!* That left a mere six days to graduate, finish my job as a resident assistant, travel home, and organize/buy/pack the gear I would need for the trip. I would not get home until late Tuesday night, giving me one full day to put together the biggest adventure of my life. All of this flickered through my mind for a split-second.

"I'm in," I replied.

"Good. See you on Wednesday." I hung up the phone and went out into the living room of my apartment to greet my grandparents.

"Scott, we are so proud of you!" my grandmother oozed.

"Yeah Scotty, we really are," chimed in my grandfather. I smiled and nodded, voicing my gratitude. Smiling and nodding was how I navigated through the graduation weekend. It was a strange time, at least at my college. Everyone was stressed out because their loving, involved, overprotective families were in town. Then there were the litany of banquets and ceremonies and other engagements to attend. Insert the desire to spend meaningful time with friends, and it became an emotional rollercoaster. Everyone reacts differently. Some cry, some get clingy. Some get defensive, while some imbibe and do things they regret the next morning.

There are also a few—myself included—quiet in nature who take a back seat and watch the fanfare play out. This led me to witness my first lizard cremation ceremony. I do not know what I will remember more vividly; being on stage flashing the pearly whites in front of 10,000 people while shaking President McCullough's hand and receiving my diploma, or watching a crowd of inebriated graduates sing "Kum Ba Ya" to a dead lizard's ashes.

Year-end responsibilities kept me on campus until Tuesday, two days before embarking on the trip. Having just graduated, I should have been in an emotionally disordered state. However, my mind was completely focused on the forty-eight hours remaining until Joe and I would be pedaling away from the Pacific.

The accelerated timeframe meant that I would have one day to accomplish the following: affix a rear-tire rack to my bicycle, improvise a front handlebar bag out of a massacred fanny pack, dig through my six moving boxes labeled "stuff" to find my cycling clothes, sift through a deep cavern of outdoor gear to locate the necessary camping tools and sleeping bag, make sure my tent worked, go to the store to *buy* a pair of "panniers" (cycling lingo for saddle bags), pick up Joe from the airport, shlep him back to my house, pack everything to make sure it would fit, repack everything when I saw that it would most definitely not, and re-repack a third time. Whew.

"This bicycle you are about to see has been around the block once or twice," I said to Joe as we stepped into the garage. I shifted some boxes and blew dust off the saddle of a light-blue Italian gem of a bicycle my father was letting me borrow for the ride.

"Twenty years ago, it cost as much as a brand-new car."

Joe appeared unimpressed.

"But where are the pedals?" he asked.

The bottom dropped out of my stomach. There really were no pedals on the bike. *How could you forget the pedals, Scott?*

"You've got a point there," I replied, trying to sound calm. My mind churned, frantically trying to come up with a solution to the problem. Riding a bike without pedals is about as feasible as eating a bowl of tomato soup with a fork.

Salvation came in the form of my younger and more intelligent brother, Jason.

"Why don't you just take the pedals off of my bike?" he inquired, obviously pleased with his problem-solving capacity. It was quiet for a minute.

"Wow. Why didn't I think of that?" I said.

"You're bringing him along, aren't you?" Joe asked.

"Unfortunately not," I answered.

"You are already two stooges—hate to make it three," Jason said as he walked inside.

Fifteen minutes later I collapsed on the couch in the "packing HQ" room.

"Did I tell you I've had time to pack and repack a full four times over the past two months?" said Joe in a cheery voice.

"Really funny," I responded. I was quietly debating whether to tackle or squirt him from a water bottle when I had a realization.

"Joe!" I said, "We need haircuts. We can't start this thing with mop tops. Picture all of the ladies flocking in our spandex-sporting direction who will turn away disgusted when we take our helmets off. We need a 'doo that will hold up under the helmet."

"You're right! Go get your clippers."

Six hours before launch time I gave Joe a sharp-looking buzz that screamed "save a bicycle, ride a Joey!" I handed him the clippers with a nod.

Although the amount of skill needed to trim hair is minor, there is an awful lot of trust involved. On the first night with my travelling partner, this was the first instance in which we put our trust in each other. Joe was trimming for less than thirty seconds before I heard a startled "oops!" and the clippers jerk away from my head. I was mortified.

"Joe! What in the world are you doing?"

"Dude, relax. I've got it all under control."

My friend Joe Matelich has an uncanny affinity for rolling with the punches and a prodigious capacity for appearing composed even when a left hook catches him off guard. In the last two months of college, he stepped into a yearlong job and somehow won the "Employee of the Year" award. He would be the one to pull the tablecloth out from under thousands of dollars worth of fine China and actually make it work. The guy decided to learn guitar during one summer break in college and came back singing "Free Falling" better than Tom Petty himself. One of the most adaptable, resourceful, and cool-headed people I know. In other words, he was the perfect accomplice.

Somehow he managed to fit all that into a skinny, pale frame no taller than 6'2".

When the cutting was done a few noticeable lines remained etched into the hair on the sides of my scalp. I will trust Joe with many things—my life included—but with hair clippers again I would think twice.

The alarm tone on my phone the next morning came too early, but nervous excitement propelled me out of bed. Before my mind was fully aware, my body had gotten itself dressed and downstairs for breakfast. As the fog clouding my sleepy eyes gradually receded, I noticed another similarly-afflicted body to my left.

"Good morning," I mumbled, but it probably came out sounding more like "hrrrumph…" Joe nodded in acknowledgement. The one person awake and chipper was my mother. Then again, she wakes up before five every morning for work anyways. And she did not have a two-month bicycle excursion looming ahead of her.

"You guys ready?" she chirped.

I thought for a second. Yes, I finished breakfast. I even brushed my teeth. The plan was to leave at 7:00am for downtown Seattle. Departure time was approaching. All signs pointed to "Go!" but there was one critical piece missing; I suddenly had no desire to go anymore. My stomach churned with anxiety and my palms were sweaty. I was not ready for a two-month mountain of uncertainty any more than Cher is likely to start singing gospel tunes on her next album. All I wanted to do was go back to bed, wake up comfortably in a few hours, and munch on some sugary cereal. Why on earth I had thought riding across the country would be a good idea was leagues beyond me.

The only thing that pushed me out the door was the beautiful, sunny day in Seattle. In the month of May that is about as common as Haley's comet. I figured it must be a sign. We loaded up in the car, waved goodbye to my father and brother (who were betting we would give up in less than twelve hours), and set off towards downtown and the beginning of the journey.

"Be careful now, Scott," Mom chided after the car was parked and we were gearing up to go. "Stay safe on the roads, and remember you can always call home if you need anything." What my mother could have done for a flat tire half way across the country was beyond me. I was nonetheless grateful for her support—Joe's parents tried to talk him out of the trip for months, enticing him with an all-expenses-paid cruise to Alaska. Their efforts were obviously futile. We were putting our spandex-clad butts where our mouths had been for two years. I gave my mother a hug goodbye and we started pedaling.

One traditionally begins a cross-country ride with the rear bicycle tire submerged in either the Atlantic or Pacific and finishes with the front tire touching the opposite. As we pedaled along the Seattle waterfront we looked for the first patch of "beach," found it, and stumbled down the rocky shore.

"Hey Joe," I said when both of our tires were submerged, "you think we should get someone to take our picture?"

"Hmm... We probably should." I climbed back up the rocks—Seattle beaches aren't known for being particularly sandy—and implored the closest passers-by to document the first moment of what was either going to be the experience of a lifetime or a monumental failure.

"Excuse me, would you mind snapping a picture?" I asked.

"Sure, no problem."

"You folks from around here?"

"...No, we're just visiting." As one of them said this, the rest of the group anxiously tapped their feet on the ground and buried their hands in their pockets.

"Well you caught us at the beginning of a journey across the country!..." My voice trailed off, lost in a sea of blank stares. They snapped a picture and quickly walked away. Our mission to make authentic connections with fellow Americans was not off to a great start. Then again, they could have been Canadians visiting from Vancouver.

The ride out of Seattle was a rude awakening. When I dreamed about our trip across the country romantic portraits of mountain vistas, wide open fields, and beautiful rivers came to mind. What did not come to mind were steep city blocks and impatient people sitting in traffic.

Within four blocks I had already heard honks, seen the middle finger, and nearly fallen into traffic losing my balance on a steep incline. We got lost trying to find the bicycle trail exiting the city across Lake Washington, found the route just before resorting to swimming across the lake, and then promptly lost it again. Further ahead, while looking for the trail, I accidentally rolled through a four-way stop on a residential road at the same time as a big pickup truck.

"Hey, what the hell! There's a stop sign there," he yelled out the window.

"Sorry!" I replied, saying all there really was to say.

"No you're not" he retorted as we rolled by. I really was sorry. Contrary to popular belief, the number-one objective of cyclists is not to make life miserable or difficult for other vehicle traffic. And a person riding a bicycle makes mistakes every once in a while just like a person in a car. The important similarity between the two is the keyword "person." People make mistakes.

"What do you think about 90?" Joe asked after another hour of getting lost on back roads and playing touch-and-go with the trail.

"Fine by me."

We merged onto Interstate 90 going uphill at about eight miles an hour and began the ascent up to Snoqualmie Pass. At first, riding a bicycle on the interstate struck me as very odd and potentially suicidal. Although very noisy, we found the interstate to be one of the safest types of road. A shoulder the size of a car lane and consistent rumble strips demarcating the boundary between us and traffic made it feel like we were riding on our own superhighway.

The one drawback to riding on the interstate is the large amount of road debris that accumulates on the shoulder. It is very difficult to see debris and upcoming obstacles when riding behind another bicycle, so it is the lead cyclist's responsibility to alert trailing cyclists when an obstacle is coming ahead. Joe was new to this practice and when he swerved to miss a large metal hook in the way I had no time to adjust my trajectory. I heard a loud "Pop!" followed by a sharp "Hissss!" as the air left the tire.

"Joe! I got a flat," I yelled. He turned around and came back.

"Sorry man, I figured you were going to miss that hook."

"Wait, you mean you saw it and didn't point it out?"

"Yeah…"

"This is a two-inch hook we are talking about!"

"Sorry…"

"Well, here we are on the freeway changing a flat tire," I chuckled. There was nothing to do but smile. Most of the time a flat tire is no big deal. Gaining a feel for when and how to signal on a bicycle takes time, and with three hours of experience there was still much for Joe to learn.

The delay did nothing to help our already slow pace.

"Next time," I said, "just try to point out that kind of stuff *before* I'm on top of it."

"You got it, man."

And that was all there was to it. Dwelling on Joe's mishaps and mistakes was not an option. The same was true of the converse. Friendship is a constant balance of give and take. If either of us were to start keeping score it would have been a tortuous relationship over the coming months.

I-90 and Highway 2 are the two main corridors running east/west across Washington State. Each winds through the Cascade Mountain Range, at Snoqualmie (I-90) and Stevens (Highway 2) Passes. Stevens Pass is higher, steeper, longer, scenic, and has better skiing in the winter. Snoqualmie, if it is known for anything, has the honor of receiving the most atrociously wet and heavy snow anywhere in the Northwest. We settled on taking Snoqualmie Pass because it was the "easier" of the two options.

The bit about "easy" is where we erred in our judgments. We struggled up to a place called North Bend, only to realize the road had barely started going up. When driving on a highway at 60 miles an hour, a mile goes by once every minute; on bicycles we saw a sign that said "Snoqualmie Pass: 5 mi" and then spent the next hour struggling to the top.

"I can feel it. It's going to be around this corner." I said over my shoulder encouragingly.

"You know, I believed you the first, second and third time," Joe replied. The top was not around the next corner. But we made it, slowly and surely. The moment of triumph at the top was delicious.

By the time we clawed our way up and over the summit it was past three o'clock in the afternoon. Another 65 miles stood between us and Ellensburg, our target destination for the first day. We were looking forward to a cathartic downhill to compensate our climbing efforts, but it never came. Snoqualmie Pass is a terrible creation that goes up but does not come down. Completely unfulfilling, like the raccoon who bites into the Twinkie and finds out some devious agent had removed all of the creamy goodness.

It occurred to me that we had just attained a lofty elevation of

3,022 feet. A decent accomplishment, until my mind wandered to the Rockies in Colorado. We would attain altitudes of greater than 11,000 feet there. After one day of madness, the prospects of the next two months seemed insurmountably daunting. *What are we getting into?* I asked myself again. I could not come up with an answer.

The rational person would have turned around and rode straight back down the pass, chalked the day up to experience, and spent the rest of their life convincing themselves that they made the prudent choice to go home. But following a dream is not always rational.

We did make it to Ellensburg, after five more hours of riding and another flat tire. It was starting to get dark and cold and we got lost less than two miles away from my great-aunt Bonnie's house. We had to call her so she could come find us and lead us to her house. Not the triumphal entry at the end of the first day I was expecting.

"You guys look tired," she remarked matter-of-factly when we pulled into her driveway.

"You have no idea." I replied.

Chapter TWO

Ellensburg, WA to Spokane, WA

I WAS AWAKENED THE NEXT morning not by an alarm, but by electrifying soreness running up and down my entire body. Everything ached. Legs, arms, shoulders, back, feet, hands, and neck. I laid motionless for a long time, transfixed, until the alarm finally did go off. Barely reaching far enough to turn it off, I collapsed on the floor in a heap of rubble. Joe was similarly struck.

"Ohh…-Ah!- Ohh…" was all he could say.

I thought getting up the previous day was hard. This was downright excruciating.

"Joe, there is nothing in the world I want to do more than lay here for the rest of my life."

"You mean that?"

"Every bit of it." I said and walked gingerly into the kitchen.

"Good morning!" said Aunt Bonnie. "You want some toast to go along with your eggs and bacon?" I had never been asked a more delightful question.

"Yes please. And Joe…" I looked into the other room. Joe was flailing about in his sleeping bag. Every time he would try to get up by using an arm on the ground he would fall back to the carpet, his back unable to tolerate such pain. It was a pitiful sight indeed. "…He'll take some, too."

We were not the first to experience the "morning after day one" phenomenon. The first pedal-powered bicycle was invented by the Frenchman Pierre Lallement in 1865. Ambitious humans have been asking themselves "how far?" and "how fast?" ever since. One of the most notable was Thomas Stevens, an Englishman who became the first to ride across the United States in 1884 and continued to circle the entire globe by 1886. This was quite a feat considering he rode an "ordinary" bicycle, the old-fashioned type with solid tires and a gigantic front wheel. On good days he followed old wagon trails and unpaved roads. He took nothing more than a few spare clothes, rain jacket, and a pistol. Funding of his exploits came in part through a monthly article published in the magazine *Outing*. The contributions were devoured by an American public newly curious about a world that was becoming increasingly more accessible.

I imagine Mr. Stevens feeling very similar to the way we were feeling on the second morning. It takes someone possessed by a maniacal spirit to get back on the road after Day One. Yet there we were, sticking gruesomely thin bicycle saddles between our legs again. It did not take long for my tender, sensitive buns to remember the pain of the day before. There is no way to find a comfortable position on a bicycle with a derriere already past the pain threshold.

Two flats on the first day convinced me to get a new back tire. I bought a tire called the "Armadillo." Sounded appropriate. And it brought the animal count on board my bicycle to two.

The first animal was the official mascot of the trip: Spike the Bulldog. Spike is the Gonzaga University mascot, and a stuffed miniature version of the ferocious canine perched atop the back of my bike for the entirety of the trip. Spike dutifully kept us company in times of hardship and scared away all the people with sticky fingers at gas stations who would have liked to lay their paws on our stuff. Spike was also a good way to break the ice with strangers.

Looking to the day ahead, there was one large obstacle between our current location of Ellensburg and the target destination of Ephrata: the mighty Columbia River. No, we did not have to ford the river, Oregon Trail-style. However, human manipulation of the environment over the past 100 years was working on this particular day against us.

Around the turn of the 20th century the U.S. Bureau of Reclamation was formed with the intent to supply water to irrigable land in arid regions of the western states. The Columbia River, the fourth largest river in the country and largest emptying into the Pacific, was a primary target. Around the turn of the century there was also a growing demand for electricity and the construction of dams that produce hydroelectric power was high on the public conscience.

These two interests collided and the result was the damming of nearly all of the Columbia River's length in the country. Today there are fourteen principal dams on the main stem of the river. The Grand Coulee Dam, the largest of those, generates enough power alone to light the cities of Seattle and Portland, Oregon. The reservoir behind the damn supplies water to over 600,000 acres of land in the Columbia Basin.

With the help of reclamation Eastern Washington has become a fertile region that reliably turns out crops of wheat, corn, and apples. Grant County, Washington, is the largest producer of potatoes of any county in the country.

Aside from the tragic relocation of many Native American

communities and destruction of salmon spawning habitat, this all sounds great economically and agriculturally. So why would this be bad for us? The continuous chain of reservoirs makes the river very wide in most places. And where there is a wide river a wide bridge is needed. This is the case at Vantage, where I-90 crosses the Columbia River Gorge.

Bridges are generally not kind to bicycles. The main reason is the shoulder becomes essentially nonexistent, leaving very little "oops" room between a riding mistake and passing vehicles. There are other factors, too. At Vantage there is a large amount of sharp road debris and severe crosswinds that enjoy changing directions at a moment's notice. I don't know whether I prefer getting blown over the guardrail into the river, or into traffic. And I would rather not make that choice in a millisecond's time.

We pulled off and stopped on the side of the road just before the shoulder vanishes and bridge begins.

"Alright, here is the plan," I began, trying to sound confident to Joe. "We book it across the bridge as fast as we can. Don't look back; don't budge from the white line. And how about we stay alive. Do you wanna go first?"

"Doesn't matter to me."

"Why don't you go first."

"You got it. And Skip," Joe said, referring to me using a name that had become a term of endearment, "I see it this way. This is a win-win situation. Either we make it across, stay alive, and the trip keeps going. Win. Or we get annihilated by a semi-truck, die, and go to heaven. Both sound like wins to me."

"I don't know whether to call you the world's greatest optimist or the most morbid man alive."

"Then let's make it the first one," Joe said with a grin.

I was uncomfortable with what we were about to do. All it would have taken is one swerve from one ditz of a sixteen-year old driver looking down at a text message to put me out of the game for good. I did not want to go forward, but I was not going to turn back.

Sometimes following a dream leads one to confront risks that are uncomfortably exposed in the open. Whether humans like to acknowledge it or not there is hidden risk in every single second of every day.

Here it goes, I thought, gritting my teeth.

We started pedaling. Joe picked up speed quickly. I can only speak for myself, but adrenaline was pumping hard. I did not breathe for the first three quarters of the span. Cars were passing us mere feet away at seventy miles per hour. Just as it was seeming like we were home free, I heard the low rumble of a semi-truck barreling up the road behind us. Nobody would slow down to let him move over. The rumble came closer and closer. My hands grasped tightly around the handlebars and teeth clenched, face contorted in complete focus.

When semi-trucks pass by, you feel them before you see them. The wind coming off the front grill pushed us a full arm's length to the right, so close to the concrete barrier that I could have touched it with my elbow. Before I had time to think, the passing tail of the truck sucked us back to our previous position on the white line. It all happened within the blink of an eye and I was left completely out of breath, paralyzed in shock. I watched the truck speed off in the distance thanking God that the former, rather than latter, piece of Joe's win-win situation came true.

We made the last few pedals to the shoulder and to safety. There has never been a shoulder that I have been more excited to see, and I have seen some very attractive shoulders in my short lifetime.

I cannot remember exactly what I screamed in elation. But it probably was not intelligible.

"Ain't no river wide enough!" Joe chimed in. A huge weight was lifted off my shoulders. That we had to climb a thousand feet out of the Columbia River Gorge was a minor detail because there was a *shoulder*. Up we went, dancing and bouncing on the pedals lightheartedly like the puppets on Splash Mountain. The Columbia River really is impressive from an elevated vantage point, so we pulled off to take one last look at the Gorge.

"Gorgeous," Joe said.
"You had to say it."
"Yep."

    The situation turned grim once again. Upon gaining the rim of the gorge, headwinds blowing out of the east began to make their assault like an invisible cavalry charge. They screamed in our ears and whistled between our tires.

    Wind wields such demoralizing power because it breaks the established exchange rate between the input of work and resulting output of speed and distance. Riding in it is a depressing feeling akin to discovering the hard-earned dollar you bring over to Europe is really only worth sixty Euro-cents. It gets loud, so loud that it is difficult to hear the person trying to speak to you riding directly adjacent.

    There is almost nothing you can do about wind. The only ace in the hole cyclists have is a technique called drafting. It requires less effort to ride behind someone than it does to break the wind in front. The concept comes into play in many other venues such as Daytona racing and the "V" patterns of migrating birds. By taking turns between breaking the wind and resting, cyclists can mitigate the wind's negative effects. If you still cannot visualize it, picture Hulk Hogan tag-teaming the "Macho Man" Randy Savage.

    Forward we trudged, agonizingly slow. By the time we arrived at my friend Amanda's house in the small town of Ephrata we were a weary, crazy mess. We collapsed in the front lawn, a heap of twitching appendages punctuated by the occasional involuntary scream.

    Over the next few days it was very windy and we spent a lot of time looking at each other's buttocks in drafting formation. So much time that we developed names for the position directly behind each other, where the buttocks was big and the drafting sweet. Joe dubbed the area directly behind me the "bosom of security." His was the "trunk." Exchanges would go something like this:

"Joe, I am getting tired. Can you spell me?"

"Yeah, sometimes."

"No! Not *smell* me—*spell* me! As in, 'give me a break for a spell?' I want to get in your *Trunk!*"

"A-hah, why didn't you just say so? Got no junk in my *Trunk* so hop on in!"

Or,

"How're ya doin' back there, Joe?"

"Skip, your *Bosom of Security* is very generous today!"

I was privileged to get to know Joe's trunk and he became very familiar with my bosom of security.

Returning to our pitiful state in the lawn, my friend Amanda noticed there were some strange people lying down outside and opened the door to investigate.

"Oh, it's you!" she said. All we could muster in reply were a few groans and a slight shift in weight. "You look like death," came the matter-of-fact reply, "but you know, my dad is cooking *steaks* tonight..." My eyes shot open. I could taste the A1 steak sauce dripping off the words. Joe was similarly, miraculously reinvigorated.

"I don't think we've met. My name is Joe..." the conversation trailed off as they walked inside. I was left on the grass with a few minutes to gather my thoughts. It hit me for the first time that we were actually making things happen. The point when you realize your dreams are becoming reality is euphoric indeed. We survived two days, and there was no reason to believe that the next two—or forty—would be any different. Although there were many miles to be pedaled, countless mountains to be climbed, and weeks of time in the saddle ahead, I could not help but think that there is nothing in the world I would rather be doing.

Amanda is an energetic and outspoken young woman with a desire to move to North Carolina and write novels on the beach. She also happens to offer counsel with regards to my pitiful pursuit of romantic relationships.

"So what is your most recent blunder, Scott?" she asked inquisitively, not long after we had settled in to her family's home. I began to explain to her that spending all day in grimy spandex had not served me well in the relationship department thus far.

"You do seem to have a point there," she replied pensively.

I was happy to be off the hook so easily this time. In the past Amanda had taken great pleasure in pointing out my deficiencies. Tuning in to a typical conversation would go something like this:

"Scott, you've gotta know that when this particular femme says she is taking a break from the dating scene, she is testing you to see if you have the wherewithal to convince her otherwise. But she knew you wouldn't have the guts, she likes the idea of having one more boy dreaming about her, and when the next boy comes around she will keep saying the same thing."

"And thus you're saying I got the whole thing completely wrong?"

"Hate to say it, but yeah."

"It sounds like I played right into her hand."

"Like you were a toadfish going after a slimy worm on a hook screaming 'obvious.' Look I am saying this to you as a friend, but I honestly don't know how you could be so clueless."

I had no idea how I could be so clueless about being clueless. Maybe this explains my poor track record with the opposite gender. And have you ever seen a toadfish?

The steaks Amanda's family shared with us in Ephrata were delicious. We devoured them, along with potatoes, asparagus, French bread, and salad. The amount of food we consumed was concerning. *This can't be natural. I don't even feel full.* Joe echoed similar sentiments the next morning. Equally as concerning was how Amanda's family would react to such gluttony, but they kept telling us to eat to our heart's content. When someone tells you to follow your heart it is a good idea to listen.

Over dinner and into the evening we got to hear a lot from Amanda's father. His name was Ed. And Ed was quite the character.

"It's a conspiracy, see. The Mormons are everywhere in big business. They own all of the biggest companies. Companies like Coca-Cola. Which is ironic in and of itself because they aren't permitted by their religion to drink the caffeine they put into each can of Coke. And they rule the Boy Scouts. Mormons are the ones really running this country…" and so the conversation meandered through the realms of politics, history, and economics among many others. Ed seemed to have something to say about just about everything, and did not hesitate to let you know it. When I looked over the table at Amanda during one particularly lengthy diatribe she rolled her eyes. Ed continued,

"The woman's vagina is like the holy grail…" (I have no idea how we arrived at this topic) "… and without it, you don't have anything."

"Dad!" Amanda had finally had enough. Personally, I was amused by his uncommon perspectives and entertaining opinions. But after a while the conversation became a bit much. In the limited time I spent around Ed, he came off as a know-it-all. It is impossible to genuinely know someone after so little time, so I can only offer conjectures and Amanda's later apologies for her father's domineering personality.

Along with those apologies and rolling eyes came some explanation.

"Even though my dad never went to college he managed to raise five kids. I am the last one and he still managed to put me through private college. He has had a lot of experiences and done a lot of things in his life."

That Ed made a point to demonstrate how much he knows makes sense, and I imagine two kids in their twenties riding willy-nilly across the country seemed quite ridiculous to him.

Believing he must know best, Ed told us exactly how our route across the country should go. The fact that we planned to angle south through Wyoming and Colorado before turning eastward was appalling to him. He thought we should stay north and pass through North Dakota and Minnesota before angling south around the Great Lakes because it would be a significantly shorter route.

"No way. Don't even try to tell me it is only 100 miles further to go the way you're going. I know my own country," he responded haughtily when we told him there was not a big difference between our route and his suggestion. We had already done our research and found that the standard bicycle route across the northern states was less than a hundred miles shorter. On the northern tier the Great Lakes require one to dip significantly south, and at northern latitudes the coast is also further to the east. At any rate, the way he negated our plans *de facto* was discouraging. Who really wants to ride through North Dakota? I was partial to the idea of Yellowstone and the Colorado Rocky Mountains myself.

That I reacted strongly internally to Ed's criticism tells me that there is a stroke of him in me, a piece of my soul that does not like being told what to do.

Families are peculiar things. I drifted off into a deep slumber that night pondering what it was like for Amanda growing up under the roof of her father. Just like I at times have weighed the odds that I was adopted by my parents. I did not have much time to think, though, because my mind was ready to start counting the sheep jumping over the fence.

"I think Ed really likes to hear himself talk" Joe said when we were out of earshot on the road the next morning. "I tried to distract him so you would have a chance to talk with Amanda."

"Yeah, I noticed that too. Thanks, Joe."

"The man can cook up a mean steak, though."

We rode away from Ephrata grateful for the nutrition and shelter, and with plenty of new, interesting perspectives. But I do not think Ed gained much from the experience. He was not very interested in our story. Not that he was obligated to learn something from us; people have every right to listen or to ignore, especially in their own home. But I do wish he would have accepted what little we had to offer, in the form of a few original and humorous stories and a break from the normality of everyday life. They say giving is better than receiving, but we never really had the chance. I could not help but imagine how civil, productive, and enjoyable family gatherings, politics, and *Trading Spouses* would be if people made more of an effort to see life through one another's eyes.

The third day of riding through Washington State was a lot like the first two: painful and windy. Spokane, our target destination, resided over one hundred miles to the east. The only difference was that this time rain accompanied the pain and wind. My mood fell along with the first few drops, anticipating the worst. And the worst happened. The skies opened up and dumped buckets, but I quickly realized that rain was nowhere near as severe a factor as is the wind.

By noon the wind had blown away the rain. It was blowing in our faces even harder than the day before. The vast expanses of eastern Washington stretched ahead for miles, giving the impression we were going absolutely nowhere. My mind went on standby mode. I stared at the mileage on my odometer, watching the tenths and hundredths place after the decimal cycle between .00 and .99 for what seemed like ages. Joe and I did not talk. We just kept riding.

Ten miles away from Spokane the wind's charge finally lessened due to increased tree cover.

"How much does it cost to stop the wind?" Joe asked, emerging from an hour-long silence. My mind was exhausted from the hours spent leading Joe in my Bosom of Security, breaking the wind for my tired partner.

"No idea..." I replied.

"Tree-99!" he chirped, chuckling at his own joke.

We staggered into beautiful Spokane, Washington as the sun was setting. Spokane is the home of my alma mater, Gonzaga University.

It was a surreal feeling to return to my college campus so soon after graduating. I opened the door to a friend's house and was greeted by a circle of people all sitting on the floor in a circle. All the furniture had been moved out, and all that was left were bare walls and a few twelve-packs of beer. I sat down, grunting in pain all the way, and began listening to the conversation directly to my left.

"Yeah man, last night I was *so* blasted."

"Dude all I remember is us pissing on the fence singing Katy Perry and then everything went *black*."

"The rest of the night must've been awesome."

"And then this morning..."

"Dude."

"Yeah man."

"Wow."

I do not know how many hundreds of times I heard similar conversations in college without a second thought. But now it seemed so foreign; *why would anyone do that?* I asked myself. *Getting up early to ride a hundred miles with a hangover would be terrible.* But then I remembered that most people are not riding their bicycles for two months at a time.

After a half hour in the circle someone asked Joe what he was up to. When he told them, nobody in the circle knew what to say. I looked at the ring of blank faces staring at us. "But so far we have only ridden three days and made it across one state," I said in an attempt to break the silence and make our mission more digestible. My attempt failed.

After another spell of silence the conversation returned to the group's plans to float down the Spokane River on inner tubes with a case of Bud Light.

Four years of alcohol dependence had made many of my friends immune to all spontaneity and originality while sober. Joe and I were learning that for about the price of a twelve-pack of Coors every day we could live our simple dream full of pedaling, eating, and sleeping.

And for as boring as some parts of eastern Washington can be, it seemed much more interesting than the alternative.

I borrowed an iPhone (because I still do not have one) to check the weather forecast. It looked ugly; a storm front was moving in and rain was inevitable. With the books closed on the first three days it did not look like things would be getting any easier—and the awareness of an impending storm hovered like, well, a black cloud over my head.

Chapter THREE

Spokane, WA to Haugan, MT

THANK YOU GOD, I THOUGHT to myself as we pedaled away from Spokane. The wind was at our backs for the first time. The predicted storm was nowhere to be found. We felt fast. Dangerously fast. The trip briefly took on a feeling of familiarity as we rode a route I had ridden a hundred times in college.

The Centennial Trail connecting Spokane and Coeur d'Alene, Idaho offers great views of the Spokane River, surrounding hills, and the Ponderosa Pine forests blanketing the Inland Northwest. We ducked and weaved along the golfcart-sized path around trees, under old railroad trestles, and alongside the river until arriving at the Washington-Idaho border. We stopped for a second to snap a picture with Spike. Then the bottom fell out of my stomach.

"Joe, turn around and tell me what you see," I said.

"What do you mean?" he responded, still looking down and fiddling with his camera.

"I mean look at those big, grey, nasty-looking clouds hovering over the city right now."

"Ohh..." his voice trailed off. The breeze at our backs was slowly dropping in temperature and came in increasingly random and sporadic gusts. I felt the tension increase, like when the scary music begins subtly in horror films just before the climax.

"I think we best get a move on."

I picked up my phone in Coeur d'Alene and dialed a friend named Anne.

"Hello Anne! Would you mind if I stop by for lunch?... No, I am on my bike passing through town... Oh yeah, can I bring a friend?" I asked with a sideways glance at Joe.

"What did she say?" Joe asked.

"She called me and idiot and asked if I knew it was raining outside."

Anne is a nurse and also was my surrogate mother when I spent a summer working in a hospital emergency room a few years back. She has the perfect blend of sarcasm and compassion for work in the ER, and writes rap lyrics to the emergency department's annual musical production. One day she approached me with a pen and an innocent request.

"Hey Scott, can you write down some blood pressure and pulse recordings for me?" she asked with a sweetness that should have put me on guard. I hurried to get a piece of paper and pushed the end of the pen—*Zap!*—instead of clicking down like a normal ballpoint, the pen delivered a nasty shock that traveled halfway up my arm.

"Anne!" But she had already turned and was walking down the hallway laughing in triumph.

This time it was my turn to surprise her.

"You're doing what?! No way!" she said, eyeing Joe and me in her living room incredulously.

"Dead serious," I replied.

Telling people we were riding across the country was fast becoming one of my favorite things, seeing the looks of indignation and disbelief on faces. She took another bite of the hearty pasta she served us for lunch, chewing thoughtfully for a second.

"You are crazy."

"I thought you already would have guessed that."

"Probably right. Never gave you the honest psychological triage you had due. But seriously, good luck out there. I don't want you to show up in the ER as a patient any time soon."

By two o'clock it was pouring outside and we were soaked within minutes of walking out Anne's front door. Fifteen minutes later we stumbled into the hospital where I worked to say hello to some other good friends.

"Shut up. I don't want to hear about it," a nurse named James said when I spotted him in the hallway. He was quiet for a second in pensive pause. I was caught off guard and had no idea what to say.

"That is the final thing on my bucket list," he continued. "I have always wanted to do it. I am so jealous."

The sight of a former intern dressed in dirty, wet cycling clothes drew raised eyebrows and tentative greetings from all of the doctors and nurses. I was even told my choice of attire for my first day back at work was inappropriate. "No, I'm actually not coming back to work this summer." Then I would explain myself. "I had no idea!" was the common response, followed by a warm embrace. Not a small gesture, considering my state of soppiness. One person went so far as to give me a list of all of her relatives between Wyoming and Kentucky, including representatives from the states of Wisconsin, Minnesota, South Dakota, and Iowa. I did not have the heart to tell her I was not going through any of those states.

When I left the hospital it was still dumping buckets outside. We made plans to stay with a friend named Christine. We rang the doorbell and dove into her house almost before saying hello. Despite the fact that we had only ridden about forty miles (compared to the hundred per day we had averaged the previous three days), I was exhausted. The warm shower, delicious dinner, and night spent watching movies with Christine felt like heaven.

"Scott, why would we ever leave this place?" Joe whispered the next morning. It was depressingly gray and rain was dripping down the windows. For the life of me, I could not come up with a good answer. Inside was warm and filled with nice people and food. Outside, the specter of a day filled with squishy shoes and cold toes ominously beckoned. Every rational bone in my body screamed *Scott, leaving this place is a bad idea!* Unfortunately bicycles do not pedal themselves and miles are not made by stretching out on a recliner by the fireplace. In a short amount of time we had said our goodbyes and were outside in the rain and wind once again, dreaming about hot showers and fireplaces.

Idaho was the last of the lower forty-eight states to be explored and it was not until 1863 that the Panhandle region of the state saw any significant non-Native American populations. The area had been inhabited for thousands of years by tribes such as the Kootenai, Flathead, Kalispel, Nez Perce, and Coeur d'Alene. In 1863 prospectors poured into Montana from the west coast to mine gold and had to pass through Northern Idaho en route. The region developed to meet the lodging and alimentary demands of the travelling gold miners.

As the stream of settlers and prospectors increased, tensions with Native American tribes increased as well. The decades following 1863 were marked by frequent confrontations between the recently arrived white settlers and the area's long-term residents. All-out massacres were not uncommon. The story of Chief Joseph and his fraction of the Nez Perce Tribe is the most well-known of its type, but it does not stand alone in history. Those tribes choosing peace were maliciously swindled out of their territory and resettled on reservation lands.

While looking for some background information of the region, I came across a book written in 1903 titled *An Illustrated History of North Idaho*. It had this to say about the conflicts between whites and Native Americans:

"Our national domain was wrested from the hands of its aboriginal inhabitants. This struggle could have but one termination. *The inferior race must yield to the superior.*"

While one would hope the views and attitudes regarding our country's first residents have evolved over the course of the past century, what will never change is the way Native Americans were systematically deceived and murdered so the nation's destiny could become manifest.

Sometimes it is challenging for me to have anything but a cynical attitude towards modern society and the past evils upon which it is built. However, some evidence gives me cause to maintain faith in the human race.

We stumbled upon that evidence in the town of Cataldo, Idaho, which is home to the first Jesuit missionary roots established in the area. Father Pierre-Jean DeSmet arrived in 1842 at the request of the Coeur d'Alene Tribe, who wanted one of the "medicine men" in black robes to be a part of their community.

Over the next decade an admirable partnership formed between the locals and the Jesuits. In 1850, Fr. Antonio Ravalli and over three hundred members of the Coeur d'Alene tribe began constructing a church that still stands today as a vestige of relations between whites and Native Americans done right. It is the oldest building standing in Idaho, despite being built entirely without nails.

So there Joe and I were, riding our bicycles up a gravel road to the grassy knoll where the church building sits. Rain fell all morning and at the moment there was a light drizzle. Turning a blind corner we were confronted with a giant yellow creature producing a steady stream of small children from its bowels: a school bus. It must have been a field trip, and now we had to navigate through the steady flux of Power Ranger backpacks on our way up the hill.

"Aw, *lucky!*" said one young boy carrying a green Ninja Turtles lunch box as we passed by. He was obviously referring to how our bicycles could carry us up a hill a bit faster than he could walk. Here is what I wanted to say back to him:

"Lucky? Us, lucky?! Have you seen what the weather is doing today, kid? You stepped off that warm, dry bus three minutes ago but I have been sitting in this rain for a full four hours already today. That is, if you consider placing my buttocks on this slim sliver of a composite saddle 'sitting.' My feet squish because they are so wet and my fingers are pruny. I ain't *swimming*, kid! So why are they pruny? Now, think about what you just said and please, please, call me the lucky one again."

It was probably good that I kept my mouth shut.

Perspective is everything. Through the kid's eyes, our bicycles were to be envied. Things were different from our point of view. I would have traded my bicycle and a day spent shivering in the rain for a Ninja Turtles lunchbox in a heartbeat.

The world looks different when viewed through different eyes. I am slightly embarrassed that it took an elementary school field trip to teach me that—at the age of twenty-two, no less. Disclaimer: if someone ever does try to see the world through my eyes they better bring with them a good pair of far-sighted spectacles, or else the world is going to look like pea soup on a foggy day.

We paid our respects to the grounds, left the Cataldo mission and continued riding towards the Montana border. The rain finally abetted as we crested Lookout Pass on the Idaho-Montana border. But the rain didn't really stop; it turned into snow. A highway advisory signal blurted out the warning "Danger: Potholes. Next 10 miles." It was hard to imagine the situation getting any worse.

Descending from a pass on a bicycle can be the most exhilarating feeling in the world. It can also be about as enjoyable as wrestling a boa constrictor. In either case you do not breathe very much. It all depends on road conditions and one's affinity for velocity and risk. On this particular day road conditions were as bad as they can get, short of not having a road at all. The only things that could have made the situation worse were snow drifts or an unhappy mama grizzly bear waking up from hibernation with a kink in her neck.

As if the falling sleet and terrible road were not enough, Joe's front brake picked up a rock and stopped functioning properly on the descent. Who needs brakes going down a mountain, anyway?

Somehow we made it down from the pass, dodging rocks and potholes for miles and squeezing the brakes (for Joe, just one brake) so hard that new meaning was given to "white knuckles." The day was aging and we were ready to enter into retirement.

"Let's stop here," I said to Joe as we saw the sign for the town of Haugan. We pulled off and slowed to a stop. I greedily gulped from the water bottle I had been too terrified to grab when descending from the pass. For the first time I could see patches of blue sky in the clouds. It had stopped raining.

"I am glad that is over," I said with a relieved sigh.

"Me too," Joe agreed.

"My feet are wet. Really wet."

"Mine too. And I could really go for a warm shower right now."

"Me t—" That did it. I realized then that for the first time on the trip we had no place to stay overnight and no plan for how to find one. My stomach turned over, but I was not sure if it was because I was nervous or just really hungry.

"Well, what should we do?" It was more a statement than question, because we both knew what we had to do. It was time to engage the local population.

"Put on the kindest 'stranger face' you've got," I said. We turned up one of the four residential streets in town and approached the nicest looking house on the block. "Block" is a loose term in the small towns of Western Montana. A dirt road curved out of view and ten houses were spread out amongst a thick stand of pine trees. It was the evening and all that was lacking to make this into the start of a horror movie was uncomfortable music.

I was worried the residents of the house would be able to hear my heart pounding in my chest as I stood on the porch. Quite frankly, I was nervous. *What if they did not like strangers?*

The first time I knocked, nothing happened. To be thorough I knocked again and was finally met at the door by a gray-haired fellow lacking a shirt. One hand was scratching his belly button and the other was holstered in his pocket. He did not verbally say anything, but the one raised eyebrow was telling me, "you have ten seconds to explain yourself before you become target practice for me'n my shotgun."

"So this is going to be a bit random..." I tentatively began. I told him our story and asked if he knew of anyone in town who is nice and could help us out. He sat in the doorway chewing cud for a full thirty seconds.

"I guess y'could try the church down that there road," he said, finally. "The pastor lives in the trailer right behind the building."

Off to the church we went, where we were greeted by a fellow similarly suspicious of us. Pastor Mark was his name, if the sign out front was correct. He was a portly fellow, the kind of person whose deep laugh amplifies in their chest cavity to fill a room of any size. His wide-set eyes peered at us through a pair of oddly stylish glasses while his hand ran through his silvery hair.

"Pastor Mark, we are recent college grads and riding our bikes across the country. We started in Seattle five days ago and now here we are in Haugan. Would you mind if we pitched our tents somewhere on the church grounds?"

Inside I yearned for some form of benevolence, because if this did not work out I had no idea what we would do next.

"Well, it is going to get a little cold outside—we could put you folks up in the motel in town."

Out of embarrassment we declined; there is no way they could have afforded to get a room for us. Mark paused and scratched his chin and gave a look as if he were sizing us up.

"Wait... Why don't y'all just sleep in the basement? It ain't much, but there is a shower and it should be warmer than outside." Now he was singing music to our ears.

Before long we had relocated indoors and were chatting like old friends with Pastor Mark and his wife Bethany. I could have listened to Mark for hours solely on the basis of the animated and thickly accented way in which he spoke. It really is a shame that Seattleites have one of the most nonexistent accents in the country.

"Y'see, we're actually Baptists from the South," Bethany said. *Baptists? In Montana?* "We came here on a mission trip ten years ago," she explained. "We finally decided to permanently relocate here last year and have been around for quite a few ups and downs already."

Mark agreed.

"Yes, it has been quite the time. This place is like a third world country. What I mean is that these people have no way of escaping the destitute circumstances which surround them. Folks who grow up 'round here don't have any reason to hope for any kind of life worth livin'. If we have a cause, this is it: to bring the light of hope to these good but troubled people. We ain't really into all the denomination mumbo-jumbo. Being a Baptist is about the fifth or sixth verse we sing. What we're about is lovin' Jesus Christ and lovin' his people here on Earth." The southern twang in the way Mark pronounced "luuv" was one of the most comforting and assuring things I have ever heard.

The thought that anyone would come to Montana in today's world as a missionary baffled me. I never thought the Northwest (my home) could be a place worthy of missionary attention. Yet here we were talking to two Southern Baptists convicted to serve the people of western Montana. It all made sense. The area is rife with alcoholism, drug and gambling addictions, and poverty. Prerequisites to a vibrant life such as hope, opportunity, and future are hard to come by.

Pastor Mark and Bethany are heroes. Not because of the souls they may be winning for some kingdom in some afterlife, but because they are inspiring people to hope and to pursue a better future here in the present. I owe gratitude to a great many individuals who encouraged me to believe in a tomorrow that can be better than today. Without that hope, there would be no impetus to dream of a cross-country bicycle adventure.

Hope changes people.

"We don't have too much to feed you, so I hope you aren't too choosy." Bethany was in the kitchen gazing at the pantry. In short time she whipped up a feast of macaroni, canned pork and beans, and a full three burger patties for each of us. Without difficulty we devoured it all.

As we unrolled our sleeping bags and welcomed sleep I could not help but be amused at the outcomes of the evening. Finding two jovial Southern Baptists perfectly content to live in a trailer dropped squarely in backwoods Montana was a surprise. That they opened up their church basement and cooked us three burger patties without any buns was pure serendipity.

Chapter FOUR

Haugan, MT to Jackson, MT

IT IS MUCH EASIER TO get out of bed when the sun comes to greet you in the morning. I peeked outside the door of the basement and sure enough, golden rays of light were just beginning to shine through the thick stands of trees surrounding the church. After eating breakfast with Mark it was time to say goodbye. It felt like we were more like old friends than strangers who came eleven hours earlier.

Compared to the day before, the ride into Missoula was a stroll through the park. Most of the day was spent on the interstate. Due to bridge repair, oncoming traffic was diverted onto lanes normally carrying eastbound traffic. We used this opportunity to ride the westbound lanes (in an easterly direction) completely devoid of cars.

Joe obtained great satisfaction from shouting at the diverted oncoming traffic.

"Can't touch this! Na na na na—can't touch this!" he sang in between mocking gestures at the oncoming cars. One of those things you always wanted to do, but normally would be killed for in a split-second.

We turned off and rode parallel to the interstate for about twenty miles. The only speed limits posted on the local highway were for trucks. In Montana alone would this be the case. Joe, being a Montanan himself, informed me that the federal government threatened to cut all funding to Montana highways unless they put speed limits on their roads. Most roads seemed to be seventy-five miles per hour and hardly anyone follows even those generous guidelines.

A tailwind pushed us into Missoula. This outdoor Mecca and general hippie town full of University of Montana students was a special stop to us for a couple reasons. First, it is home to Joe's aunt and uncle. Second, it is home to the headquarters of Adventure Cycling Association. The ACA is an organization unknown to many, but was of great significance to us.

It originally was founded as BikeCentennial in 1974 by Dan and Lys Burden, two cycling enthusiasts attending the University of Montana. Their dream, conceived while riding from Alaska to the tip of South America, was to organize a mass bicycle tour in the summer of 1976 to commemorate the United States bicentennial. Dan contracted hepatitis in Mexico, which forced him and Lys to abandon what they had dubbed the "Hemistour." Another couple riding with them, Greg and June Siple, continued on to the Tierra del Fuego in Chile as Dan and Lys returned to Missoula.

By New Year's Eve in 1976 both couples had been reunited and Adventure Cycling Association employed more than a dozen full-time staff members. Their tasks included, but were not limited to, publicity, route-finding, and building community support along the entire trail (which had by now become known as the TransAmerica

Trail). In the summer of 1975 Gary spent two and a half months driving a motor home across the country putting together a series of guidebooks that would serve as roadmaps and provide local history for the ride's participants.

We owed a lot to the mapping efforts begun by Gary. To date the organization has assembled 92 maps detailing 40,974 miles worth of various routes that traverse the country north/south, east/west, and just about every other direction imaginable. Like many touring cyclists, we used the foldable, waterproof maps for the majority of our travels. They contained every piece of useful information imaginable to the traveler mounting a bicycle: distances between towns, amenities offered along the way, an elevation profile detailing major climbs and descents, and useful phone numbers.

The most incredible part of the story in 1976 was that the trip actually happened. With the support and organizational work done by BikeCentennial, over 4,000 individuals hailing from all fifty states and abroad embarked on the journey. Just over 2,000 successfully completed the entire TransAm. Although they have acquired a new name, a spacious HQ, and a membership base of 44,700, the ACA of today remains committed to their mission of "inspiring people of all ages to travel by bicycle... for fitness, fun, and self-discovery."

Adventure Cycling seemed like the coolest group of people based on their mission statement alone, and that sentiment did not change after we visited HQ in Missoula. Upon opening their doors (which were made from bicycle handlebars, of course) we were greeted by smiling faces, an office abuzz with energy, maps galore, and a freezer full of ice cream sandwiches free for cyclists. They take Polaroid pictures of touring cyclists who come by the office and put them up on the Wall. I looked at the Wall, populated with over a hundred pictures from the last season, and felt for the first time like I was part of something bigger than myself. Here were other people who had done and were doing the same thing we were. I was excited to get to know these people and hear their stories.

Up until Missoula we had been traveling "off-route" and largely alone, but heading east from Missoula we would be on the same roads used by many other cyclists making the same pilgrimage (or the reverse direction). Using maps had its benefits and drawbacks. On the one hand, having a set of maps detailing every single bend in the road was nice. It helped to know how many more miles remained between us and the next quart of chocolate milk, and I felt more secure with phone numbers to the local fire departments in every region.

On the other hand, the maps make the art of bicycle touring so simple and explicit that it is easy to use them to avoid every possible uncertainty and deny any impromptu adventure. Joe and I occasionally deviated from the route for anywhere from a couple miles up to a few days. That is not the way it works for the majority of cross-country tour groups. Telling fellow cyclists of our off-the-route exploits was entertaining. Reactions ranged from amazement ("You went *off-route?* No way!") to incredulousness. But I had trouble deciding if the people who just stood there looking at Joe and me with quivering lower lips were stupefied by such originality or were irate with a righteous anger. How dare we wander away from the straight and narrow path that has guided faithful cyclists across the country for nearly forty years!

I found it was touring cyclists we saw on a daily basis who were the hardest to engage on a deeper level. The most interested people were those who had absolutely no clue what we were doing. Most memorable conversations happened with people not riding bicycles. Very rare were the times I remember actually getting to glimpse into the soul of another cyclist. One of the exceptions is a Scotsman we will meet later in this chapter.

I think our fellow cyclists assumed to know most of what there was to know about Joe and me solely because we were undertaking similar pursuits. It is hard to transcend the threshold of superficiality with people who already believe they know most of what there is to know about you. Nine times out of ten, this would be the exchange between us and other touring groups:

"You going to Yorktown?" they would ask, naming the most common start/endpoint to the east.

"Yes," I would respond.

"Huh. Well, we are going to Astoria." That was no surprise either, because Astoria is where most rides start/finish to the west.

"That sounds about right," Joe would say. Before we had a chance to ask them about the ways in which their experience has shaped their character or expanded their life-perspective, they were long gone. People who stuck around to converse longer tended to be solely obsessed with talking about cycling gear. Those monologues went something like this:

"These Ortileb panniers have been just *great*. Really glad I went with the deluxe bicycle multi-tool because, well, I don't really know how to use everything it has, but I am ready for anything that comes up on the road. And I am *stoked* I went with the liter and a half-sized Nalgene bottles instead of the standard one-liters. I can carry, err, another half liter per bottle with those! Did I mention the rain jacket I just picked up at REI..."

Sound like a riveting conversation? By this point I would be deciding whether the cloud pattern forming overhead looked more like a whale or Chris Farley. It was a surprise to discover that materialism can exist even in outdoor pursuits. More surprising was the fact that the majority of interactions with touring cyclists reminded me of talking about the weather at office parties.

A branch of Joe's extended family lives in Missoula, Montana. His Uncle Louie and Aunt Melanie were outside to greet us at their house after a smooth day of riding through western Montana. Within seconds the royal treatment began. Outside was a balloon, originally of the "Happy Birthday!" sort, that had been modified to read "Welcome Wayward Cyclists! Joe, Scott, & _____." The blank was reserved for Oliver, Joe's friend from high school and the third musketeer who joined us for four days as we finished riding through Montana. Wren, Joe's cousin responsible for the balloon, had forgotten his name.

"Hey guys! ...Oh my goodness, you look exhausted!" Melanie was almost hopping up and down, bursting with energy. "Hold on a sec—okay Joey, lie down on the ground," she ordered, "I've got just the thing for you two."

"But—"

Before Joe had time to think, he was lying on his back and getting a shake-out of his legs.

"Ahhh..." came the contented response.

"It took you guys long enough!" a new voice said. By this point I too was lying in the grass. I tilted my head just enough that I could make out a skinny, blonde-haired preteen coming our way. That must be Wren.

"Oooh, you don't look so good," she clucked while looking down at the sweaty, sunburned heaps that were Joe and me. "You don't look good at all."

I was about to thank her for the sarcastic welcome when a van pulled into the driveway. The passenger door opened. Enter Oliver Santin. A stout man of about five feet and nine inches, with hair and a personality that continually reminded me of Ben Stiller. He graduated from Carroll College in Helena, Montana with a biology degree. Originally planning to continue to medical school, he considered revising his career plans to be a firefighter and worked in the wakeboard division of a sports shop for nine months. When he had finally arrived at a point of clarity in his life he settled on—of all things—the priesthood. Oliver can be summed up in four words, confessed to me by multiple members of the feminine race: "Father What-a-waste." And it was true; his humor, kindness, and charm quickly endear him to just about every young woman's heart. The same qualities made him a perfect addition to our trip.

The three of us enjoyed a delicious salmon dinner with Joe's family. After stuffing our faces it was time for a dessert of apple pie and ice cream. I always forget to reserve space in my stomach for dessert and was already busting at the seams. But I was not one to turn down apple pie when it could be the last real food in days.

"Hey, I've got something for you," Wren said to me as we all walked inside from the patio. I followed her upstairs, wondering what a teenage girl might have up her sleeve. She disappeared for a second in the bathroom and came out wielding a stick of Old Spice.

"Here, this is for you," she said while handing it to me. "I heard you say you didn't bring any deodorant with you. And, well, when you and Joe pulled up today, you guys *stunk*."

"Gee, thanks Wren," I said. I didn't know whether to be thankful or insulted, but was getting good at thinking one thing and saying another.

We started out from Missoula the next day heading south towards Chief Joseph Pass and the Big Hole area of Montana. Oliver was sprightly and always pushed the tempo with his fresh legs. Joe struggled to keep up and yo-yoed between catching us in the draft and falling back. After the fifth time I had to drop back and help Joe catch up I set Oliver straight.

"Oliver, I think we should tone this down a bit. Marathon and not a sprint, you know." What Joe and I had learned over the previous week was that the saying "less is more" is the gold standard for bicycle touring. It became obvious the faster we tried to go, the slower we actually went due to the frequent breaks to eat and recover. Although counterintuitive, the best thing to do is to find a comfortable pace and dial it in for as long as possible.

Along we plodded on the highway through the Bitterroot National Forest, stopping along the way occasionally to ogle at the beautiful vastness of southwestern Montana. I understand now why they call it the Big Sky State.

Chief Joseph Pass lies on the Continental Divide, and I was elated to cross the threshold. To me it seemed like a rite of passage or a sign of progress. As we struggled up to the top of the 7,241 ft pass all I could think was *divide, divide, divide!* When we arrived at the top I looked around for some sort of sign or elevation marker that could validate what we just accomplished.

There was nothing there besides three pairs of burning legs and a ski resort. In my imagination I envisioned a grandiose sign declaring "This is the Continental Divide! Congratulations for making it up here, you studly cyclists! Now when you urinate alongside the road it is going straight into the Gulf of Mexico."

As we descended into the Big Hole—a tremendous combination of vast plain and surrounding mountain—all I could think about was how disappointed I was to not get a picture in front of a Continental Divide sign. What seemed to be most important was having a picture I could use to impress friends. The experience behind the picture was just a means to the end of being "cool" in the eyes of others. Navigating through this image-driven culture and existence I tend to want others to notice me, instead of taking time to appreciate the things that honestly merit attention.

The beauty of having to pedal a bicycle is you are always looking into the future. There is not much time to think about what happened in the past (whether good or bad), and within an hour I was laughing at the irony that there was no sign to cross the Continental Divide. Image-driven culture is very ironic.

Continental Divide or not, we were thrilled at how lucky we were for the entire day. We should have been drenched on numerous occasions by rainstorms to the east, west, and south. At one point there was a storm ahead dumping buckets of water travelling at exactly the same speed as us, and in the same direction. Although the road was inundated, we stayed completely dry.

We spent the night under a lean-to at the American Legion Park in the town of Wisdom. Before falling asleep I revisited every time we narrowly escaped storms headed our way. It seemed impossible. Then it all made sense: there was a priest on board. *They say you make your own luck. Thank you for coming along, Oliver.*

The temperature dipped below freezing at night to 28°F. Bundled up in my sleeping bag and warm clothing I was still cold. In the morning I woke to a drop of water landing directly on my nose. *The roof is leaking!* I thought. But it was just condensation on the ceiling from the moisture in our breath. I exhaled and watched as the wispy strands of airborne droplets curled and danced and faded into nothing.

Sounds of approaching footsteps interrupted the morning tranquility.

"Hello? Anyone there?" I questioned nervously.

I mustered up the courage to exit the relative warmth of my sleeping bag and peeked over the wall of the lean-to. Standing on the other side of a barbed wire fence, no more than five feet from my face, was a large heifer. She looked about as surprised to see me as I was her. A couple of her friends sauntered over to see what the hubbub was all about. I felt an odd sense of solidarity with the cows, having spent a night in the cold just like they did.

"It was heifer so cold last night, wasn't it, Betsy?"

She snorted, then stared back at me blankly. Curiosity does not kill too many cows. I again tried to break the ice.

"Yeah, I think I started shedding my winter coat a little soon, too."

The blank stare persisted.

"Why the silent treatment, Betsy?" I started to feel guilty for devouring a three-quarter pound hamburger the day before.

Spending the night in a lean-to on a cement floor after riding over one hundred miles did not refresh us in the way that a bed and apple pie can. Only nineteen miles down the road was the town of Jackson, Montana, home of (locally) famous hot springs. It all added up to a perfect easy day to relax.

There is not much to Montana's town of Jackson besides a few houses, a Mormon church, a mercantile store, and of course, the hot springs. We made a beeline directly to the front counter.

"So how much to use the hot springs?" Joe asked, resting his elbow on the counter. The woman behind the desk was on the back nine, her face a contorted mess of wrinkles that said she had dealt with one too many customers in her day. When she spoke her voice was raspy.

"Seven dollars a head to use the hot springs. Two-person rooms are forty-five dollars. If y'all want to camp, that'll be ten for the site plus ten a head." After a quick conference of the triumvirate Joe said,

"Alright, we'll take a two-person room," figuring an extra five dollars to get a bed for two and carpet for one was better than camping. Forty dollars to camp seemed ridiculous, anyway.

"You know only two people are allowed in the rooms," she responded in a tone that was more of a statement than question. Joe placed his elbow on the counter and negotiated,

"So... would there be a problem if an extra person just happened to show up?"

"Sorry, rules are rules," the woman stated plainly.

"Listen," Joe lowered his voice, "is there any way we can slip you a little extra tip and you just happen to look the other way, if you know what I—"

"—You heard me. Rules are rules. Now what can I do for you?"

"Nothing, I guess." Joe was noticeably disappointed.

"Alright, you folks have a nice day now." There was ice water in those words. I walked out the door with a sour taste in my mouth.

"Whaddaya think was wrong with her?" Joe inquired.

"I dunno. All I know is that this is highway robbery. Forty bucks, to camp?!" Oliver added. My eyes were drifting towards the Mormon church up the street. There was a truck and a civil-looking man working on the church's fence. Within five minutes I had obtained permission to camp on the church grounds for free, by asking nicely and being respectful.

I walked back to Joe and Oliver, who were still talking about how frustrated they were.

"Guys, don't worry."

"Don't worry about what?" Joe.

"Just don't worry. We've got a place to crash tonight. Just say thanks to the Mormons for this one."

"You are the man," said Oliver. And so we paraded triumphantly back to the hot springs counter.

"We'll take a *day* pass for the hot springs apiece, please."

"That'll be twenty-one dollars." It was as if she was immune to emotion.

Interesting people show up at hot springs. We were reclining in lounge chairs, working to tan the areas of our bodies that don't get too much sun in biking attire. I got up and was gone for five minutes. When I came back outside there was a man staring at a sleeping Oliver and Joe from the pool, not more than seven feet from them. One elbow and arm was resting on the side of the pool. He was rocking back and forth slightly. The strangest part was there was nobody else in the entire pool area. It wasn't like he was forced to plant himself close and stare directly at them.

I was uncomfortable, and what do uncomfortable people do? They talk about the weather.

"Great day out today, isn't it?" I said. The man was startled.

"Oh, uh, yeah. Sun is great," came his choppy response. By this time Joe and Oliver had woken up and rolled over to face our company. They did not have the slightest clue he had been staring at them.

"So where are you from?" Oliver asked.

"Bozeman…" and so on and so forth. Our new friend was named Sebastian and was a potter by trade. He said his work is highly renowned and is sold in places like Yellowstone and Jackson, Wyoming. He was travelling west to visit his daughter on the Hood River in Western Oregon.

"How long have you been driving?"

"Well, today I had been at it two hours and decided to call it quits here because of the hot springs. I hear there are some in Lolo so I am going to end up there tomorrow. And I always wanted to try a hot springs in Idaho…"

"Hold on. How many days is it going to take you to get to Oregon?"

"I was planning on about five." Sebastian was obsessed with hot springs. He was going to visit his daughter for a weekend, but was taking five days to get there. To me, it begged the question: is it about your daughter or the hot springs? Later, at dinner, a lonely and intoxicated Sebastian joined our table.

"You know, what you guys are doing is pretty cool," he drawled. "Hey," a sly look came over his round face. It was humorous because his eyes could not focus. He then he continued: "how you all getting back home? You gonna ride?" He smiled and was looking pleased with himself. We acknowledged his joke with a smile and a nod.

The only thing that made talking with Sebastian bearable was the delicious bison burger I was in the process of eating.

Out of the blue another man came up and started talking to us. He looked about sixty, with a hollowed and weather-worn face. His hair was gray and his chin was covered in motley stubble. When h spoke, he sounded exactly like Sean Connery.

"I made the most incredible discovery today!" he began, before even introducing himself. "Submarines! I discovered submarines!" At this point I thought this man was crazy. The Scottish accent did not help his case. But he was undeterred, and continued:

"They are the greatest thing ever. And *huge!* Did I mention cheap?! I got one for five dollars at, uh, how do you call it…" I was clueless, but Joe had been following him from the start.

"At Subway!" he echoed, with the same enthusiasm as our new friend.

"Yes, Subway! I couldn't even finish the thing. So guess what: I wrapped it up and am saving it for tomorrow! Oh, you fellers are the ones with the bikes out back, right?"

"Yeah, that's us," we all agreed. The man held out his hand.

"Peter MacDonough's the name. Pleased to meet you. Mind if I sit?"

"No, not at all," Oliver said.

We were already four people sitting at a four-person table, so we had to make some space. Over the next hour we were enlightened to the experience known as Peter MacDonough. He came from Scotland to ride his bike across the United States. He had already been at it for two weeks, and was going to continue alone until the Atlantic Ocean. We swapped stories and he spoke of how deeply touched he had been by the kindness and generosity of every single person encountered on the way.

"Why in the world did you decide to do this?" Sebastian piped in, a bit intrusively. Peter immediately turned somber.

"Me wife was diagnosed with dementia in 1999 and passed away in 2005. It was the hardest thing in my life to see my own wife look at me with a blank look on her face. My mum slowly started showing signs of Alzheimer's ten years back and has been in an assisted care facility since last year. I finally decided that this is something I need to do. Now I am raising money in support of Alzheimer Scotland and trying to use this trip as a way to spread awareness of how terrible it is and how much support is needed for both those suffering from dementia and their caregivers."

I was speechless. Peter opened the window to his heart and it was an incredible sight.

"So, where are yew lads sleeping tonight?" he finally asked, apparently not nearly as affected by his own words as we were. He followed us to the Mormon church and pitched his tent alongside ours. The next morning just before parting ways, he left us with motivating words that have stuck with me ever since.

"If yew dream of something, don't wait for tomorrow to make it happen. Just go dew it."

Chapter FIVE

Jackson, MT to Yellowstone Nat'l Park

SALON DOORS SWUNG WIDE OPEN and the silhouettes of three dusty, weather-worn cowboys stood in the doorway. The trio took metered steps forward into the light. They walked in unison, hips swaying gently and shoulders see-sawing confidently back and forth. Their bicycle cleats tapped out a subtle clickety-clack rhythm on the floorboards.

The sound almost passed for spurs on cowboy boots.

Joe meandered his way up to the bar. The dark wooden walls were covered in antique decorations alluding to a frontier rancher past. The venue was void of patrons, save for one couple sitting at the bar who had already had much too much to drink.

"We'll have pasties, please. One apiece," Joe said with an air of haughtiness that I did not hear very often.

"Joe, what in the world are pasties?" I asked when he sat down at the table.

"You shall see, unenlightened one."

"Genuine, blue-collar Montana tradition," Oliver began to explain, impatient with Joe's sudden air of haughtiness. I realized I was flanked by two Montana diehards who bleed Big-Sky blue.

"Goes back to the mining days over a century ago," Joe said in a didactic tone. "The men going to work all day digging for gold would put these things in their pockets until it was time to eat them for lunch. So they had to be durable and filling to satisfy the miner appetite."

"…So what exactly are they?" I inquired.

"Right. Cross a meat pie with a calzone and you have got yourself a pasty."

I could not come up with a better description. Our server brought out three large wads of what looked like solid dough. But a single bite was all it took to reveal the delicious and hearty treasure inside. The mining lifestyle had to be more tolerable walking around with pasties in hand.

On this particular night Joe, Oliver, and I quit in Virginia City, Montana after riding 114 miles. The history of the once-bustling town of 10,000 is steeped in mining, beginning when gold was discovered in nearby Alder Creek in 1863. Now the population hovers around 130 and the largest draw for the settlement is tourism. The nearby waterways, including Alder Creek, bear the permanent scars of dredging. Tons of overturned earth lined the streambeds as a reminder of prosperity's past.

Outside it was drizzling and the temperature was approaching freezing. I did not want to leave the warm confines of the restaurant but we could not stay there forever. The female member of the tipsy couple across the bar offered a suggestion.

"Why don't you just head on over to the Episcopal church up the road a few blocks? It's really big so you can't miss it. And they never lock it."

"Do you know the pastor or someone in the church we can talk to?" Oliver asked.

"Oh no, but I'm sure they would say it's totally fine. Small town, you know," she clucked.

"So we just walk up and go in?" Joe did not sound convinced, either.

"Well, that's normally what I do when I want to get into a building."

We found the church exactly as she said it would be. A side door led down to the basement, where two foldable tables set up in longitudinal fashion gave the impression of a meeting hall. Completing the arrangement was a small kitchen and restroom in an adjacent room. It was almost too good to be true.

Half an hour later we had unpacked our sleeping bags, changed into street clothes, hung up wet spandex to dry, and were readying to hunker down for the night. Our belongings were strewn out across the entire floor looking as if we owned the place. I was finishing up reading a few pages in my book when I heard a loud "knock knock!" on the door.

My blood froze.

The same side door we used to enter squeaked slowly open. As it did I could hear the *thud, thud, thud* of my heart pounding in my ears. And then the tension left my body in an instant; it was just our friend from the bar. Her hair had become more frumpled since we parted ways at the saloon and she held a can of Pabst Blue Ribbon in her hand.

"Just figured I would check in on you guys!" She said rather loudly. "I see you found the place. You going to be alright?"

"Ye-ah," I responded. My voice cracked. "I think we're going to be fine."

The following evening we again found ourselves in a restaurant making conversation with local residents. Again were offered a place to spend the night. This time it was Butch, the motel owner in West Yellowstone, who gave us a one-night stay in his motel for five dollars apiece.

It was high time to wash clothes, so we set about town trying to find a laundry mat before returning to Butch's motel. It did not take long to locate one, and soon quarters were jingling and the machines were spinning.

As I sat there waiting for laundry I stared idly at two large industrial dryers not in use.

"...Do you think?" I said aimlessly.

"Think what?" Joe responded. But I was already inside one of the dryers spinning cartwheels.

Riding in the dryer was the closest I have ever come to being in outer space.

I used to think concepts such as generosity and goodwill were so far removed from everyday reality that they might as well exist in outer space. Five bucks and a motel owner named Butch were now telling me otherwise. I bet there is a lot of generosity and goodwill up there in outer space. But there is also a lot down here on Earth. The problem is that many people manage to live their entire life without ever experiencing it.

We were lucky to have so much benevolence come our way, but that is not always the way it goes. Touring cyclists advanced in years often made remarks about how it seemed people looked at them suspiciously on account of their mature age and scraggly beards. I guess we had youth on our side. Also, there were some situations (including the one with Butch) that I would have avoided had I been female.

Then there can be ulterior motives behind acts of goodwill and generosity. At least there was with Butch. We gradually meandered our way back from the outskirts of town to the motel. Turning the corner into the parking lot we were startled by Butch's voice coming from the garage.

"We was wondering when you was goin' get back," he said. That struck me as an odd greeting from a motel owner. His voice held a deliberate tone indicative of extreme intoxication. A friend who was with him at bar, now equally drunk, chimed in:

"Yeah, where was you doin'? Chasin' girls, or lightin' your farts on fire?"

"Neither, actually," Oliver replied. "We got some ice cream and did our laundry."

The uninteresting and highly plausible nature of Oliver's response caught both of them off guard.

"Well, you want to play a game?" Butch asked, stumbling out of his chair and slapping Joe on the back. He didn't give anyone a chance to respond before blurting, "Foosball. We're gonna play foosball."

Teams were selected and sides chosen. Luckily I was the fifth man and sat out. My atrocious Foosball skills would have been ill-suited in the West Yellowstone Cup.

Butch and Oliver squared off against Joe and Butch's friend, Frank. Within two minutes of kickoff it became clear Oliver had withheld a key piece of his life from us. He was a wizard at the table, a Foosball virtuoso. And Butch loved every second of it, frequently interjecting with crass and insensitive comments.

"Oh, yeah baby! You see that one go in?! Your goalie is useless like your girlfriend was for me last night. Haha! Is that all you got? Go ahead and start trying now."

And that was just the first game. After Team Vulgar won by a score of 10-2 both Oliver and Joe stepped back from the table, thinking the formality was finished and we would be allowed to retire to our bedroom and catch some much-needed shut eye. Unfortunately that was not the case.

"Again!" Butch shouted.

"Yeah, c'mon buddy! Let's not let 'em steamroll us this time!" Frank yelled encouragingly at Joe.

Fearing our fifteen-dollar good fortune was in jeopardy, Joe and Oliver obliged and stepped up to the table once again. At times it is necessary to strike a balance between the expectations of others and one's own incompatible intentions.

Frank dropped the ball into play. Round and round the players spun to the tune of Butch's gloating. After snapping some rather humorous photos of our new friends playing Foosball, I began to walk around the garage. It was a large space with white walls. There was stuff everywhere. Snowmobiles, refrigerators, a pile of wood, and what looked like a bar table off to one end. The crowning piece to the ensemble was a human-sized inflatable resembling a bottle of Jagermeister.

"Whoohoo! Winners again!" Without looking I knew who it was. The door between the lobby and garage opened, and a rather unhappy-looking woman poked her head around the corner. I guessed that it had to be Butch's wife, working the late shift at the lobby table.

"Butch! You be quiet now. The customers will be kept awake by all this racket."

"Yeah, sure, whatever."

The door shut with an emphatic *slam!* The volume returned to its previous level within minutes. Joe and Oliver were not going to get off playing only two games of foosball. I continued wandering around the garage and started reading the (literal) writing on the wall. It was covered with messages like:

"Thanks Butch! Best parties in West Yellowstone ever! Love: Donna, Michelle, and Kirsten."

"Butch = party animal. Golden West motel = the shit."

"Butch you are the man! Thanks for the good time, mate. From: your Australian brothers."

When he offered us a room so cheaply, Butch was really looking for some party buds. I do not blame him—there is not a whole lot happening in West Yellowstone in the month of May. After an playing an hour without losing a single game, Butch finally stepped back from the table and said,

"Alright, time for some halftime refreshments! So who wants a shot?"

"You know I do pardner!" Frank was quick to reply.

"Maybe a bit later for me, but thanks Butch," Joe kindly declined.

"Yeah, I think I am gonna sit this one out, too." Oliver was equally as unenthusiastic about the possibility of a wild night.

"You folks sure? This one's on me."

"Yep, we are sure."

"More for me, I guess..." He opened the freezer and pulled out a bottle of Jagermeister, pouring generous shots for himself and Frank.

"To a good time! Let's party!" he said and tilted the glass back. Without missing a beat he continued, "Man! I am hungry. Let's get some food goin' in here!"

Joe had the misfortune of standing close to the fridge. Butch threw open the door and pulled out a package of boneless ribs. They were the instant kind claiming to be ready in three minutes right out of the package, the kind that make me wonder from what kind of monster the meat actually came. Joe was tasked with cooking the ribs. Butch dove back into the fridge and started tossing out packages of chicken wings and lasagna, which Oliver and I deftly caught until our hands were full.

He emerged with two packages of egg rolls in his hands.

"I tell you what," he said somberly. "I'll make you three another offer. One that you can't refuse. I know you're thinking you don't want to stay up too late tonight because you have to get back on the road tomorrow..." His voice became louder and mouth broke into a huge grin. "...But you stay up tonight and *rage* with us, sleep in, and stick around tomorrow. Room tomorrow night is free. So let's *party!*"

I had never been asked to "rage" by a man in his fifties.

"Listen, Butch," Joe began, "we have had a really good time tonight. Thanks for everything. But we are here to ride bicycles. We aren't going to party with you or anyone tonight, and it is probably best that we get a move on over to bed soon."

It finally occurred to Butch that we were not going to succumb to his rambunctious intentions that night. I was silently cheering Joe on with every word he said. The time for sleep had long passed. We quickly signed our names on the wall, shook hands, and walked through the (still open) garage door with a cooked package of insta-ribs in hand. I swear I saw one of those ribs wiggle like it were still alive.

"Guys, I forgot my backpack in the garage," said Oliver.

"It seems like the logical solution would be to go get it." Joe said.

"Yeah…" his voice trailed off. He turned around, entered the garage briefly, and remerged with pack on shoulder. "That was awkward," he said when we were safely sound-proofed in our room.

"What was awkward?" I asked.

"Oh, nothing…" I guess sometimes things are so traumatizing they are better left unspoken.

In the morning we had to say goodbye to Oliver. He was a groomsman in a wedding and needed to get back home for the bachelor party. It was a bummer for us, but something we always knew was going to happen when he showed up in Joe's aunt and uncle's driveway in Missoula.

"O-to-the-Liver," as Joe called him affectionately, "you take care of yourself now."

And that was that. Oliver's brother picked Oliver up in a beaten minivan and the two sped away while Joe and I continued our ride towards Yellowstone National Park. It was not long before we reached the "Welcome to Yellowstone" sign, snapped a picture, and rolled up to the toll booth at the entrance to the park.

"Ten dollars, please. Each of you." The voice coming from the other side of the glass was expressionless. I was dumbfounded. *I'm going to be here for four hours, and you want me to spend ten dollars so I can ride my bike on the side of the road?!*

In 1872, President Ulysses S. Grant signed the act of Congress that brought the 2.2 million acre Yellowstone National Park into being. However, the park's history began many years before its official existence. Native American tribes such as the Crow, Shoshone, and Nez Perce had already been around for thousands of years when the first white explorers and trappers began to trickle into the area in the early nineteenth century. The earliest evidence of human occupation dates 11,000 ago. Before official geological surveys commissioned by the government in 1869, the general American public did not believe a place such as Yellowstone could exist. The "tall tales" of erupting rivers, steaming lakes, boiling mud, and petrified trees told by the likes of mountain man Jim Bridger failed to captivate a skeptical citizenry.

The early history of the park is a feel-good story gone awry. A writer named Cornelius Hedges, among others, proposed the area be set aside as a reserve protected from human development. Those sentiments were echoed by many of the early visitors to the area, who feared the pristine and fascinating wonders would be destroyed if humans were left to their own devices. Instead of succumbing to the pressures of tycoons thirsting for Yellowstone's vast natural resources, Congress declared firmly that the lands be "dedicated and set apart as a public park or pleasuring ground for the benefit and enjoyment of the people."

The declaration was not realized instantly; between 1872 and 1886 poaching laws were largely ignored and vandalism ran rampant. In 1886 the Army took on the role of overseeing the park. During thirty years of oversight the Army developed and enforced policies which allowed the public to access and enjoy the land while protecting the ecological health of the area. The Army finally relinquished control of Yellowstone to the civilian National Park Service in 1918.

Over the years, Yellowstone has been the subject of much controversy. Fire management policies of the National Park Service came under, well, fire, after the blazes during the summer of 1988 roasted 36% of the park lands. To the dismay of neighboring ranchers, wolves were reintroduced to the park in 1995. Use of snowmobiles in the park has been hotly contested since the 1960s, when it was reported that air quality in the park nearly violated the Clean Air Act due to snowmobile emissions. At times the air quality in Yellowstone was worse than downtown Los Angeles!

As a federally funded operation, Yellowstone and other national parks are constantly struggling to stay afloat and provide adequate services to park-goers.

What is fuss over, really? Absolutely magnificent and unabated natural beauty. After just minutes in the park, ten dollars seemed like a reasonable price to pay. The roads were extremely well-maintained, weaving between river valleys and cresting bluffs overlooking snow-dusted meadows and canyons. Taking it in from an unobstructed vantage point atop a bicycle at a slow pace of fourteen miles per hour made the experience all the sweeter.

At one point I was startled by a rustling noise in the trees not more than five yards off the road. Instinctively, my head swiveled to the right and my eyes met those belonging to a gargantuan buffalo camouflaged in the trees.

"Joe!" I shouted, "I just stared last nights' dinner in the eyes."

Ironically, Yellowstone can be an awful place to ride a bicycle. During peak season the roads are jam-packed with tourists from all around the world more concerned with spotting an elk in the trees than watching where they drive. Luckily for us, we happened upon the park early in the season. Lingering snow cover in May keeps away most visitors until at least Memorial Day, but still some brave souls planned their park visit to coincide with our trip.

Homo sapiens have got to look ridiculous in the eyes of other animals, especially in Yellowstone. Driving extra-slow, the slightest rustle of leaves in the distance can trigger an observer to pull their car aside and stand with eyes peeled for other animal species that are quite frankly uninterested in anything human. All it takes is one car to pull over and then *everyone* has to stop and get out of their cars to see if there is a creature to be seen.

I can imagine what Bullwinkle the Moose and Yogi Bear would do if they were somewhere in the park.

"Alright, five bucks—I mean dollars—say our theatrics will cause at least one car accident," Bullwinkle would wager.

"You've got a deal. But if you lose, you have to serve as a decoy while I raid the picnic baskets up at the Lewis Lake Campground."

"Yogi, you drive a bear of a bargain."

"What can I say? I don't horse around. Now on the count of three, you jump out from behind this rock and take off running across this here meadow. I'll give you a five second head start. Once you get to that rock over there out of sight, we can stop and catch our breath. There should be a perfect view so we can see the vehicular carnage."

"You are a devil."

"No dear Rocky, I am but a created being. Some call me a visionary. I just like to think I put the 'wild' in *wild*life."

"So what was the plan again?"

"You moose never learn. Just run on the count of three. One… Two… Three!"

To find the most concentrated population of vertebrates in Yellowstone National Park one has to look no further than Old Faithful, the most famous geyser in Yellowstone and I would imagine therefore the world. It was named in 1870 by members of the Washburn Expedition, a month-long effort of a group of Montana residents to explore the region that would later be incorporated as

Yellowstone National Park. In the early years, before park regulations and the environmental conscience, the geyser served as a laundry machine. Clothes placed in the geyser's mouth were expelled by the steamy eruption and emerged completely clean.

Old Faithful erupts about every ninety minutes. It is not the most spectacular of the park's geysers. That distinction belongs to Steamboat Geyser, the largest in the park. The problem is that Steamboat Geyser has erupted a mere eight times since 2005 and was dormant for a full fifty years between 1911 and 1961. Unsurprisingly, park visitors do not line up to ogle the Steamboat.

Consistency as embodied by Old Faithful has a way of sedating. Consistency convinces one that reliable mediocrity is palatable and even desirable compared to the fear of being disappointed.

We made it to the geyser site with a few minutes to spare. It erupted right on schedule, just like it has for only God knows how long. A crowd of hundreds beheld the spectacle along with us. It was an average eruption by Old Faithful standards.

Watching the geyser is like watching reruns of *Seinfeld*. Everyone already knows the punch line. But the laughing-track crowd always seems to be amused well enough, and Old Faithful is no different. I rode away from watching the geyser satisfied in the same way that watching reruns is satisfying. But is this type of satisfaction everything, or is there something more to it?

Many people become content with "satisfied" instead of striving for "enchanted" and "awestruck." Being satisfied is easy and reliable and scripted, like Old Faithful and *Seinfeld*. But it seems to me there is more to Life than only watching reruns. There is more than routine geyser eruptions. There are a whole lot of experiences out there to be had, so many that doing it all is impossible. If I find myself living a life that has already been lived, I am a prodigal son wasting away my inheritance. I might as well stop calling it "living" and refer to it by its true name: decomposing.

On the other hand, when curiosity drives me to ask a "what if?" question and I commit to see where the answer takes me, that is really living. Contrary to popular belief it does not cost very much.

Enchanted and awestruck—that is what two wheels, five dollars, and a cheap motel can get you these days.

Chapter SIX

Yellowstone Nat'l Park to Saratoga, WY

"Joe, I'M DREAMING TONIGHT WE end up with a roof over our heads and pillows under them. Maybe a shower too. Think that is too much to ask?"

Yellowstone was in the rearview mirror and we were riding across central Wyoming—exposed, barren, and angry central Wyoming. The sun was shining weakly between gaps in the clouds, but that would not be the case for much longer. The wish list of showers and pillows was a way to deflect the anxiety about the solid wall of gray-black clouds looming on the horizon.

At a fork in the road Joe stopped to double-check the map. Yes, we had to take the right-hand turn angling straight into the storm. The clouds hung there beckoning, daring us to move forward.

"You want to ride across the whole country?" they taunted. "You're going to have to go through us first!" Watching a plains storm materialize before my very eyes *knowing* there is no escape is one of the most intimidating things I have ever experienced.

All at once it was upon us. Visibility dropped to nearly zero. The wind picked up and howled in my ears. Within seconds the road was inundated with standing water and fenders were rendered useless against the watery onslaught. My shoes squished and my pants plastered to my legs. Water dripped down my forehead and off my nose. The one item that worked to my favor was a technical mountaineering jacket from Mountain Hardware. I was thankful my core remained moderately damp instead of soaked.

I looked up at the sight that was Joe and could not hold back a chuckle, despite the nasty weather. Instead bringing a quality rain jacket, he elected a (very permeable) windbreaker, poncho, and shower cap. The windbreaker went on first, followed by the poncho. The poncho hood he wore underneath his helmet and stuck out like the bill of a hat. The shower cap went over the top of his helmet. It all gave him the look of a super hero in costume; the poncho flapped in the wind like a cape and the hood worn under the helmet blocked all view of his eyes. As for the shower cap, it was just icing on the cake. He was a real-life Darkwing Duck. How he managed to see anything—let alone ride a bike through a rain storm—was far beyond me.

The storm's fury persisted half an hour longer than I would have preferred.

When we pulled in to the gas station in a town called Fort Washakie two hours later my shoes were still sopping wet. People talk about "getting cold feet" and "one's feet wet." I for one prefer the former rather than the latter. Wet feet are about the most uncomfortable thing I know. After being soaked for eight hours, the soles of my feet were so pruny they blistered from rubbing up against themselves. Cold feet, on the other hand, go numb and that is about all you hear from them.

Wet feet and all, we walked into the gas station and perused the aisles for sustenance. In one refrigerated aisle my eyes were immediately drawn to the "Mondo Burrito XXL." It was wrapped in psychedelic purple, orange, and yellow tin foil. Nothing suggested any shred of nutritional value. On the contrary, I thought about the consequences: high sodium and bad gas.

I have been sweating like Richard Simmons at a hot yoga session, so maybe I could use some extra salts... I looked over at Joe *...And I don't have to smell me; he does.* The best part about the burrito? It cost one dollar and seventy-nine cents.

Another two hours went by and it became apparent the burrito was a dollar-and-seventy-nine-cent mistake. My insides were rumbling like a '69 Mustang. It was too much to bear, so I shifted my weight in the saddle and blew off some steam. I heard Joe choke behind me.

"What the hell was that?!" he screamed. "Man, I could *taste* it. Do you mind giving me a warning next time?"

"Sorry, didn't mean to fumigate you..."

Joe and I spent every waking hour with each other. I knew by heart every one of his favorite phrases, eccentricities, and what he sounds like talking with his mouth full. Despite the fact that we were around each other twenty-four seven, we never got on each other's nerves. Never did a misunderstanding become malignant or blown out of proportion. The average person does not eat flatulence and have a good attitude about it. One would expect the figurative air to need clearing in a situation such as this, but not with Joe. There was something special about our dynamic that I cannot precisely identify. It might boil down to having a shared goal that we needed each other to accomplish.

People asked how we got through frustrating times. The best and only answer is smiling and laughing. It was a conscious choice we made every day. Being able to laugh off anything and everything made even the most disheartening and desperate situations manageable. In extreme cases it was necessary to bring out Burt Bacharach. "Raindrops keep fallin' on my head, but that doesn't mean my eyes will soon be turning red…"

Our next stop was Lander, Wyoming. The only places in the Cowboy State I knew previously were Yellowstone and Grand Teton National Park. Talk to just about anyone and they will tell you there is *nothing* else in Wyoming worth seeing, but travelling through central Wyoming on Highway 287 proved that notion wrong. I was pleasantly surprised by the rolling hills, red cliffs, and green trees lining the route.

We had yet to figure out where we would be sleeping.

"Excuse me sir, this is going to sound random…" I began telling our story to a passerby on the street.

"Hmm, let me see," said the man, lips pursed in thought. "Nope. Can't think of anyone who can help you out."

"Well can you at least recommend a good place to get some grub?" I pleaded.

"Sorry, I have no idea."

We stared blankly for a few quiet seconds.

"Wait, I know. Go to the Gannett Grill. They have good burgers. Just go up two blocks, take a left, and it'll be on your left."

At the very least our acquaintance tipped us off to a great place to eat. Despite the fact that this was the tenth burger in two weeks, Joe and I grabbed a corner table at the bar and happily went to work. Although the food was pleasurable distraction, the thought of spending the night on the street bugged me. I told Joe as much.

"Don't worry about it, Skip," he said with green pepper and feta cheese falling out of his mouth, "somethin's gonna happen. It's *got* to happen." I wanted to believe him, but my soul was shrouded in doubt.

Sure enough, within five minutes a lone man holding a beer came up to us and started chatting away.

"Where you folks coming from? Seattle? No shit! Where did you start this morning? Dubois! That is a long ways—you must be all kinds of sore." And so the conversation continued for some five minutes.

His name was Mitch. In grimy construction clothes, and with hair in a loose pony tail that terminated at the small of his back, his appearance did little to put us at ease. That he was alone did not help, either.

The more we talked, the more my initial impression of him proved wrong. He was just off from a hard day of construction and came to grab a fermented beverage before heading home to his wife and kids. He showed himself to be educated and personable.

"I used to own a bike shop with my brother in Casper," he recounted. "We were doing damn well. He still runs it. My wife and I moved up here when she found a job opening as the director of the Lander Art Center here. Those kinds of opportunities are hard to come by, so we decided she had to jump on it."

"It had to be hard to let go of the shop."

"You know, nothing about the whole ordeal was too bad. I still get updates about how the shop is doing. And the move was easy. Well, most everything was easy besides moving the teepee."

"Hold on, did you just say 'teepee?'"

I was baffled. First I thought this guy was going to be crazy. Then I began to believe otherwise when he started talking to us about having a family and owning a bike shop. But now I could not help but regress to my previous suspicions.

"Yessiree-bob, eighteen feet tall and floor space is ten feet across. You can fit a bed, a stove, and a rug in there and still have room in the middle so your head doesn't touch the ceiling. Well, I guess I wouldn't call it a ceiling..."

"So do you, err, live in this teepee?" At this question Mitch smiled.

"Do I look crazy to you? Naw, I don't live in it; we just have it pitched in the yard." *That is good, I was wondering for a second.* "Say, speaking of teepees, you two found anywhere to stay tonight?"

It was the golden question.

"Why don't you just come on down to our digs and we'll see what we can do for you. We're the grey house at the corner of Beverly and Third."

With that, Mitch bode us a temporary farewell and proceeded home. Joe and I finished up our hamburgers in silence, contemplating the complete randomness of our encounter with Mitch. We paid for our food then exited, anxious to see this teepee in person.

There are not many houses with teepees in the front yard, so finding Mitch's home was easy. We dismounted our bikes and I walked up the stairs to the porch and knocked on the screen door. Everything was quiet for a second, then the door swung open with a jerk.

"I was wondering when you were gonna find us. C'mon in."

I anticipated a house with chipped paint and flowers growing out of a rusted pickup truck in the backyard, but once again my preconceived notions were ill-founded. Everything was normal, if normal actually exists. The inside of the house was gorgeous. Beautiful paintings of landscapes, flowers, and children at play were complemented by handsome cabinets and counters. Some homes emit an aura of enthusiasm and life, and this was one of them.

We were introduced to his wife, Wendy, who happened to be the formal cause of all of the paintings in the house. His two boys, Kramer and Fletcher, made themselves scarce. Fletcher was young, and I think when I went up to give him a high-five he about wet his pants in fear. Kramer just turned thirteen and was in a rebellious stage. He quickly said "hi" and returned to his room, I suspect to text message his love interests.

"I went out to the teepee to check things out for you guys, but we haven't been out there to clean it since winter let up. I am going to put you two in our guest bedroom. Hope that's alright." I was a little disappointed, if only because spending the night in a teepee would make for a cool story to write about in a book. However, the dangerously comfortable guest bed more than made up for any reservations.

When we emerged from the guestroom Mitch was blowing dust off the cover of a faded old book. It was a first edition print of *Around the World on a Bicycle,* the book Thomas Stevens wrote after being the first to ride a bicycle around the world. I felt an odd sort of connection to this long-dead man, until I remembered his journey was completed in 1887 atop an "ordinary" bicycle (with an enormous front tire and without a chain) on unpaved roads. He would look at the relative luxury in which Joe and I traveled and scoff.

Mitch flipped open to a passage detailing a brief run-in between Stevens and some locals in the Middle East, who did not stop bothering him until he fired some shots from his pistol in the air. At this point it dawned on me that we were nowhere near as sensational or "hard-core" as our bicycle-touring predecessor. Riding atop wonderfully crafted machines on paved roads suddenly seemed rather pedestrian.

Just before I crashed out on the guest bed Joe said matter-of-factly,

"Scott, today we learned a very important lesson: if you stop dreaming I will slap you." I remembered back to when I dreamt about a roof, pillow, and shower earlier in the day. Dreams come true sometimes, even though it may be necessary to ride through a storm before they do.

Although the time spent with Mitch and Wendy was short, I left their home feeling like family. The difference between them and others was how open and candid they were with us, allowing a genuine glimpse into their lives. Mitch did not hesitate to share his authentic self, even on the porch getting ready to leave.

"Yeah, sometimes people look at my long hair and don't take me seriously. My dad hated it. But here's my opinion: screw them! I don't really care what anyone thinks who judges on appearance anyway."

Lander was the city of faulty first impressions. I am embarrassed at how easy it was for me to judge people and places based on hearsay and outer appearance. I am also undeservedly lucky in that I got to see just how wrong my stereotypes were. This happened because I was blessed by individuals who were willing to share their authentic selves with me, a complete stranger. Authenticity has a way of destroying stereotypes. A week after saying goodbye, Wendy sent me an email that said,

"We were excited to have you over to our house because we wanted Kramer and Fletcher to be exposed to what you are doing, so that they will be inspired to go out and invent adventures of their own." Mitch and Wendy get it. I thought about how oblivious Kramer seemed towards his marvelous parents. *One day, Kramer, you will see how lucky you are to have a mother and father who love you enough to encourage you to think for yourself.*

As we left Lander, Mitch left us with a few last words of advice: "Get on the road and do not stop until Rawlins, because there is nothing in those 120 miles 'sides a coupla skinny cows and enough tumbleweed to build a bonfire the size of Texas."

"Joe, I think Mitch was right," I said as we plodded into Rawlins that evening, 120 miles later. There really was almost nothing on the portion of highway connecting Lander and Rawlins. The scenery was so yawn-inducing I nearly fell asleep riding.

The sun was setting and cast a golden glow on what would otherwise be an unattractive assortment of mobile homes, warehouses, and fast food restaurants.

"We rode 120 miles today for *this*?" was all Joe could say in response.

Rawlins was named after an Army general who passed through the area with a survey team establishing the route for the first transcontinental railroad. Over the years the city has also found itself on the Overland Trail, Oregon Trail, Mormon Trail, and Lincoln Highway. Now the major trail passing through the city is a four-lane divided highway that goes by the name "Interstate 80."

The visionary behind the interstate system was President Dwight D. Eisenhower, whose signature on the Federal-Aid Highway Act of 1956 authorized $25 billion to create a system of linked superhighways across the country. Aside from being one of the largest accomplishments of Eisenhower's presidency, the interstate project has been termed the greatest public works project in history.

The interstate system revolutionized American life. It is known to many Americans as the route to work, the airport, and just about everywhere else. Most every item available at the grocery store travelled in a semi-truck on the interstate. The network of interstate freeways also plays essential roles in national defense and evacuations due to natural disasters. Easy automobile travel on the interstate affects the lifestyle Americans lead. Efficient and accessible highways have facilitated suburban expansion and the spread-out nature of many of the nation's cities.

The cynic will now point out the dark side of interstate culture. It tends to erase local identity in favor of established culture. Familiar entities such as McDonald's, Taco Bell, Denny's, and Best Western are easily distinguished at intersections by their tall neon signs, but local small businesses are sparse. After a cursory glance at interstate culture, it seems the quest for familiarity and ultimate efficiency is drowning the idea of small business in a triple-shot non-fat two-pumps-vanilla extra-hot latte from Starbucks.

There Joe and I were, two starving travelers taking a pit stop at Interstatesville, U.S.A. *I have been here before*, I thought. *No wait, can't be; last time the Burger King was on the left and the McDonald's was on the right. Must have been a different exit.* I sniffed the air. They say smell is more closely tied to memory than other senses. The suspicious-yet-alluring odor of Big Macs and French fries filled my nostrils and I was home.

"Joe, I would kill for a McFlurry right now."

"Your wish is my command," he replied, beckoning me towards the golden arches.

"Alright, Genie," I concluded our impulse decision with the usual banter.

That Oreo and ice cream concoction tickled my taste buds in ways they are rarely tickled. Forbidden fruit is always the sweetest.

We began to chat it up with other restaurant patrons about such non-intrusive topics such as local churches and fire stations, not informing them we planned on pitching a tent in the back yard. The only problem was nobody in the entire restaurant was from Rawlins.

"Wow, that's incredible! But no, sorry, I don't know anything. We're just passing through on the way to my parents' house in Utah. But you goin' to D.C., and then what? You gonna ride home, too? Haha." We moved on to the next table.

"Nope don't know a thing about this place. I'm from Sacramento." Third time the charm? Think again.

"What is this town called again? Ralfings? Isn't that a bit nasty to name a town after vomit?" What could ever be behind door number four?

"Right on, man. Ridin' to the Atlantic. That has gotta be one far-out experience." *Excuse me, sir, but we asked you a question.* "Oh yeah. Sorry bro, I've got no info for ya. Hey, you figure out how you're gettin' home? You gonna ride back t…"

Before we let any other passer-by make a joke about riding back home we escaped from the restaurant and set about finding a place to call our temporary home for the evening. The whole place seemed fleetingly alive, as if the city could disappear tomorrow if traffic from the interstate were to dry up.

"I see some steeples over there," Joe said, "let's go check it out."

It was a Catholic church. Always a good sign, because that meant there would be a rectory and—we could only hope—a priest who lived on church grounds.

Joe walked up to the door and knocked. Nothing. After a minute he knocked more forcefully. Still nothing. I walked around the building and did not see a single light or shred of intelligent life.

"I've got an idea…" There was a twang of mischief in his voice. "Bring your bike and follow me. But move quickly because we don't want too many people to have the chance to see us."

Within minutes we had pitched the tent in the side yard of the rectory under cover of a waist-high fence and tree-bushy-thing. From the road we were hardly visible.

"This is the first time I have ever stealth camped."

"Yeah, me too."

I went to bed that night thinking about what I would say if I were startled awake by a police officer shaking the tent. My sleep that night was fitful at best. But if it were not for the smelly, snoring, farting body to my left I probably would not have slept at all. Joe had almost been incorporated as part of my being, and I leaned on him when I was uncomfortable or unsure of myself. Spending a night as a vagrant was one of those times.

Luckily, no police officers bothered us that night and we woke up early the next morning to pack up before anyone would show up at the church. My back developed a gnarly knot during the dark hours of tossing and turning. Incognito camping is not something I particularly enjoy.

There was no love lost when we packed up the tent and departed Rawlins the next morning. Fittingly, our route led us down the interstate for twenty miles. Those were some of the windiest, bleakest, and least interesting miles of the entire trip. When we turned south off of I-80 towards Saratoga the wind worsened. At one point the gusts topped 50 miles per hour.

Like I said before, there is nothing more demoralizing than the wind. Today it was hitting us in the face from the one o'clock direction, and it was so strong that no amount of riding in any "trunk" or "bosom of security" could make a difference. Our riding pace was cut in half and by the time we had ridden forty miles into Saratoga we were about ready to quit for the day.

At one point Joe started into a conversation that had been going on in his head for some time. He had a funny way of doing that. Here is where I picked up:

"…and then my friend Danielle, you know the one who rode across the country last year, was telling me about how one day in Wyoming it was really windy and the group was getting blown all over the road. She was in one of those tour groups where you pay a lot of money to have a guide take care of you. Anyway, one day in Wyoming when it was really windy one of the riders in their tour group was riding with one hand—could've been reaching for their water bottle for all I know—and not really paying attention, well, at the same time a wicked wind gust comes up and blows her into the lane at the exact same time a semi truck was passing by and *wham!* The truck driver didn't have any time to react and she was killed on impact. Tour group was in limbo for a few days while they grieved but decided she would want them to keep riding until…" His monologue again dipped below audible levels, drowned by the incessant wind buzzing in my ears.

For the rest of the day I kept a tight grip on the handlebars.

Chapter SEVEN

Saratoga, WY to Kit Carson, CO

THE SIGN READ "WELCOME TO Colorful Colorado," but it was false advertising. Low-hanging clouds blanketed the surrounding mountains and a thin fog obscured all objects past a hundred feet. Snow was falling thickly. The only color was white.

It was cold. I had on all my layers and was still uncomfortably cool when I pedaled hard to generate some body heat. All feeling had left my toes and the fingers were not far behind. "This little piggy went to the market, and this little piggy, it just went numb…"

"Alright, let's get a move on," Joe said through chattering teeth, after stopping to snap a picture at the sign. "I don't want to be discovered frozen in an ice block here in another thousand years." I did not want to become the next woolly mammoth either, so we hopped on the bicycles and started again into the white abyss that blanketed the road and surrounded us on all sides.

We had dealt with the cold that comes from being sopping wet, but this cold was different. It cut through layers of clothes and skin to the core, shaking my morale and sending uncontrollable shivers up my spine. Riding faster simply meant more cold air and snow in the face.

The plan was to make over a hundred and ten miles before sunset. Knowing only thirty of those were complete and the day that showed no indication of getting any warmer, my attitude was not positive. Joe was uncharacteristically quiet, meaning he was similarly poor-spirited or just thinking up the next corny joke to say when we reached stages of delirium. Something told me he was not thinking up any jokes at the moment.

The only sounds breaking the silence were labored breaths and the gentle squeaking of gyrating bicycle wheels.

It was about fifty miles before we saw any sign of civilization, when the town of Walden was supposed to welcome us. When we were fifteen miles away I began checking distances on my speedometer to see if we had inched another mile closer. Time and distance do not fly when your lower extremities lack sensation and fingers cannot even close around the shift lever.

When only five miles remained to Walden, I heard a familiar "Pop! Hissssss..." that could only mean one thing.

If there were a worse time to get a flat, I could not think of one. Snow was falling in a very passive-aggressive manner. I was cold, hungry, and it took me a full three minutes to remove my gloves with uselessly cold fingers. The rear tire popped, meaning all of my gear had to come off the back of the bike. It sat in a pile on the shoulder of the road, getting wet in the falling snow.

After ten painful minutes my poorly functioning fingers managed to maneuver the bad tube from underneath the tire and insert a fresh tube. Using Joe's small pump I brought the tire pressure up and replaced my panniers and sleeping bag to their proper places.

We rode no further than half a mile when I noticed to great dismay that the rim of the wheel was bumping against the ground without any cushion from the tire. *You have got to be kidding*, I thought. I was disgusted. But sure enough, the rear tire was flat for a second time in five minutes.

The second flat was a dagger to the soul. I yearned deeply to be done riding, find a Jacuzzi, and sip on coffee and Kalua until a plane could pick me up and take me home. Joe lent me a hand and a new tube as I went through the whole ordeal once again.

But this time I was smarter; my father always told me to check for glass lodged in the tire before putting in a fresh tube, otherwise the fresh tube may pop on the same sharp edge that caused the first flat. In the whitewash and frustration of the first repair I completely forgot to heed Dad's advice.

I ran my finger around the inside of the tire and felt a prick from a piece of glass. It was amber, the kind of color that comes from beer bottles. I could not decide whether to be furious at this inanimate and insignificant shard that managed to cause two flats and draw a drop of blood from my finger. In the end I decided "no" and tossed it aside. It is easier to go about life without holding grudges.

Despite the "welcome" from Walden being a snowy one, it was welcome indeed. Joe and I located a café, locked our bikes together, and walked inside through a heavenly rush of warm air. Within seconds sitting down I removed my frozen feet from their shoes and rubbed them so as to accelerate circulation. Our waitress approached and gave a strange look when she saw me rubbing my feet.

"Vat I can get for you?" she said with an Eastern European accent. She was young and I noticed a thread of nervousness in her voice.

"I'll take a hot chocolate," said Joe gratefully.

"Make that two," I quickly added.

"Hmm?"

"Sorry. Yes, I would like a hot chocolate, also."

When she returned with our steaming beverages she was followed by what looked to be her preceptor. They spoke briefly and then she said,

"Vat you vould like to order?"

Joe went with a Reuben, but I had scanned the menu carefully and noticed an "unlimited soup and salad bar" option.

"What is your soup for today? Clam chowder? Alright, I will take your soup and salad bar combination."

Clam chowder is proof there is a God that loves mankind. My favorite day in college was Friday, just like it is for many. But while most would attribute this to nighttime activities, it was the highlight of my week because it was clam chowder day in the cafeteria.

Our waitress, probably on the job for less than a week and in the country for mere months, must have thought I was crazy. In the hour we spent at the café I tucked away six bowls of chowder and multiple trips to the salad bar for heaping plates of potato salad, pasta salad, and vegetables. Every time I flagged her down to ask for another helping, her look of astonishment increased. It was worth it to keep eating just to see what her next facial expression would be.

The wind picked up during lunch, but for the first time in a long while it was working for us. It blew the clouds and snow away and started pushing us up and over the Colorado mountains looming ever closer on the horizon. Willow Creek Pass, with an elevation of 9,683 feet, was a breeze. My belly was so stuffed with chowder that I did not need to eat for four hours (which is a feat, considering we were normally eating every hour or two). I stopped riding to dial a friend, happy as a clam.

"Hey, Stephanie? This is Scott. Yes, I'm doing great! Now this is going to be on the random side. Do you happen to be at your place in Fraser this weekend?"

I am lucky enough to have a friend whose family owns a cabin nestled in the woods just outside of the Winter Park Ski Resort in the Colorado Rockies. But "cabin" is a loosely defined term; I prefer "estate-home." Joe and I were double-lucky because they happened to be up there for Memorial Day weekend.

After a friendly greeting from Stephanie and her family, we walked downstairs to the guest bedroom.

"Is this really happening?" Joe said, ogling the posh digs.

"No, Joseph, you are not dreaming—this time."

"And the beds have *sheets!* I have been craving sheets since Dubois."

Two nights prior, Joe and I were stealth camping in Rawlins. Then I felt like a fugitive, now I was feeling more like an honored guest of the royal family. Stephanie's father spent half an hour hand-drawing us a detailed map of the route to Denver and we dined on brilliantly cooked steaks and baked potatoes.

A cyclist herself, Stephanie escorted us the next morning eleven miles to the base of Berthoud Pass. We had been anticipating this climb for a week because at 11,307 feet, it was the highest point on our route and the last major ascent until the Appalachians on the East Coast.

"Guys, I'm just *heartbroken* that I've gotta turn around here," she said, sizing up the steep incline. The road wound in and out of sight, following the contours of the slope, until it disappeared from view far off in the distance. It was not an encouraging sight, despite the stunning scenery surrounding us.

No matter how pretty a mountain is, it always hurts riding to the top of it. Within minutes I was huffing and puffing, but felt like I was getting nowhere in the thin high-altitude air. I looked over my shoulder and Joe was also gasping like a fish out of water.

"Hey Scott!" he yelled in between gasps, "how do you eat an elephant?!"

When we were struggling up Snoqualmie Pass on Day One Joe asked me the same question. Gruesome pictures came to mind; fried elephant trunk, anyone? But before I could vomit, Joe gave me the answer to his question:

"One... bite... at... a... time!"

Many people were amazed when we explained our spandex odyssey across the country. I cannot count the number of times they would interject with a comment that essentially said,

"Wow... That is really great. I could *never* ever do that type of thing."

Those who assumed themselves incapable of performing a feat such as ours were missing the point. They needed to ask the elephant question. It is easy to be dazzled and intimidated by the "big picture" of things while failing to see the hundreds of tiny small pictures that all contribute to form the bigger whole. It was as if we had ridden the first 1,400 miles all at once. It is much easier to ride one mile and repeat 1,400 times than it is to ride 1,400 miles without a break.

To tell myself that I am not going to be able to put down the elephant all at once requires patience and perseverance. But it is the only way to get things done.

After munching on the proverbial elephant for a few weeks I was surprised by the amount I could consume. Although in the moment it always felt like we were going nowhere fast, in retrospect the amount of ground we covered was formidable. At the top of the pass Joe and I took a moment to reflect; seven major passes, crossing the continental divide six times, racking up almost 1,500 miles—and we had only been eating the elephant for two and a half weeks.

Every person in the world, no matter how incredible, is confined to living one day at a time. It is the truly extraordinary ones who figure out how to weave those singular days into a remarkable lifetime. The rest of us sit looking at the tapestries of the "greats" and convince ourselves we are incapable of such mastery. Yet it always starts with a single thread, a single day, a single bite.

The descent off of Berthoud Pass was astounding.

Despite the good intentions behind the hand-drawn map from Stephanie's father, there were times when Joe and I stood at the side of the road scratching our heads.

"See, we are looking this way and this road jogs off to the left here... err... would that be a right instead? Dude, beats the heck outta me."

We wrong-turned our way into Denver and eventually ended up at our friend Dana's apartment in a satellite city named Arvada. Joe had big plans for the first rest day:

"Last time I was here Greg, Ron, and I tried to tackle a seven-pound breakfast burrito at Jack n' Grill. But we failed. Tomorrow, my friends, we are gonna take it down." My stomach knotted up in nervousness and pain.

We showed up the next morning ready to take on the seven-pound monstrosity. Brave souls who conquered the burrito in ages past watched us from their Polaroid perches on the wall..

When the burrito arrived I just about fell out of my chair. It filled an entire serving platter and rose at least half a foot off the plate. The outside was drenched in sauce hot enough to singe my nose hairs and the inside was chalk-full of potatoes, eggs, and chicken.

"How do you eat an elephant again, Joe?" I said.

Dana, Joe, and I began methodically consuming the burrito. It seemed like an eternity before I noticed any progress. The biggest challenge was not the copious amount of food, but the spiciness. It was tempting to gulp down glassfuls of water.

"If you drink too much water, you're done for," Joe advised. "That's what happened to us last time."

While I love her to death, our friend Dana was useless at eating burritos. Joe and I filled each other's plates incessantly with the challenge, "I will if you will."

About half an hour after we started eating I looked at the serving platter that held the burrito. The mountain of food was decimated and all that remained was a mere fifteen bites.

"Alright, if we split this up there are five more bites apiece. All we need to do is finish what's left on our plates and a tiny bit more. Then we are victorious!" I was ready for my fellow warriors to rally around my raised arm and greasy fork pointed in the air. However, my fellow warriors had other intentions.

"I dunno man. My stomach is feeling kinda sick," Joe replied. *Sick?! Mine too—but that isn't going to change with five more bites. Let's do this!* But Dana was similarly unenthusiastic.

"Yeah Scott, I am done too."

I realized it was pointless to argue, and any sort of last-ditch effort was going to come down to me. The heroic thing to do would be to wield the fork and put down all the remaining food, but I was no hero. I sheathed my fork and flew the white flag; sometimes the elephant is just too big for one sitting. It was hard to see the last remnant of burrito be taken away.

We did not eat again until dinner, and even that meal was a dainty one.

The next morning we said goodbye to Dana and headed south through the city to another Denver satellite named Parker. Riding through the city was stressful in a way that pedaling through sparsely populated areas was not. Everyone was in a hurry and wanted to take out their aggression on us.

From Parker we got on the road headed south to Colorado Springs. The impressive foothills of the Rocky Mountains, known as the Front Range, thrust vertically to our right. To our left eastern Colorado stretched for miles and miles. I felt sandwiched between the past (mountains) and the future (flat expanse). After a few seconds of thought, I realized I was always sandwiched between the past and future.

In the present, the ride into Colorado Springs was arduous due to brutal headwinds. We got lost in the city shortly after arrival. Somehow we stumbled upon our friend Lilly's house, our planned destination.

"I know you're going to laugh when I say this," Lilly began as she led Joe and me down to the basement where we were to sleep, "but my family is going downtown tonight to do the Irish pub run. Wanna come?"

I hesitated in answering and looked over at Joe. He shrugged his shoulders in an "I dunno" gesture, leaving the decision up to me.

"Sure, what the heck? A little jogging after riding a bike 1,500 miles never hurt anybody, right?"

Wrong. Those slow, painful three miles were some of the worst I can remember. My back was tight, legs felt like deadweights, and I did not have the slightest clue what to do with my arms. By the time I figured out they are supposed to go back and forth in alternating rhythm with my legs, my calves were cramping. I do not know how I looked to the casual observer, but I felt like Bambi taking my first steps out of the womb all wobbly and disoriented.

To make matters worse Lilly belongs to a running family. Both her older brother and sister ran on Division I cross country and track teams. Lilly was no slouch of a runner on the trail herself.

This was your one chance to make a good impression and relive some of your high school cross country glory days, Scott, and quite frankly you're blowing it. A generous head start was not enough to keep all of the family from speeding past us.

"See you guys at the finish line!" Lilly's sister shouted back encouragingly. I felt everything but inspired.

By the time we had finished running our three miles most everyone else had finished and Lilly's father was drinking a beer.

"I was wondering when you guys were gonna get back here," he said and slapped my back jovially. I almost fell over because I had lost all control of my legs. Sleep came effortlessly a few hours later.

We spent the next day and a half traversing eastern Colorado. If the region was an infomercial, its sales pitch would go something like this:

"Hello, my name is Eastern Colorado. You may might have thought I was beautiful like my mountainous and colorful twin to the west, but you are gravely mistaken. I am covered in brown so drab you'd think I was a faded picture. I like to take long walks out in the dirt and pretend like it is a beach and always go for a swim when it flash-floods. I promise you will be able to appreciate anywhere else in the country after visiting me. So come on down and discover how great your everyday place of residence is!"

The eastern half of Colorado was mind-numbingly dull.

How did Joe and I make it across this forsaken wasteland? By dreaming about Kansas. The flatness of the state had us drooling ever since we entered the Rockies. And Dorothy could not have said it any better so many years ago.

"There's no place like home."

Chapter EIGHT

Kit Carson, CO to Buhler, KS

SUMMER IN KANSAS IS SCORCHINGLY hot and exceedingly windy. It was as if God turned on a fan connected to a heat lamp.

Within the first hour in the state I felt like I had excreted every ounce of water and grain of salt through my pores. The temperature was 95°F but it felt like Dante's inferno. Joe was struggling.

"I gotta stop and get some fluids, Skip," he said. "I'm drier'n a turd in the Gobi Desert."

"A what?" I replied.

"Don't worry about it. Let's just get some water."

Everyone in Kansas loves to talk. I found myself speaking to a rotund farmer at the gas station while Joe was filling his water bottles.

"Although the theoretical zone in time-space known as Kansas was admitted as a state of the Union in 1861," the farmer began, "it was actually not discovered until the first commercial airlines began flying in 1920's. While above Kansas a passenger looked out the window and asked 'Where are we?' The stewardess had no idea. She asked the pilot, who said the same thing. An official inquiry was filed and a joint expedition was commissioned by the government and William Frederick 'Buffalo Bill' Cody. It was deemed the largest national exploratory operation since Lewis and Clark. What they found was a humble and down-to-earth people (not a big surprise, given the flat nature of its topography) partial to buckin' hay, chicken-fried steak, and twisters."

I looked at him in disbelief.

"Alright, you got me. That story is pure baloney."

I walked into the food mart and was greeted by an instant rush of air-conditioning that felt refreshing like the cool side of the pillow multiplied tenfold. Making a bee-line for the soda fountain, I downed two bottles of cool water in the blink of an eye. Joe was looking at a red Gatorade through the refrigerator glass, drooling like an eight-year-old surveying Christmas packages underneath the tree. It really is the small things in life.

"Hey! Where you folks ridin' from?"

I turned to face the voice addressing me. It came from a blonde guy with boyish features who had turned away from his group to ask me the question. The eagerness with which he spoke, coupled with eyes permanently stuck in the "wide" position, made me instantly uncomfortable.

"Well, this morning we started just to the Colorado side of the border, but originally we pushed off in Seattle."

"Gee, man, that's great. I really like to ride bikes. That's what I'd be doin' right now if I could. Except it's so *hot* outside…"

"…So what exactly are you doing, then?" I asked.

"Oh, right. I go to college at University of Florida an' study meteorology. These are my classmates and professor, and we're here on field trip *storm chasin'!*"

My heart skipped a beat. *Storm chasing? That is the last thing I want to hear right now.* But he continued, unfazed.

"Yeah, we're lookin' for the *big* ones. Y'know, thunder 'n lightning 'n all. Did I tell you—" a thoughtful expression came over his face, and his mind made a quick calculation, "—I'd give you at least an eighty percent chance of survival. The storms we're goin' after are a few miles to the southwest so they should be outta your way. But y'know what they say about the weather 'round here, right?"

"No—what's that?"

"If you don't like it then just wait five minutes because it's a goin' to change..." He paused again, this time to blink. "...Although I don't know if I'd like to hear that at the moment if I were in your shoes. Whelp, looks like this ship's a sailin' so I best be getting' a move on."

With that, my new buddy turned and followed his group back out to their cargo van. The female student exiting in front of him did not make any effort to hold the swinging door as she passed through. Distracted by one of the free advertisement newspapers situated next to the door, the unfortunate kid did not see the door coming and it smacked him in the face. He stepped back, slightly started, and rubbed his forehead. No one else in front of him seemed to notice, so he opened the door himself and was the last one to jump into the van.

Despite the ridiculous comments about storm-chasing, I felt sorry for him. It seemed like the other storm chasers were avoiding him. It was the same at my grade school and high school; no matter how well-intentioned, some people are branded as outcasts. The innocent and pedestrian interaction we had might have been the first one of the day for him. It always pays to be nice to people, because you never know who may be aching for an act of kindness.

Like I said, Kansas is windy. I was a bit stronger in the saddle than Joe, which meant on blustery days such as this I spent most of the time breaking wind. The combination spending twelve hours in the 95°F Kansas heat and breaking wind for ten of those hours obliterated me. Pain became my entire existence. A throbbing headache spread down my neck and I was sick from dehydration. My legs were ablaze and my rump could not find a comfortable position. The miles ticked by with agonizing slowness.

At a certain threshold of pain the mind separates from the body. This happened to me during the final hour of pedaling. I felt like I was floating, feeling my heart pump and legs turn circles. The resolve to push onward came because Joe was in tow. He depended on me, and I did not want to let him down.

When mile one hundred and ten arrived my legs no longer recovered when I stopped pedaling to coast. Even at rest they screamed out in pain and throbbing soreness.

"Joe, I'm being attacked by the permasaur right now!"

"Huh?"

"You know, when you get to the end of a long day and your legs are permanently sore no matter what you do? The permasaur is a devilish creature."

"That a dinosaur called the permasaur would resurrect itself in invisible form and attack your legs at the end of strenuous days of cycling, I find highly unlikely."

"Fine, Mr. cynical. By the way, Santa Claus isn't real, either."

That night in my journal I drew a picture of a dinosaur that said,

"I am the permasaur and I'm here even when you stop pedaling because you are permanently sore." The permasaur seemed so humorous in my state of late-onset delirium. That is another one of the permasaur's tricks, making ridiculous things seem more comical than they actually are.

Our first stop in Kansas was Scott City. I hoped it would live up to expectations it had going for it based on the name we share. We arrived with nowhere to stay and no clue what was going to happen. On the edge of town there was a rather impressive-looking house with an older man parking a motor home in the driveway. We waited for a minute so he could disembark. Filling out a fairly thin frame, the creases on his face suggested he had spent a good part of his life laughing.

"What are you folks up to?" he asked inquisitively.

Funny you should ask, I thought. *I would love to tell you.*

"We started this morning in Kit Carson," I began, "and are riding our bikes across the country. Ended up here in Scott City tonight."

"Kit Carson? I'll be. You know that's over a hunder' twenty miles from here?" He did not seem to believe us.

"My legs do. You wouldn't happen to know any good places around here to get lots of food for a small price, would you?" Joe asked.

"Hmmm…" He scratched his chin. "You like Mexican?"

"I was born with a burrito in my hand," Joe replied.

"Alrighty then. There are two mighty fine Mexican restaurants in town. Just go up the street three blocks and take a right. Anything else I could do for you?"

"A shower." Joe instantly realized his statement in jest may have been a bit too forward. Our new friend's brow furrowed in thought.

"I don't think the city park has any showers… Hey! Tell you what. You come back this direction and you can use the shower in my garage. Not gonna be the cleanest shower you ever seen, but it should do the trick. By the way, name's Allen. Pleased to meet you."

After exchanging handshakes and other pleasantries we followed Allen into the garage. I looked over at Joe and gave him a wink.

"You two didn't know what you were getting into when you came here through Kansas, did you? Consider yourselves victims of Kansas Hospitality."

I ate a burrito that night that was all kinds of delicious. Savoring every morsel of cheese and sauce and bean in blissful silence, I was halfway startled when the father of the three-member family sitting in the adjacent booth turned around and spoke to me.

"Where y'all from?" he asked. It was a second before I realized he was addressing me. I sputtered a quick response.

"I'm from Seattle and my friend Joe here is from Montana. But the story—if there is one—is that we're riding our bicycles across the country."

"No shit! Did you hear that, hun? These two are ridin' 'cross the nation!"

By this point in the journey we had become accustomed to others' surprise and to answering their questions. Joe and I took turns rattling off the quick answers so the other could take a bit of food. After about five minutes of questioning the family was finished with their meal and stood up to leave.

"Good luck to y'all! I'm glad we bumped into you this evening," the mother said while she shouldered her large purse.

"They were really nice," Joe said, watching the father pay at the register and exit the restaurant. Then their daughter reentered the restaurant and walked back to our table.

"We just wanted to let you know we are very impressed with your journey and happy you have the courage to go out and pursue your dreams. You are an inspiration, and I hope you enjoyed your dinner tonight *on us*. See ya later!"

In my flabbergasted state I could not muster an adequate response to the generosity shown us. Joe was tongue-tied as well.

Having our dinner paid made me think about how our adventure impacted others. There was some force compelling this family and other strangers to act generously. The notion that one's wildest dreams are attainable is powerful and contagious. Seeing the two of us genuinely pursue our dreams brought others face to face with the notion that they could follow theirs.

Kansas is not as boring as people think it is. As we rode through field after field of wheat, corn, and soy it felt as if we were in the middle of something *productive*. Kansas ranks eighth among oil-producing states as well, and small oil wells were not an uncommon sight. While I would not call Kansas "drop-dead gorgeous" like I would describe Montana or Colorado, the state certainly has charm.

Then again, maybe that was because Scott City was named after me and a nice family paid for our dinner.

We were drained from two consecutive one hundred and twenty mile days in the Kansas heat. Our mileage the next day reflected the exhaustion, rolling into the settlement of Rush Center that evening we had accumulated a modest eighty-seven. The population of Rush Center according to the 2000 census was 176 and there was only one restaurant.

A healthy dose of skepticism accompanied me as Joe and I walked into the dusty establishment. Little did I know the best chicken-fried steak I have ever tasted was waiting for me on the inside. Normally eating chicken-fried is accompanied by nutritional guilt, but the calorie debt accumulated during the day's riding erased all sense of gravy-soaked remorse.

"What you folks been up to?" a stranger from a couple tables away asked as he approached. He walked gingerly with a cane, and required twice as long as I anticipated to reach our table. Joe answered,

"The short answer is we've been riding our bikes for a long time."

"Oh yeah?" His eyes narrowed. "Then how far you been ridin'?"

"Not exactly sure, but we started in Seattle twenty-three days ago."

"And how many flat tires you got?"

"Right now we don't got any," I said and Joe choked back a laugh, then added "but so far on the trip we've had four."

"Well that doesn't sound too bad. Now listen, I been lookin' at you two from my table over yonder since you sat down and I knew what I was goin' to do from the get-go. Pardon my assumption, but you two don' look like you have too much money. So I thought I would give you this." He slapped his hand down on the table and kept it there for a second. "Dinner's on me tonight, boys!"

With that he turned and sat back down at his table. When he lifted up his hand he revealed a green bill christened with the likeness of Ulysses S. Grant.

"A Fifty?! No way!"

"I don't even know what to say."

For the next twenty minutes I kept looking up at the generous man sitting at his table. He conversed and laughed like nothing had happened. When we were ready to leave we walked over to him and Joe started a conversation.

"You know, we didn't introduce ourselves back there. My name is Joe and this is my friend Scott."

"I was wondering what your names were goin' to be. Name's Vern Jenkins and this here's my wife Susan and daughter Leslie."

"Pleased to meet you all," Joe continued. "We just wanted to say thank you again for all of the help. We aren't really made out of money and this is huge for us."

We continued talking for a time and realized Vern and Susan's house was on our route the next day, some thirty miles up the road in a city named Larned (pronounced with two syllables, as in "Lard" without the "d" and the name "Ned"). We promised to stop by the next morning and say hello.

That night we were planning to sleep in the city park. Out of pure curiosity Joe walked a block over to the fire station. I was laying down in the shade, quite comfortable, when he came back excited.

"Dude we just scored! There was a guy coming out of the fire station and I asked him if we could use the shower. He said sure and left the door open for us. Never specifically said we weren't allowed to stay inside overnight, so it looks like we've got a roof over our heads!"

We slept on the concrete floor of the fire station in the shadow of a big, red fire truck.

The next morning we had no trouble finding Vern's house. He was waiting by the window and opened the door before we could knock.

"You guys getting' soft, or what? It's nigh ten o'clock already!"

"Hey it takes some of us longer to get from point A to B than others, especially atop our noble steeds," I motioned to the bikes.

"Yeah, y'do have a point there. Well c'mon in and I'll show you around. My wife and I have lived here over thirty years. She's out to breakfast with some of her girlfriends right now. Anyway, over those years we've had each of our rooms custom furnished by a man who lives up on..."

And so we received the tour of his house, which ended up being a tour of his life as well. The two are inextricably linked; ask anyone about the photos and magnets on their refrigerator and you are bound to hear their tidbits of their life story.

When we arrived at the shelf containing photos of the early years between he and Susan, Vern's nonchalant tone became metered and somber.

"You probably noticed that I don't have a whole lot of hair at the moment. Well this is when we got married. See all of those wavy locks? And this was on vacation when Leslie was in between second and third grade. This one was on a family road trip with my grandkids to New Mexico just a few years ago. Still had plenty of hair.

"Last January I started having terrible pain in my neck. I kept getting sick and felt weak, but the doctors were at a loss to figure out what was going on. After so many months without answers my attitude was becoming very terrible. I didn't have my strength and couldn't do the things I used to like to do. The only thing that helped me keep my sanity was doing things like sewing. See, for Christmas this year I am working on embroidering sets of hand towels for each of my kids' families.

"Anyway, I went into the doctor again after I started noticing lumps in my neck. They did a biopsy and found out I had non-Hodgkin's lymphoma. I was devastated. And scared, too. That was at the end of last year. Then the rounds of chemo started, and later the radiation. I lost a lot of weight—not your typical diet, I know. Susan was saying I needed to slim down a little bit and ever since then I've been telling her I was sorry I followed her advice.

"Anyway, my hair fell out and people hardly recognized me. Never thought that something like cancer could happen to me. But, praise the good Lord, the doctor said I was in remission and the last time I went back for a checkup he said everything looked good. I'm just glad I still had health insurance on my teacher's retirement pension, else I don't know if I would be showing you through this house at the moment.

"All you can do is trust in the Lord and sometimes you gotta push hard to get through. You two bicycle riders should know exactly what I mean..." His facial expression changed from thoughtful to mischievous.

"...You gotta push hard, like with your *dick*."

There is a clause written into the fine print of the aging process which allows the elderly to occasionally make inappropriate and vulgar comments without reprimand. Vern was highly qualified as a candidate for this exception. Joe laughed uncomfortably, as did I. A few moments later, Susan walked in through the front door.

"Oh, there's my wife comin' back to keep me in line," Vern said.

I quickly moved to greet Susan. We stayed another fifteen minutes, long enough to receive a recommendation on where to go for breakfast. Vern was already nostalgic about the night before:

"I bet you two had no idea what that ol' turkey Vern Jenkins was going to do for you. But one day, when you are on your way to make history, I am going to see your face on the news and I'll say 'I threw down a twenty dollar bill to pay for them varmints' dinner before they was famous!'"

A pit opened in my stomach. *Did he say "twenty dollar bill?"* Joe had a perturbed look on his face. Just like he had done so many times before, he shrugged. As if to say *meh, he's not going to miss it. Let's thank him in spirit when we use the extra thirty to buy dinner tonight.*

"Alright, we best get going. But you're right, Vern—if we are ever famous, it all started with you."

"I'll be watchin' for you two," he replied, shaking each of our hands.

"Y'all take care now," Susan added as we rode away.

The way Vern spoke to us about his life—and kept speaking and speaking—told me that he does not have the chance to be heard very often. That is a shame, because he has a story worth hearing. I think everyone just wants someone to listen to them, because that way their life-experience is validated.

Susan recommended a café ten blocks up the road. It was eleven o'clock and we had yet to eat a real meal. I was ravenously hungry. We walked up to the front counter and surveyed the menu. I ordered a full stack of pancakes. At five dollars I figured I was in for a solid flap-stack.

The server came out a few minutes later with an underwhelming plate. I looked at the meager arrangement—which does not deserve to be called "stack—" and my heart sunk. The pancakes were small. They were thin. And they were gone in two bites apiece.

My stomach rumbled. It warmed up with those pancakes and was ready for the real thing. Unfortunately there was no meal to come, so it idled there loudly with impatient grumbles.

"Those four-inch pancakes would fill you up great—if you were a gnome," I said under my breath to Joe.

A talkative local introduced himself and the ancient-looking man sitting with him.

"This is Dr. Brotherton," the local explained. "He fought in World War II and became a POW when he was captured by the Japanese. He was forced to participate in the death march, but survived. He's 96 years old. Worked for decades here as a doc but retired just a bit ago."

All of a sudden complaining about small pancakes was embarrassingly trivial. Something tells me Dr. Brotherton was not fed pancakes of any size on the death march. He could barely hear what we were saying to him, so our conversation was short. We did manage to ask him what advice he would give to young men twenty-two years of age.

"Work like the devil, and keep your nose clean," he said. As I walked out of the café I sneezed violently thanks to Kansas allergens. I opened my eyes to find the back of my hand covered in dirty, green snot. *Wonder if he was making a point...*

"Looks like we got sixty miles between Larned and the next civilization." Joe was simultaneously looking at the Adventure Cycling map and riding through town traffic. "I'd say we better load up on some lunch and extra water."

I filled a water bag with an extra gallon of water and packed it away in my rear pannier, hoping we would not end up like cartoon characters mistaking stands of cactus for an oasis in the desert. *Better safe than sorry.*

At lunch, however, I was regretting all the extra weight.

"Joe, let's just pour this out. I'm sick of lugging this burden and I think we're going to find some water in another thirty miles."

"That sounds like a bad idea to me," he responded dryly.

I looked at the clear liquid in the bag, despising it at the same time as worshipping it. Joe's tone took on a mockingly frantic character as he said,

"Master Frodo you *know* you have to keep carrying it. The whole world is depending on us. We can't just leave it here—think about the Shire!" Joe was impressed with his impersonation of Samwise Gamgee.

"Alright Sam, that's enough out of you."

Thirty miles further along the road there was no water and nothing besides scorching asphalt and treeless fields stretching for miles. All my bottles were empty, the water in the bag had been consumed, and I had ridden thirsty for an hour. Without the extra water, the situation would have been dire. Thanks to Joe, who stopped me from dumping it out. I was disappointed in myself for being so careless.

I looked over Joe, who was studying the map intently. My recklessness would have prevailed were it not for his voice of reason. Sometimes you need a good friend, one who is not scared to say "You know [Scott], you are full of smelly brown stuff right now." Joe was that friend for me. In all of the hours and days spent together, not once did he cease to stop watching my back. I did not stop watching out for his.

It is so easy to take trust for granted. It had not even been three weeks on the road, and I was already taking it for granted. This makes me wonder how much more I take it for granted in my normal life. They say it is easier to give than to receive, but I am not so sure if this is true when it comes to trust.

I would ride my bicycle off a cliff for Joe—even if I was not allowed to pack a parachute. I could not begin to comprehend life on a bicycle alone. After sharing every meal, every hill, every joy, and every storm with my friend oft-mistaken for brother, I did not care to find out.

We committed a major error in showing up to the town of Buhler, Kansas at half past four on a Saturday. Nothing was open and it looked like we would be dining on leftover bread and peanut butter for dinner and breakfast the next morning. That is, until Len McIntyre showed up and saved our skin. He flagged me down within five minutes of riding through town and immediately set to making things right.

"Ooh, ah, well there is nothing in town open at the moment. Hmm, ah, everything closed at four. Small towns on the weekends… Why don't you, ah, head over to the park over there and I will meet you in a few minutes. Goin' go talk to my wife and, ah, see what she says."

I could not stop looking at him because he was the spitting image of my grandfather. His full head of graying hair was sharply combed backward and to the side. Although his face was a road map of wrinkles, it belied a handsome past. His mannerisms were amusingly eccentric, featuring many pauses, shifts in posture, and darting glances left and right. At first I thought he might be slightly mentally handicapped, but I soon learned it was the exact opposite; his mind was moving a thousand miles an hour and the body had the unfortunate task of trying to keep up.

We went to the park as instructed, where we were very content to find the municipal pool open and free to touring cyclists. After a few jumps off the high dive and a much-needed shower, Len pulled up in his car.

"Alright fellers, you hop in the car because I am goin' to drive you up the road to a pizza joint that is still open. Your things should be just fine the way they are while we are out."

I turned around and surveyed our bicycles. Everything had been unpacked and strewn about a picnic table. My inner feeling screamed *Scott, leaving your things out like that is a bad idea.* But this was Rural America, and they play by a different set of rules.

Len, Joe, and I devoured pizza slices at an alarming rate. It was an all-you-can-eat buffet that we had every intention of utilizing to the fullest. What is more, Len offered to pay and I did not want any of his dollars to go to waste. After what had to be twelve slices apiece, Jim took us back to his house to meet his wife Ella.

"We built this place from the ground up and been livin' here ever since. That's gotta be," Ella paused to count, "over fifty years now. This is just our home, and I couldn't picture living anywhere else or any other way. I'm 'fraid our kids would stop visiting us if we moved, because it wouldn't be home anymore."

That Len and Ella would stay in the same place for over fifty years is astounding compared to today's norm of frequent moves. The U.S. Census Bureau reported in a yearlong period between March 1999 and February 2000, 16% of the population moved residences. And that figure is not out of the ordinary compared to years prior or after. One out of every six Americans moves each year. In the Midwest, the average duration of residence among homeowners in 2008 was only nine and a half years, more than forty less than Len and Ella. As more and more people migrate from rural towns to metropolitan areas, this number only looks to decrease.

What are the consequences of moving frequently? Len had an answer.

"I used to know every single person in this town. Now that I haven't been working for some years there has been a couple new families who have moved in I haven't met yet. But there is something to be said about knowing everyone in town by name. Some of the people here we have known for forty years."

People today do not throw down roots like they did in the past. It is much less feasible to maintain small, agriculture-based communities today than it was fifty years ago, because much of the sweat equity required to raise crops or livestock is now replaced by mechanized labor. Farmer John does not need to hire the village boys to plow the field or milk the cows anymore and the village boys are forced to move to the city to find work.

The traditions and lifestyle of rural communities around the nation are dying as the exodus continues. We passed through uncountable numbers of rural ghost towns, streets lined with windows of formerly prosperous businesses now boarded up. I am not the expert who can figure out a way to stop emigration away from rural towns, but aspects of the former rural life can be translated into modern terms.

For example, I have yet to meet my next-door neighbors—even though they have lived there for almost an entire year. In Buhler and small towns like it, this would be unheard of. The community where I live is largely unknown to me, filled with people whose existence (proven by their cars parked in the driveway and the garbage truck that comes to pick up their trash) is as mysterious as a foreign-language film. Does my community have to be so disconnected?

The sun was setting on the third consecutive day that a complete stranger paid for our dinner. Never had this happened to me before, and I do not expect it to happen again in the future. Small-town "Kansas hospitality" seemed to be second nature; none of our gracious benefactors had to think twice about offering a helping hand. This basic look-out-for-each-other mentality is a product of life in small, close-knit communities. Do people look out for each other in suburban neighborhoods or high-rise condos as much as they do in rural Kansas towns?

I can only hope my life in the future will retain the connectedness of the small-town existence. It is the counterbalance to the anonymity and alienation of urban life.

It was pitch black outside when Joe and I returned to our bicycles in the park. Although we left our belongings strewn about in plain sight, everything was exactly as we left it. Not one item had been stolen or moved.

Chapter NINE

Buhler, KS to Eureka, KS

"You two are showing up a little late," said the gruff man through a small gap in his thick goatee. He was clad in leather from head to toe, save for a cotton bandana decorated with skulls and flames which covered his bald scalp

"Must've missed the memo. Ran out of gas back in Wichita," I replied. The man laughed. "Is there anywhere around here we can get some water and food?"

Joe and I had stumbled upon a motorcycle convention. Bikes—the Harley Davidson kind—lined both sides of the street. Flocks of leather-clad men and women walked up and down the sidewalks pawing through merchandise, eating greasy food, and checking out each others' cycles. In spandex we stood out like sore thumbs.

Not too worried about bicycle theft at a motorcycle convention, we parked our brazen steeds without lock and went about searching for food. It did not take long to find a truck-trailer barbeque stand. We asked for sandwiches.

"Sure thing, fellas, just sit tight for a second," the man behind the counter said. Five seconds later he came from around the trailer with two sandwiches for us. "Here y'go you two. Enjoy!"

"Wait—what do we owe for these?" Joe asked.

"*Nada*. You been ridin' a mighty far ways, I presume. Unlike the rest of us..." He motioned towards a stand of men with rotund bellies. "...So you deserve it. And next time you see us caterin' to anybody, you just remember how good them sandwiches were and tell all of your friends."

I am ashamed to confess that now the name of the barbeque truck escapes me. Any truck in Kansas with BBQ and smiling pigs on the side could be the one, so now I have to recommend them all.

This was the fourth day in a row Kansans had gifted Joe and me a meal.

We had ridden twenty-five days. From what we had heard from other touring groups, it was high time to start getting sick of bicycling. Almost every pedaling adventurer said something along the lines of,

"Yeah, I used to care about how fast and far I rode. But then I realized it doesn't make any difference. Fifty, sixty, eighty miles, it's all the same. I'm gonna get there, but I am just sick of riding hard and getting tired."

Fueled by hearty Kansas barbeque, riding slightly uphill, into a headwind, with thirty-five pounds of gear apiece, we made seventeen miles in an hour—a respectable pace without those qualifications, but all things considered, it was savage. Did we have to do it? No. Did it save any time? Not much. Then why did we do it? Either the mind-numbing hours were turning us into masochists, or there was something addictive about doing something for nothing more than the sake of doing it well.

Eureka! And so a town in southeastern Kansas was named. Seriously: a thirsty pioneer shouted Newton's famous word upon finding a spring of water and the rest was history. The town has about 2,600 residents, but we were interested in one specifically. The head lifeguard at the public pool regularly shelters cyclists in her house or front yard. Naturally, we moseyed on over to the pool to do some investigating.

At the pool there were no less than five bicycles loaded down with touring equipment parked against the fence. We were not the only ones who heard the scoop. Inside the pool office I asked about this lifeguard who could hopefully help us out.

"Oh yeah, that's Renee. She's over yonder talkin' to those kids who were divin' in the shallow end."

It looked like Renee was busy. Given the smelly condition of our bodies, we decided to take a dip in the pool ourselves. When Joe took off his bicycle jersey I noticed the past days of Kansas sun had drawn some impressive tan lines. I was about to tell him so, but then I caught sight of my own terrible lines in the mirror. A razor-sharp boundary demarcated the end of the shirt sleeve of my jersey, and the backs of my hands had an odd line where the glove fabric did not cover.

My neck had acquired a healthy dose of color. I thought back to the shirtless man who answered the door on our first night in Montana, and how we now looked very similar. The next time I see vicious tan lines, an adapted form of Martin Luther King's famous words will echo in my head: "...that Man will be judged not by the evenness of his tan, but by the stories of which his tan lines are a consequence."

Tan lines are interesting, because they happen to people who get out and *do* something.

I struck up a conversation with Renee when she had a free moment.

"Yes! C'mon over!" she said enthusiastically. She looked about forty-five, with creases running across her deeply tanned face. Her raspy tone and weathered features belied a boisterous nature. "There's already gonna be quite a few of you, but if you don't mind then feel free. My house is on Fifth Street. Turn right at the old café and you'll see it on your right. The one with the trampoline and shutters that are all crooked."

Her house was exactly as she said it would be. There was a large crowd of people, bicycles, and tents in the yard. Kids of all ages were running left and right throughout the house, opening the fridge in the kitchen and bouncing on the trampoline. It reminded me of *Home Alone*, before the family leaves McCaulay Culkin behind.

"Just make yourself at home!" Renee said and hurriedly walked by. Joe and I found some chairs outside and sat down. Removed from the heat and madness, I had a moment to catch my breath. Out of nowhere a beautiful young woman emerged from the house and walked over to the trampoline. She seemed oblivious and uninterested in the seven new visitors to her house.

I almost choked on a bite of string cheese.

"Joe, am I wearing biker goggles right now or is she very attractive?" I asked quietly.

"What do you mean?" he whispered back.

"I mean, we have spent weeks living in an exquisitely primitive state. Is that clouding my judgment?"

"No, Skip, I'm right there with you. I was thinking the same thing—very attractive." That was all Joe had time to say because she was fast approaching.

"You must be Renee's daughter?" I asked after she finished a couple acrobatic flips on the trampoline.

"Yep. Name's Hilary."

"Then nice to meet you, Hilary. My name is Scott."

"Alright."

She was impatient to get back inside, and I spent the rest of the evening hopelessly trying to come up with something else to say. It is hard to be witty under the gun.

There were seven cyclists including us staying at Renee's house. Then there was Renee and her four children, along with what seemed to be half the neighborhood's adolescents. I wondered if there is always this much chaos at the Renee family household.

Among touring cyclists there exists no archetype describing the majority; at Renee's house there were two men in their late twenties from Great Britain, a young couple from Alaska, and a college student named Adam from Loyola Marymount University. The chaps from across the pond had some of the thickest accents I have heard. The Alaskan couple seemed uncomfortable in social situations. Adam was taking a semester-long leave of absence to ride his bike across the country. I doubt many of his friends coming back from summer break will have stories that top his travel tales.

Renee approached the patio table and collapsed into one of the lawn chairs. She gestured those of us seated in a circle.

"Whew! Running a hotel out of your home is a full time job. There's some watermelon inside if you want, and the burgers you guys picked up should be on the barbeque soon."

"Is this a normal occurrence, to have so many people over for the night?" Adam inquired. Renee thought for a moment.

"Y'know, I think this is the most at one time, ever. And y'all are the first ones this summer, at least at my place."

"How did you get started with all of this?" one of the Brits inquired.

"Two years ago a boy named Ernesto knocked on my door. I guess I shouldn't say boy, 'cause he was about your age. Hardly spoke a lick of English, and very shy. But he was riding across the country like you all and his bike was broken. I looked at it and had no idea how to fix it. It was late, so I told him he could stay the night in our house. The next day I drove him over to the closest bike shop—

which 'round here ain't very close, y'know—so he could get his bike repaired.

"He got everything all fixed up, but by the time we got back home it was getting late again. So he stayed with us another night. Kept on eatin' what I put in front of him. God, he had to weigh a hundred pounds soppin' wet. I'll be an unckie's muncle if he did not end up staying with us nearly a week. Kinda became part of our family. Ever since I've been offerin' to help you folks in any way possible."

"There really isn't much happening in small towns like this," she continued. "I've been all over Kansas in my life and seen a fair amount of other states, too. But growing up here you don't ever get to see what life is like on the 'outside.' I want people like you to come and share your lives with us so my kids know somethin' about the world. And maybe one day they'll go out and experience it, too."

It seemed like the perfect marriage between a rural lifestyle and a rapidly changing and globalizing world. Renee took a breath for what seemed like the first time in three minutes, then expired slowly. She shifted her weight in the chair, and then made to stand up. The side conversation between the Brits and Alaskans died down.

"There's one other thing I wanted to mention before y'all head off to bed. I just wanted to say thank you everyone for coming tonight. You spice up life around here, whether you know it or not. I'm not gonna say much more, but I just wanted to share a bit 'bout who I am. I'm a believer in God and in Jesus Christ, and I'm a believer in welcoming the stranger. It is what He says to do, and so it is what I do. I have no intention to say anything else about my faith, but I hope you know the reason I try my damndest to be generous and hospitable is that He first welcomed me as a stranger."

It took a minute for anyone to speak, or even move. Renee's words were so genuinely sincere that no action or response seemed adequate. There is something refreshing about actions that line up with words, but the talk is walked so infrequently that this is a serendipitous occasion. Unfortunately it is not people like Renee making the headlines. The "news" is reserved for the likes of gunmen and fanatics waving signs saying "Aids Cures Fags" and Martha Stewart.

There are plenty of people like Renee out there, so why does negativity dominate the news? Our guardian angels of society go largely unheard and unseen amidst highly-publicized instances of hypocrisy and hate.

Later I was in the kitchen, bent on satisfying my craving for watermelon.

"You going to put salt on that, or what?" It was Renee, swinging open the screen door with her foot because both hands were carrying plates loaded with hamburger patties and cheese.

"So how much am I supposed to put on?" I asked.

"Just a quick shake. Like this," Renee replied, grabbing my slice of melon and the salt shaker. Stretching out her arms as if she were Indiana Jones about to swap a talisman for an equally weighted bag of sand, she readied the watermelon slice and salt shaker. After giving the salt shaker a slight jiggle, she looked up and asked "Did you get that?"

"I think so. Let me see…" I went about imitating her, temporarily assuming the persona of Indy. My hand pretended to quiver. I gave it an accentuated jerk. "Was that right?"

"Y'know, with a little practice you're gonna go places."

Salted watermelon is delightful. The small flecks of sodium chloride unlock flavors previously hidden amongst the red flesh and black seeds. Sure, an unsalted watermelon is sweet. But throwing in a salty tang gives the melon infinitely more dimension; sweet can become even sweeter.

While happily munching away at a thick slice of melon, my eyes wandered around the kitchen. A mountain of dishes piled in the sink rose a full two feet above the counter, which itself was a battlefield littered with dirty pans, half-eaten pieces of toast, and a delicious plateful of half-eaten cookies. The door to the refrigerator was ajar and I do not know how the milk stayed cold. A kitchen like this would drive to insanity those even mildly affected by obsessive compulsive disorder.

Above the cabinets a plaque a foot tall and two feet wide was nailed to the wall. It had three simple words: "Enjoy the Journey." I stood there speechless, looking at those three words for a long time. I cannot come up with any three words that more accurately characterize a bicycle adventure or a life well-lived.

When gingerly perched atop a nefariously slender bicycle saddle for two months, "journey" is really all there is. In Kansas it still felt like the Atlantic Ocean was a world away. *The journey is all we have so by-golly we better enjoy it*, I said to myself numerous times. Those who navigate through life with the sole purpose of arriving at destinations are inevitably and invariably disappointed because the journey is what makes any destination worthwhile. If the whole process is not valued, it is only a matter of time before reality ceases to live up to expectations.

Life is a watermelon. It can be sweet, but it's truly astounding depth is unlocked only by those who make the conscious decision to appreciate living for the very sake of living. Enjoying the journey is like munching on a crisp, cool watermelon *and* putting salt on it so the flavor in its entirety can be fully enjoyed. Living for the destination, confining one's satisfaction to the fulfillment of arbitrary expectations, is like eating unsalted watermelon in a shadowy cave, convinced life cannot get any better. Before I tried adding salt, I thought unsalted watermelon was the best thing in the world.

"Do you think Plato ever tried watermelon?" I asked Joe. We were both looking up at the stars from the trampoline.

"Hrrrrm? Play-do doesn't try to wadder mellll… Hrrrrm." Half-asleep Joe was an amusing character to talk to. Out of nowhere he started giggling.

"Hey Scott."

"Yes, Joe?"
"Waddaya call a biker riding behind a car?"
"I have no idea."
"Exhausted."
"Nice one, Joe."
"Hey Scott."
"Yeah, I'm still listening."
"Waddaya call a biker riding in front of a car?"
"You got me again. What do you call 'em?"
"Tired."

"Joe, that's not very funny…" But I rolled over and saw he was already breathing rhythmically, mouth contorted in a contented grin.

Chapter TEN

Eureka, KS to Sedalia, MO

After leaving Renee and the town of Eureka, my interior monologue went something like this: *This whole enjoying the journey business is great. Look at the field over there; it is full of corn, just like back home. Think of all the people it will nourish in the form of processed starches and corn syrup.* Enjoy the corn field; check. *Wow! Check out the drilling rig pulling oil out of the ground. Suck in the smell of sulfur and rotten eggs.* Enjoy the drilling rig; check. *Wait, don't tell me—did the driver of that Ford Ranger just flip you off?* Enjoy being told to get the f*** off the road; check.

It may be circular reasoning, but everything is more humorous when you allow yourself to laugh.

Following God's example, we steamrolled over the rest of

Kansas. Crossing the border into a new state is always exciting, and entering Missouri was no different. However, Kansas was hard to leave. No other state blessed us with swimming pool access, multiple restaurant-quality meals, camping at the city park, and a great number of saintly people with which to interact.

This next story will illustrate the awesomeness of Kansans.

We spent the previous night in a town called Pleasanton with a woman in her fifties named Janet. She was kind enough to offer Joe and me two unused guest bedrooms in her house. Seconds after entering the residence, she implored us to get glasses for water out of the cabinet.

"Just make yourself at home!" she shouted sprightly from the living room.

I swung open the cabinet door and found a row of old-fashioned Coca-cola tumblers, one of which I elected and pulled to the edge of the cabinet. When the vessel was clear of the cabinet's edge I was mortified to discover it was actually *two* vessels stacked on top of each other. In my left hand I still held the top one, but my attention shifted downward to a falling piece of glassware. In sickening slow motion I watched it tilt and twist towards a tragic collision with the floor. My attempt to catch the tumbler was unfortunately confined to slow motion as well. After grazing two of my fingers it shattered on the floor with a loud *Crash!*

At the same time my insides shattered in embarrassment.

"Are you okay?!" Janet said with concern. "What happened? Oh, pulled out a double glass, I see. Don't worry, happens to the best of us every once in a while. Let me go grab a broom and sweep this up. You don't want to cut your feet on that." The average person would be thinking *this guy has only been in my house five minutes and he already is destroying things. What is going to happen next?* I felt like leaving. I did not have any idea where I would go, but I needed to go. I told her as much.

"You'll do nothing of the sort. I am serious, everything is fine," she responded sternly. If it were possible, I think she was nicer to me after breaking the glass. That is Kansas. However, I do not recommend breaking glassware as a reliable way into another's heart.

We were only riding in Missouri for a short time when Joe said matter-of-factly,

"Scott, this ain't Kansas no more."

He was right. It was getting more humid by the minute and hills were increasing in frequency and intensity. At lunch we discovered good barbeque was one thing that remained the same across the state line.

While sinking our teeth into some devilishly tasty cow and pork, a crew of firefighters sat down next to us. We asked them if there was a bike shop nearby, because our tires needed some air. The portable pump we carried with us was good for a quick fix of a flat tire on the road, but it could not inflate tires to optimal pressure.

"Hmm... I don't think we got a bike shop in town. But I always taken my kids down to see Shawn at the saw shop when we need another bike. He's quite the cyclist and I guess everyone in town just knows to go to him when they want anythin'. But I'm telling ya, you gotta see him ride. I heard he rode three hunder' miles in *one day* without stoppin'."

We found the saw shop, called the Clinton Chainsaw and Mower, and were greeted by a gruff and portly man at the door. He looked to be about sixty-five and did not have anything close to a biker build.

"Shawn?"

"Nope. What do you want?"

"Does Shawn work here?"

For a few seconds it was awkwardly silent. Then a gray-haired woman poked her head around the corner and interrupted the impromptu stare-down.

"Hello there! Where are you from? You're probably lookin' for Shawn, aren't you? Let me go grab him... Shawn! There are two young men here to see you."

A tall, slender silhouette emerged from the back room of the store, rounded the counter, and stepped into the sunlight at the front door. *This looks more like Shawn,* I thought to myself. He appeared to be in his thirties, with a sinewy frame and attentive eyes. His entire head was bald, either by choice or necessity.

"What brings you folks here?" he asked while he finished wiping chainsaw grease off his hands with a rag. As we explained why we needed a bicycle pump—which turned into a narrative of our entire journey—a gleam twinkled in his eyes. He kept asking question after question. The conversation finally lulled and Shawn took a thoughtful breath.

"Well that is really something," he mused.

"And we hear you're no slouch on two wheels yourself," I said, shifting the focus of the conversation. He beamed.

"Who told you that?"

"No idea. Some firefighters eating lunch at the barbeque joint. We asked them where we could find a bike shop and they said to come here and find you." He was thrilled.

"Ha! Well I'll be... Yeah, I guess I have put in my time on the saddle. There's this race that starts here at this end of the Katy Trail and finishes in St. Charles. I won it. Did all two hundred and thirty-eight miles in just over seventeen hours on a mountain bike." *Holy cow, that is impressive.* "I qualified for the Race Across America, but didn't have the money and couldn't afford to stop working."

The Race Across America is a feat of human endurance. Teams of eight cyclists traverse the nation's east-west axis in under two weeks, riding hundreds of miles per day on four hours of sleep each night. To qualify, a rider needs to possess the endurance of an ox, speed of a hare, and mental resolve of a barnacle. Anyone who has ever tried to dislodge a barnacle from a pier knows what I mean.

"We had the tour of Missouri start a stage here a few years back," he continued in his musings, "and there were some big names. You heard of Levi Leipheimer, right? Anyway, I was helpin' organize everything and just before the stage started one of the race officials asked me if I wanted to ride in the VIP car. Does the name Johan Bruyneel sound familiar? Back in the day he was the director of Lance Armstrong and the US Postal Service team, and he was riding in the car.

"Well, I turned the offer down because I already told some friends I was going to ride out and meet them to watch the stage at the halfway point. But I really wanted to go in the car, because that was a once in a lifetime opportunity. So I called up my friend asking if it was alright that I ditched and he said 'Shawn, get your ass in the car before I come and tan it so bad it bleeds.' That was all it took for me to jump in, and I ended up spending the day talkin' to Lance Armstrong's coach."

Shawn is one of the most down-to-earth people I have ever met. He was powerful-good on two wheels, but it did not seem to go to his head. He almost turned down a ride with Lance Armstrong's coach because he had already made a commitment to his friends. Instead of running away from the small town of his youth, he stayed to help his father run the family business.

They don't make character like Shawn's very often.

"Are you gonna hole up here in Clinton for the night, or do you plan on making some miles this afternoon?" There was a look of longing in his eyes when he asked this question.

"We were thinking we would continue on to Sedalia this afternoon, because we're shooting for St. Louis in two and a half days."

"That sounds about right. You know what they say 'bout the Katy Trail, right? They say it's so flat that it looks downhill both ways." *Shawn, you are singing music in my ears.* "Say, what were you comin' here for to begin with, again?"

"Oh, right! We were going to ask you if we could borrow a floor pump. Ours doesn't have a gauge and won't get up to a hundred p.s.i."

"You got it." He regressed to the back room and returned with the pump. "Here ya go. Gotta be careful because it is a little rough on your valve stem."

As Joe and I pumped each of our tires in succession Shawn stood there pensively, with one hand holding the elbow of the opposite arm and hand stroking his chin. He let out a deep breath.

"Two young guns, ridin' bikes across the country... I'm jealous; you fellas are livin' my dream."

In that moment I felt for him. The wavering tone of his voice betrayed an intense yearning to jump on a bicycle and follow us. We were the embodiment of his still-unrealized aspiration, a reminder of the dream yet to manifest itself in the physical world. If there is anyone who deserves a chance to make their dream happen, it is Shawn. The story of pursuing an untamed dream with unbridled passion is so universally contagious because most people have already muzzled their ambitions and forgotten that which makes them come truly alive.

"...And you said you're sure you plan to keep on up the road today?"

"Yeah, that's what we're gonna do."

This was ripping Shawn to pieces. Only after we left I realized he wanted us to spend the night in Clinton so he could ride with us the next morning. Knowing this at the time may have changed our course of action, but we kindly said goodbye and thanked him for letting us use his pump.

Of the many individuals I interacted with over the entire trip, I think about Shawn the most. It bothers me that he has not had an opportunity to pursue his dream, and I hope one day he gets a chance to ride across the country. Joe and I were very lucky to have the chance to turn our dream into reality.

The Katy Trail mentioned by Shawn is a trail following the route of the old Missouri-Kansas-Texas Railroad, which for some reason became known as the "Katy." The railroad fell out of use in 1986 and the trail was created within the next year. However, the groundwork in place which permitted the rapid conversion was set years earlier. Passage of the National Trails System Act (1968) and the Railroad Revitalization and Regulatory Reform Act (1976) in Congress allowed and encouraged the conversion of unused railroads to public space. The National Trails System Act outlines a process known as "railbanking," by which a railroad company allows a trail agency to "borrow" an out-of-service corridor until they decide to use it again as a railroad.

Both sides are served by the arrangement. Obviously, the trail agency and general public enjoy recreation and transportation benefits. The railroad company also benefits, because they can lease or lend out their obsolete holdings instead of the properties reverting to adjacent landowners. Railbanking procedures are usually opposed at first because landowners believe newly formed trails will increase crime, decrease property values, and increase spending by the local government. However, research shows just the opposite: crime rates do not change and proximity to public-use trails actually increases property values. Furthermore, easements granted to utility companies permitting them to use a corridor for their electric, water, and fiber optic lines often turn trail projects into money-making ventures for local government.

A conservancy group called Rails to Trails was formed in the same year as the Katy Trail, with the mission of facilitating these rail-trail transitions. While in office, Missouri governor John Ashcroft began the Katy conversion process by signing 185 miles of the old Katy railroad for railbanking, and the organization has not looked back ever since. In its 25 year history it has seen the rail-trail network in the U.S. blossom to nearly 20,000 miles of trails.

Our encounter with Katy began with a bit of a surprise. She is an unpaved thoroughfare. In my imagination I had envisioned a two hundred thirty-eight mile paved superhighway that whisked us eastward towards a St. Louis beckoning with open arms. Her arms were still open, but a bit more gravelly than expected.

"What do you say?" I asked Joe.

"Meh," he replied with a shrug of his shoulders.

"Then let's give it a go."

And so we started up the trail. Riding on gravel was not terrible because the Katy is well maintained (in most places) and features fine, hard-packed rock. Within minutes we experienced the benefits of being off the pavement.

"Aw man, the traffic is terrible," Joe said sarcastically

"I know! I keep having to look over my shoulder to see if anyone is coming," I responded.

"Wait, I think I hear something... Nope. Just quiet enough to hear myself thinking."

"Wow. That was deep."

"She sure is great, that Katy."

"Yeah. I'd date her."

"Me too."

Later in the afternoon we encountered a second unforeseen aspect of the Katy when a swarm of swollen, reddish bugs covered the trail. Specifically, the bugs were periodical cicada of the genus *Magicicada*. With a habitat range stretching across most of the eastern United States, cicadas are often confused with locusts—although the species are only distantly related. Cicadas subsist on a steady diet of plant and tree sap and pose little (if any) threat to humans or large-scale agriculture. They are big, oafish, and *loud*. The loudest of the cicada family is able to produce audible sounds of 120 dB at close range, intense enough to cause hearing damage.

Periodical cicadas, as opposed to annual cicadas, emerge less than once per decade. There are some 13-year and some 17-year varieties. Groups of each variety are staggered such that the emergence of periodical cicadas happens once every three to five years on average. Adults live for about six weeks above ground. Within this window of time they must molt, mate, eat, and lay their eggs in a variety of deciduous tree species. What does a periodical cicada do during the other 99% of its life? It crawls around underground hijacking tree sap. Quite the existence, if you ask me.

Joe and I came to Missouri *exactly* when a particularly populous brood of 13-year cicada was due to come out of the ground. A couple other tidbits I found while doing research for this story: "the [Cicada's] singing begins at dawn and ceases at evening. As the temperature rises during the day the volume of the singing also increases." But it gets better. "Brood XIX is expected to be quite large when it emerges again [in 2011], promising a noisy spring across most of Missouri. *People planning weddings and other outdoor social events in May and June 2011 will want to take this emergence into consideration.*"

"Hey!" I tried to get Joe's attention. "Whatever is making that noise is really loud."

"What?!"

"I said, something in the trees is *really* loud."

"Skip, can you say that again?"

"It's really noisy!"

"Ah, yeah, noisy! I could barely hear you."

We were riding within five feet of each other.

This is how I see a wedding going down during the din of Cicada-Fest 2011.

"Do you, fairest Leslie, promise to love and treasure Jim for the rest of the days of your life?" asks the Pastor.

"What?!" replies the Bride, unable to hear anything besides buzzing cicadas.

"Do you, fairest Leslie, promise to honor—"

"What?!"

"Gah." The pastor is frustrated. "Do you say I do?!"

"I do!"

"What?!" The Groom is now interested. "Did she say I do?"

"She did say 'I do'."

"Great. I do too, honey!"

"What?!"

"Jim, you may now kiss the bride…"

"Good form, Jim! Make your papa proud!" says the Excited Father, taking full advantage of the fact that nothing could be heard besides buzzing cicadas.

"Jim! Show some decency," implores the Incredulous Mother.

"...Oh my goodness did you see that?! She just got all wide-eyed and pushed him away!"

"I think it was 'cause a cicada flew up her skirt!"

"Who needs adult magazines when you got this?!" shouts the Inappropriate Uncle.

Maybe the last comment crossed the line. Everyone has an Inappropriate Uncle in the family.

The Katy brought us forty miles to the city of Sedalia. I almost stopped at a walk-in clinic to get my hearing checked, because phantom cicada songs were ringing in my head.

We arrived without a plan and defaulted to the plan *de facto*: meet our needs in descending order of urgency. This brought us first to a gas station to gulp down a quart of chocolate milk. After that we tried to find lodging, and finally, went about obtaining a dinner meal.

"I don't know if that house is such a good idea," said Joe, eyeing the wide porch and ominous knocker on the front door. The house was situated next-door to the Catholic Church, and I had a sneaking suspicion this house was the rectory. I lifted the knocker on the door, halfway expecting it to take the form of a spooky Marley brother from *A Christmas Carol*. A startled-looking woman in her middle ages opened the door.

"What can I do for you?" she asked. Her face was obscured by the screen door.

"You see, my friend and I are riding our bikes across the country and..." Now in the seventh state, telling our story was like turning an airplane on autopilot. "...we were wondering if we could pitch our tent in the yard, just for tonight, and be gone tomorrow morning."

"I better go talk to Sister Erma, because she is the one who lives here overnight." Sister Erma waddled around the corner. Her stocky figure was dressed in a black shawl and high heels, and the top of her head still did not reach my shoulder.

"You see, my friend and I are riding our bikes across the country and..." It felt like the story remained the same, word for word, every time I told it. "...we were wondering if we could pitch our tent in the yard, just for tonight, and be gone tomorrow morning."

Sister Erma's wide-set eyes narrowed in suspicion.

"How do I know you're not going to hurt me?" she asked.

"Well, there's not really too much we're carrying that could be of harm," Joe reasoned. "We are two recently graduated college students on an adventure, but if you are uncomfortable we can go elsewhere."

"No, you're not going elsewhere. Go ahead and pitch your tent over by the church there, in the corner. After you get cleaned up I will drive you into town for some dinner."

I could not decide which was the colder, Sister Erma or the frigid shower I took in the rectory. I walked downstairs to see if she would warm up to us. She was sitting at the kitchen table eating a plate full of Brussels sprouts and carrots.

"Thank you again for helping us, Sister. We know nobody in Sedalia and had nowhere to go."

"It is part of my job, welcoming the stranger and all."

"Well it is much appreciated. How long have you worked as a nun?"

"Probably thirty years by now."

"And how did you end up here, in Sedalia?" At this question her back straightened and her drab tone of voice perked up.

"Y'know, it might be surprising but there is a large Hispanic community here. They come to work in the fields doing agricultural work. A lot of them are second and third generation now, but some have recently arrived from Salvador and Mexico. I fell in love with the Hispanic community years ago when I was placed at an orphanage in El Salvador. After returning to the States, I realized that I missed participating in their culture. So I asked to be transferred to Sedalia, and have been happily involved in this community ever since."

"Y ¿hablas español?" I asked. *So do you speak Spanish?*

Upon hearing Spanish she became a different person, infinitely more present in the conversation.

"Pues claro que sí. Aunque todavía hablo como gringo." *Of course I do. Even though I still speak like a gringo.* As we continued conversing in Spanish I could tell she was gradually taking a liking to the idea of having us around for a night. Joe walked down the stairs and I said enthusiastically,

"Nuestra amiga habla español!" *Our friend speaks Spanish!* Fortunately Joe can defend himself well enough in Spanish as well. After a few more minutes, Sister Erma decided we needed to visit the best Mexican restaurant in town for dinner. We loaded up in her van and she drove us a few miles down the road. My stomach spoke to me in rumblings that transcend language.

Two weeks before we arrived in the state, Missouri was devastated by severe storms and tornados. One of the tornados, touching down in Joplin, tied for the worst on record as it claimed 116 lives and an caused an estimated $3 billion worth in damage.

The annual threat tornadoes pose to the Midwest was foreign to me. A less-severe twister hit the city of Sedalia around the same time as Joplin. On the ride home from dinner, Sister Erma showed us some of the wreckage. Entire storefronts and mobile-home parks were obliterated. I was grateful the storms had fizzled, because on our bicycles we would not stand a chance.

The next morning Erma cooked us breakfast, a great scramble of eggs, potatoes, and peppers.

"How far have you gone 'til now?" she asked us at breakfast during a transition between how she decided to enter the convent and her work in the orphanage. Joe and I were thrown off guard.

"Let's see," Joe did some quick addition, concluding with "I think we have ridden at least two thousand miles at this point."

"Hmm."

That was the extent of her curiosity. She lost no time in changing the subject back to the orphanage. She shared plenty of her experience with us, and probably appreciated the open ears we turned to her stories. But it seemed that Joe and I were nothing more than a good deed to her. Grateful for the food and shelter, we said our goodbyes and made our way eastward.

At times it was very difficult to leave the people we had met along the way. What made it so hard was the feeling that we had become family. This immediate sense of belonging came about when we reciprocally shared life experiences with our hosts. Mitch and Wendy from Lander, Wyoming come to mind. They made a genuine effort to experience the world through our eyes, in the same way that our mission was to embrace their life-experience.

Sister Erma was not as interested in our story, seeing only the charity case that we certainly were. There is absolutely nothing wrong with that, but it brings to mind a story I remember from Sunday school.

When Jesus shows up at the house of two sisters, one of them is running frantically around the house, fretting about every tiny detail of their guest's visit. The other sister chooses to simply sit in the presence of her Lord, an encounter that would alter the course of her life.

Joe calls meaningful interactions such as this "reminiscible shared experiences," memories that each person will remember and treasure for the rest of their lives. In the story of the sisters, one walked away from that day having touched and been touched by Jesus' soul. The other sister walked away with her back sore from scrubbing the floor.

We is all that we have here on Earth, and it is about time we started *being* with each other in this place like we understood what that meant. We are human beings and not human doings, after all.

Chapter ELEVEN

Sedalia, MO to St. Louis, MO

IT WAS A FEELING AKIN to when the bottom drops out of your stomach. I had taken my helmet off and was mortified to discover a dragonfly two inches long, caught in the one of the helmet's ventilation holes. One wing flapped weakly and its legs struggled to find purchase amidst the maze of Styrofoam and padding.

Cicadas were not the exclusive insect life on the Katy. There were also bees, flies, dragonflies of many colors, and probably lots of other bugs I do not feel too bad for missing. The dragonflies liked to bask in the sunlight that filtered through the trees onto the gravel trail, waiting until the last minute to fly out of our trajectory.

We rode ninety-five miles in ninety-five degree heat and ninety-five percent humidity, fueled only by an ice cream cone and a peanut butter sandwich. My hunger was so severe that I was tempted to ingest the twitching dragonfly whose broken wing I pinched between my index finger and thumb. Luckily for both the dragonfly and me, just two miles remained between us and nourishment in a town called Tebbets.

In Tebbets there is exactly one business, a bar whose storefront left much to be desired. Nearing the door I confronted my reflection in the reflective glass. It was not pretty. Dust covered my face and a twig had managed to lodge itself in my short, greasy hair. My arms were covered in a pasty mixture of sweat, sunscreen, bug repellent, and dead gnats. Joe and I looked like a drawing straight from *Where the Wild Things Are*. I supposed based on the decrepit state of the building that appearances were not going to be an issue.

"Joe, it is our lucky day," I said looking at the front door.

"Yeah?"

"This place is only open from three to eleven on Wednesday, five to midnight on Friday, and two to ten on Sunday. Twenty-three hours out of the week, and we happened to land here at just the right time."

The bartender gave us a strange look when we walked through the swinging door. I could not blame him, given our unusual attire and condition. His facial expression only became more perplexed when we asked for some food. Not very many people frequented this establishment to eat.

"Well, I guess we can make hamburgers. Yeah, a hamburger."

"Anything else? Can we see a menu?"

"Ah, no. We don' have no menus. But what else we got is beef stew with vegetables."

"…And how much for each?"

"Hmm… Three for the hamburger and, ah, two-fifty for the stew." He was making up those prices on the spot. I was nervous. Visions of rotten soup and rubbery burger patties filled my imagination.

"Then I'll take two burgers," said Joe.

"And I'll have a burger and some stew." *Here goes nothing.*

The food at this hole-in-the-wall establishment rocked my world. Inch-thick burger patties laid the foundation for towering buns too tall to fit straight into my mouth, so I had to alternate bites on top and below. The fact that they were served on paper plates only made it better. And the stew! It was thick, salty, and delicious. The quantity was generous, even by starved cyclist standards.

Two locals wandered into the bar while we were at work devouring our prey. They directed their conversation at us, but we never really had the opportunity to add anything to their dialogue.

"Where you folks goin'? Washington?! Tha's some trip."

"I did some travelin' when I was about your age. Best trip was when we made it clear up to Ohio."

"Say, you two really be somethin'. So how do y'all plan on getting back home? You fixin' to ride the other ways, too?" The two locals shared an approving laugh, chuckling together for a full minute. Knowing the great many individuals along the way who had made similar jokes, I could only shake my head.

I licked my plastic spoon for the last taste of stew. The only evidence of the food we left behind was a pile of ten saltine wrappers and a stack of paper plates.

"Did he say Missour-uh, or was it just me?" Joe asked when we were out of earshot.

I grew up in a small town in Washington called Snohomish. Try saying that five times fast. In similar fashion, the dialects and names of places along the way were continual sources of fascination to me.

At our retiring point in the afternoon, a Baptist minister and his wife offered to drive us to their house and return us to the trail the next morning. His name was Griffin and he drove a mini-van. His hair was white, but looked to be in his mid-fifties. Darlene, his wife, was short and whimsical. What the two had in common was their affinity for speaking. They are the kind of people who could in theory talk forever, because one thing always reminds them of something else. We heard about where they grew up, how they met, and their life as a pastor-and-wife. Their voices were slow and bobbing, like two people enjoying a stroll with nowhere in particular to go. I was slipping into a lethargic trance.

In my head I was vacationing on a remote beach, sipping on a margarita and tossing rocks into the ocean. I failed to register a sudden shift in tone and quickening pace of conversation.

"What do you two think? Lookin' for the Rapture to come pre-tribulation or mid-trib? Or you thinkin' it's going surprise all of us by being post-trib?"

Joe was staring at me wide-eyed, like a raccoon illuminated by passing headlights. Obviously his Catholic upbringing left him ill-prepared to answer Rapture and Tribulation questions. It was up to me to save face in front of the pastor and his wife, or bring shame on ourselves for lack of Biblical knowledge.

"You know I can't say I am an expert on the subject. Maybe I should look into it a bit more. What are your thoughts on the matter?"

"Well I go back and forth," Gene reasoned in a didactic tone, "but I have thought a lot about it and I think the rapture is comin' pre-trib. I mean, when you look at—" but Dana interrupted Gene before he could finish.

"I think it's gonna be mid-trib because…" and that was all I heard before returning to sipping my Corona on the beach.

A well-timed question can be the perfect way to mask the sorry truth that one does not know a single thing. Later Joe asked me from where that saved-from-the-jaws-of-embarrassment response came. *Joe, sometimes questions can be the best defense.* It is convenient when one's conversational foil has a propensity for speaking, because the more time they spend speaking the less time they have to figure out you really are a clueless buffoon.

The night was subdued and balmy. I stood outside on a hill in the darkness, looking for enough wireless reception to call home and remind my parents they have a son and he is still alive. A flickering of light out the corner of my left eye caught my attention. I turned to see what it was but the phantom photon was nowhere to be seen. Then another flicker drew my attention to the right. I turned clockwise to investigate, but again, nothing. I heard a faint buzzing. Then, as if a shooting star came down from the sky to give a personal display of dazzlery, a twinkling darted across my entire field of vision not more than three feet away. *Fireflies!* It was the first time I had seen them in my entire life. I turned around slowly and realized the hill was alive with fleeting bursts of light. All was quiet, save for the lazy buzz of a bug that flew close by. This entomologic serendipity became a sort spiritual experience, a time when the internal ruckus died down and left an opening to listen. In this void I heard my inner voice say *"this* is why you came on an intimidating, unknown, and at times frustrating adventure. Bask in the feeling."

Everything made sense on the hill and all was at peace. If not for self-equilibrating experiences such as this, days like the next would be intolerable.

Our Day of Tribulation started early. We started at seven o'clock in the morning, five yards away from the banks of the Missouri River. An invisible drone filled my ears, one that I knew all too well; there is no better place to be a mosquito than on the banks of the Missouri River.

"Man, these mosquitoes are all over me this morning."

"Yeah. Like we were the John McEnroe and they were a Wimbledon referee." Joe was sharp even at the early hours of the morning.

"As long as we keep on riding I don't think they will bother us," I reasoned. "And why does John McEnroe have anything to do with this?"

Minutes later I felt the rim of my back wheel hit hard against the ground. That could mean only one thing: a flat tire. I sensed the mosquitoes licking their suckers around us, ready to descend at the first possible moment.

"Hey, Joe," I said quietly.

"You say something?" he replied.

"Yeah."

"What?"

"You're going to hate me right now. But I've got a flat."

"Oh man…" He was deflating just like my tire.

"I'm gonna need your help so we can get this done quick…"

"Yep."

"…And hopefully we won't get eaten alive."

I slowed to a stop and within seconds dozens of little blood-sucking devils covered my arms. By some act of Providence I had placed the bug repellent where it could be accessed easily. I tore it out of the pouch, squirted myself down, and quickly handed the bottle over to Joe, who was doing a comical jig-step in a futile attempt to keep the mosquitoes away.

While he lathered up his exposed skin I went to work removing my panniers, loosening the rear wheel's quick-release axle, finagling the wheel out from between the rear stays and chain, changing out the old tube, putting in a new one, pumping up the tire, replacing it between the stays, and returning the panniers to their place on the rack. The deafening drone of mosquito wings drowned out all other noise.

The dirt and gravel of the Katy Trail had gradually wore my tire down to the threads and I did not realize it until it was too late. I could hear Katy laughing mercilessly to the tune of ten thousand mosquitoes buzzing, as the price of our passage on her trail was paid in blood and itches.

I got bitten twenty times through my shirt and spandex, bug repellent and all. If not for the bug repellent I do not think I would be writing this right now.

"You can say it now, Joe. 'You are a *genius* for getting the bug repellent, Scott'."

"Hey, I wasn't the one who made it necessary."

"Ah, but it was only a matter of time, my friend."

We got off the trail and started riding on roads again. I was surprised at how much of a relief being back on solid ground and away from the creatures of the forest was. *This is so great, I'll even share this modern thoroughfare with a car every once in a while,* I thought to myself. It is easy to get used to one way of doing things, oblivious to the possibility that things could be done better or different; I am never riding my road bike on gravel again.

One benefit of riding a railroad grade like the Katy trail is that the inclines are never too steep. On roads it was back into the hills for the approach into St. Louis. They were steep, constant, and it got hot. Just the same, this section had one of my favorite stretches to ride of the entire journey. The twisting and turning road snaked up and down through thick tree cover, until finally arriving at a high point. From there it was an exhilarating white-knuckle descent through alternating stands of trees and views which reminded us of the significant elevation we had gained over a short time.

Unexpectedly, a half-empty beer can flew at us from the window of a rusted pickup truck. The thrower had terrible aim and the can sputtered into the grass along the side of the road, but I did get a little taste of warm beer as it spun past. I would have loved to sit down for a chat with him, over a beer.

We had no idea how to enter St. Louis. Navigating through unfamiliar metropolitan areas is intimidating because it is nearly impossible to know which routes are bike-friendly and which are not. The one constant is the interstate. Looking at the map of St. Louis and its sprawl, Joe and I decided to ride I-64 eastbound as far as we could.

The most precarious class obstacles in interstate riding are bridges. Having survived the bridge encounter way back in Vantage, Washington, it seemed high time for fate to come knocking. I-64 crosses the Missouri River some twenty-five miles outside St. Louis. It has four lanes going each way and not an inch of a shoulder.

"Joe I don't want to hear about any win-win situations this time. Let's just get across this thing alive."

There was nothing to do besides pedal, and pedal fast. I tried to empty my head of everything besides the immediate road ahead. Cars and trucks screamed past and the sixty seconds spent crossing the bridge were some of the longest in my life. Upon making it across safely I looked up and said "thank you."

Twenty-five miles were all that remained between us and the Gateway Arch, and my spirits were soaring. That is, until I heard a sharp "Pop! Hiss!" two miles after the bridge. It was another flat tire, but Joe and I had both ran out of spare tubes. I went through the last extra tube on the trail earlier in the morning.

I was frustrated. Crossing a ditch that separated the exit ramp from a parking lot, I lost control of my bike and it toppled over. It fell at least five feet, concluding with a heavy "thud!" I didn't care. I sat down on the curb, flustered. If I were a cartoon my face would have been red with steam whistling out of my ears. Midday temperature was pushing one hundred and the humidity was not close behind; sweat poured from my brow and off of my arms in rivers. I wanted nothing more than to time-warp to the end of the day and be finished with flat tires, heat, and mosquitoes.

Joe walked up to where the ditch was not as steep, crossed easily, and came back to the spot where I sat fuming.

"Nobody said it was gonna be easy."

"Yeah."

"And we're gonna make it."

"I hope."

"Even if it takes ten more hours and it is pitch black by the time we get there, we are going to get there. So get up and let's go."

Sometimes a friend has to state the obvious when the obvious is not so obvious.

The parking lot belonged to the Chesterfield Mall. We walked over to a department store called Dillard's. Two sweaty, stinky men with bicycles and gear spread all over the ground next to the entrance doors was a peculiar scene to those exiting the store dressed in crisply ironed khakis and polo shirts. I had the front tire off and patch kit out, deciding which of the popped tubes had the more patchable puncture. Joe walked in to the mall and went about procuring submarines while I stayed outside and worked on patch repairs.

During the half hour I spent sitting alone outside the department store, looking like a desperate mess, nobody stopped to ask if I needed help. The department-store-browsing individuals in this suburban offshoot of St. Louis wanted nothing to do with me. A few curious children leaned towards me like dogs testing a leash, until their parent's hand jerked them back.

"Honey, we don't talk to strangers," I could hear the parents lecturing.

The manner in which passersby systematically ignored me sharply contrasted the reception Joe and I received in every smaller town we visited. What if I really needed help outside Dillard's? Not a single person would have known. Our friend Len McIntyre back in Buhler would be appalled at these people, much too busy and suspicious of strangers to go out to a pizza buffet with grungy nobodies like us anytime soon.

Stopping for a moment to inquire if I needed assistance would have occupied five seconds. When people become obsessed with optimizing every part of their lives, there is no room left for distractions like stopping to help a stranger.

"For a second I couldn't tell if you were you, or an angel," I said to Joe as he exited the department store doors with a pair of submarine sandwiches. As I sunk my teeth into the harmonious stack of tuna, pepperjack cheese, honey mustard, tomato, and toasted oat bread, all the cares of the world seemed to melt away. Two cookies for dessert all but erased my memory of the day's hardship.

Riding on a patched tube is full of second guessing because you are never sure if the patch will be airtight. But as I pumped up the refurbished rubber it appeared to hold its pressure. Five minutes after resuming the ride it did not seem to be leaking and I was pleased.

Scott, you are a patchwork professional, the purveyor of pro-bono, a player in the realm of practicality.

Temporary triumphs could not hold the Day of Tribulation at bay. After making ten more miles, with St. Louis proper painfully close, the Motorboat got a flat. This time there was no conveniently placed exit ramp off the highway and all we could do was pull off to the side of the shoulder and hope the hundreds of drivers passing by every minute would be paying attention.

"Y'know Skip, today is kinda like the final boss," Joe said while hunched over his back tire.

"Huh?"

"Like in Super Mario, when you get to the end of the game, and you have to win the battle against the biggest bad-daddy of them all."

"I mean, I guess so."

"No! You don't fully understand," Joe said emphatically, now distracted from his tire. "The final boss is the culminating test, the coming-of-age trial. All of the skills you learned along the way come into play, to see if they have been fully mastered. This is the final showdown to see if we deserve the glory of accomplishment." I could tell Joe had been contemplating the final boss metaphor. He continued,

"Think about it: all of the flats, the mosquitoes, the heat, the hills, the bridge, even the beer can… This is the test."

"When you put it like that, it feels like we are doing something momentous."

"Exactly. But not just in the mass-times-velocity sense. I mean *momentous* in the 'epic' sense." He took a deep breath, reveling in the momentousness.

"But here we are, just changing an ordinary, flat bicycle tire on the side of the road," I countered.

"What kind of road?"

"The interstate."

"How many pounds are we carrying extra?"

"Almost forty."

"How long have we been riding?"

"Twenty-eight, nine… Thirty days."

"And how many miles have we come?"

"Over twenty-five hundred." When I said this Joe smiled and nodded his head.

"That's right—momentous. And you just told me why."

"…And now you're making it more momentous. You've got to let the glue dry before you put the patch on!"

The tire patch leaked after Joe's failed repair attempt and he had to redo the procedure allowing extra time for the glue to dry. But we would not be stopped on this self-appointed final-boss day, and stoically mounted our bikes after the tire tube was successfully repaired.

Out of habit I reached into my jersey pocket to check the time on my cell phone. It showed "one new message from Ethan Patterson." He was a friend living in St. Louis who I planned to see. I opened his message, which read:

"Dude! I just saw you riding on the interstate. You guys are f***ing insane!"

The chances of him seeing us, out of all the roads in St. Louis and all the possible times we could have been travelling, were astounding unlikely. The message made my day.

The Gateway Arch has towered over the city of St. Louis since its completion in 1965. It is the tallest man-made monument in the country and the largest stainless steel structure in the world. Designed by the Finnish-American Eero Saarinen to commemorate President Jefferson, Lewis, Clark, and the rest who made westward expansion possible, the design was originally the winner of a contest to determine exactly what structure would best fulfill this objective.

It is impressive to behold in person. Even as Joe and I gazed from a distance of two miles, my jaw dropped.

What I have failed to mention up until this point is that Joe called this day the "final boss" day because this would be his last. For weeks he had been see-sawing back and forth with his future employer over his starting date, and they had finally settled on the thirteenth of June.

If that comes as a surprise to you, it did to everyone else as well. Call it emotional weakness, but I did not want to acknowledge Joe's departure. Informing others it was time for Joe and I to part ways was entirely unappetizing. I dreaded saying goodbye to my dear friend and partner-in-bicycling-crime.

For us the Gateway Arch was not the door to the West, but instead a gateway to the East. To Joe it was a glorious finish line to what had been a month of crazy, testing, amusing, and exhilarating experiences. *And the Arch was so close.*

"Hey, Skip! Guess what we got!" My attention diverted away from the Arch and back to the present. I could hear a tint of sarcasm in Joe's cheery shout.

"What's that?"

"Flat *number four* on the day! Whaddaya think about that?!"

"I think that sounds delightful! Whaddaya say we do about it?" There was nothing left to do on this day of tribulation besides happily welcome each new development with cheer. Call it positive pessimism.

"Well I was thinking we could patch it, seeing as we haven't had any new tubes in over a week!"

"You are smarter than you look."

We pulled over to a park bench less than a mile away from the Arch. It was painfully close. Every ounce of my being longed to be done with the ordeal, to say *sayonara* to the struggle and bask in satisfaction. But it was not time yet.

I split off in search of a grocery store while Joe again went about patching the tube. It did not take long to find one and I made a beeline for quarts of thick, brown, liquid goodness also known as chocolate milk. I snaked through aisles and dodged customers with my bike in tow. It was awkward, but I was not about to leave my bike outside of the store in downtown St. Louis. That sounded like about as good an idea as giving Nicolas Cage the leading role in anything besides the next *National Treasure* movie.

Many curious eyes followed me navigating the narrow aisles. The *clickety-clack* of the plastic cleats on my shoes did not help my conspicuousness and it made the floor very slippery. What with limited visibility and difficulty maneuvering, the store felt like a jungle. After a few wrong turns I slipped around a corner and my fully laden bicycle fell into a stack of cereal boxes. I watched helplessly as ten Lucky the Leprechauns precariously swayed back and forth. How the tower of Lucky Charms managed to stay upright was magical. Magically delicious.

As I approached the checkout area, an incredulous look spread across the cashier's face like the plague.

"What are you doing with that *in here?!* No vehicles allowed! Take it outside *right now*," she snarled through clenched teeth. I had all of two quarts of chocolate milk and two bagels in my possession, as well as a bike's worth of sweaty and dirty things necessary for long-distance travel.

"Are you sure you can't just ring me up quick? I'll be out of here in a jiff," I proposed, trying to sound reasonable.

"Maybe you didn't hear me the first time," she snorted, "I said get that *thing* out of here."

I was livid. There had been too much adversity on this day for me to take her attitude in stride.

"Fine," I grunted, and set my bagful of milk and bagel down in the middle of the checkout area. I walked around the corner, still inside but out of sight, and stashed my bike. I had to exit and walk all the way around the store again in order to arrive at the checkout line. The cashier was waiting. When she saw me she rolled her eyes and did her best to look offended.

"Sorry I didn't know the rules in this store. I didn't mean any wrong, it's just that my entire life is on that bike and I am a little wary of losing it."

"Oh yeah? And how do I know those sacks you got there aren't full of stolen food? Rules are rules that *you*," she paused to throw a disgusted look my direction, "have to follow. *So get used to it.*"

The ire this bitter woman possessed was unpleasantly surprising, like a sudden whiff of sulfury-rotten eggs accompanying the oil wells in Kansas. If she wanted to check, I would have been more than happy to open up my panniers and shove her face down into the smelly abyss. I put down three dollars as fast as I could and made to leave. I hope the rest of her day went a little better than mine had been. I said to keep the change.

We have no idea the burdens others carry in their souls. I would have appreciated even the slightest shred of understanding from the bitter cashier, because it had been one of the most exhausting days of my life. I was tired, sore, and hungry, and wanted nothing more than to make a quick exit from the store and return to Joe. The negative interaction with her was like getting my teeth kicked to the curb by a passerby after tripping and falling on the sidewalk.

But then I think about how frequently I fail to consider the stories of others. There are many times when I am quick to judge and to become impatient. I play the part of the bitter cashier more often than Simon Cowell on *American Idol*—and I don't walk around with a Paula Abdul to soothe my seething.

"Scott, hands-down this is the best chocolate milk I have ever tasted." *And you don't even know who I had to go through to bring it to you*, I thought. Joe continued, "But seriously, this is it. There is not a place I would rather be than right here, right now."

I looked at him from head to toe and glanced down at my own hands and feet. Our bodies were covered in a film of sweat, dirt, bug repellent, sunscreen, and squished gnats. I was hungry and exhausted. It was not yet six o'clock in the evening, but I felt like I aged a year in the last twelve hours.

Joe was right. Call me a crazy and him a glutton for punishment, but sitting on a park bench in downtown St. Louis gulping chocolate milk was a defining moment. After going through periods of great adversity, most people say they would not change anything—even if they could go back and rewrite history. I now understand why; it is the moments when you have to choose between perseverance and failure that go straight to the core of being. One discovers their true essence when everything is on the ropes—not when things are easy and effortless. There were plenty of moments of great joy and happiness on the trip for which I am grateful. But none so closely approached my inmost self like the Day of Tribulation in St. Louis. Maybe I should have thanked my bitter cashier friend for contributing to a character-defining day.

I relished every swallow of chocolate milk and bite of bagel in a heightened state of awareness. We mounted our bikes, Joe having repaired flat number four on the day, and resumed the approach to the Arch. As it got closer and closer, a feeling of giddiness welled up in my chest. The area surrounding the monument is a park largely covered in grass. By the time we broke free of the downtown buildings Joe and I were in full song.

"God bless America, land that I love…" we bellowed.

There was a group of men in business suits to our left who looked over when we rode by yelling. It must have looked and sounded very strange, but I was far beyond worrying about what some stiffs in business suits would think.

"…Stand beside her, and guide her, through the night with a light from above…"

Now some Korean tourists to our right stopped walking and pointed at us. A father dragged his young son clear of our trajectory.

"…From the mountains, to the prairies, to the oceans, white with foam…"

The finish line was mere yards away. The Arch towered above and mighty Mississippi stretched from left to right. We had finally arrived. Passing under the Arch we belted out the last line,

"…God bless America, my home, sweet, home!"

America had treated us very well thus far. I felt a sense of solidarity with the places I had recently been and former strangers I now knew. Although I was thousands of miles away from my house, I was still home. Our bikes fell to the ground and I grabbed Joe's hand. Images of the first day with our back tires submerged in the Puget Sound flashed through my mind. That was a month ago. *We made it, buddy, we really did it.*

At this point you may be thinking, *but Joe, you did not really make it. You had to stop early and did not finish the coast-to-coast ride.* This is an understandable reaction, but one tainted by the results-oriented nature of modern society. If all that mattered was arriving in St. Louis—or the Atlantic Coast for that matter—it would be very easy to get on an airplane and make the journey in a few hours.

It is the means and not the ends that are important. Joe successfully arrived at his destination after a solid month of adventure and I reached a transition point. He will say to this day that he does not regret having to quit before seeing the Atlantic. I do not doubt he would have continued if it were possible, but that does not mean he left loose ends untied. From start to finish, the journey was about experiences and people. Motivation to reach a destination was of little concern.

Renee would say, "enjoy the journey…"

To this Joe would add, "…because the journey is all you have and you don't know when it will finish."

Joe's journey finished a little earlier than expected, but he made the most out of every minute and for that reason it was a success. Seattle to St. Louis is not an easy trip.

After basking in the moment of arrival at the Arch we backtracked a few miles to the Saint Louis University campus to meet up with my friend Leanne. Leanne and I met two years earlier studying abroad in Spain and quickly became travel buddies. This was the first time seeing her in our own country.

"Leanne!" I shouted when I saw her half a block away. She

walked up and wrapped me in an embrace. "I don't know if you want to do that. We are just a bit smelly and dirty." She paused and I heard a sniffing noise over my right shoulder.

"Wow. You're right, you do stink," she said with a laugh. Her good-natured sarcasm was a breath of fresh air. "Did you have a tough time getting into town?"

"You have no idea."

Chapter TWELVE

St. Louis, MO to Murphysboro, IL

I WOKE UP TO A ROOM much too bright for 6:30am, the time at which my alarm should have sounded. I rolled over to check my phone. I had been assaulted with messages and four calls from Leanne. A text sent at 8:27am from her read, "So are you still alive? I would be really bummed if you left without saying goodbye." The unassuming clock on my phone declared the current time was 9:18am. We overslept by almost three hours.

"Oliver... Hey, Oliver!" Oliver stretched and yawned.

"What's up, man?"

"It's a quarter after nine."

"Hmmm..." he mused. The he stretched again, chuckled, and said "That's real professional."

"Yeah, embarrassingly professional. Not a bad way to start."

Waking up late is not the end of the world on a bicycle trip, but getting a late start typically means finishing later and riding fewer miles. The heat gets worse as the day progresses, and it was always harder to find a temporary residence at dusk compared to looking in the afternoon. We were planning on making some big miles coming out of St. Louis, but it was going to be more complicated starting three hours late.

It was Monday. The day prior I said goodbye to Joe. It felt like saying goodbye to a part of my being and quite frankly I had no idea what I was going to do in his absence. We had spent the weekend in St. Louis visiting old friends, ascending the Arch, and touring the Anheuser-Busch Brewery. I thought I was going to die when atop the Arch swaying in the wind. Unfortunately the St. Louis Cardinals were out of town. I really wanted to watch Albert Pujols play in person, to see if he really shimmers like Moses coming down the mountain with the Ten Commandments.

They don't have storms on the West Coast like they do in Missouri. One night a storm warning was issued over the entire city because the sky was illuminated every fifteen seconds by a burst of lightning followed by a chorus of thunder. I tried to hide my concern, but had to ask Leanne if this happens often. Atop the Arch she had pointed out her apartment because it is connected to a large radio tower. Being connected to a radio tower is a harmless detail until a lightning storm comes around and you realize the tower is one of the tallest structures for miles. We did survive the storm, despite the fact that the building attracted lightning bolts like my smooth brother attracts cute women. Why he was blessed with the "radio tower" genes and I was not is beyond me.

The transition between Joe's departure and Oliver's arrival went smoothly. Oliver grabbed a plane ticket and continued on the Motorboat in Joe's absence. Joe saved money by not shipping his bike back to Denver, and the Motorboat was going to make it across the country after all.

I was surprised at first that Oliver wanted to come out and ride for two weeks across the hot, stuffy belt states. Then again, who would not want to have an entirely unique, random, and eye-opening adventure through unknown and unpredictable territory atop the faithful Motorboat?

By the time we said goodbye to Leanne it was eleven o'clock. Not long after waving goodbye, we started questioning our route exiting St. Louis. I spent an hour the night before on Google Maps outlining a route which sent us through the dangerous part of town—I simply could not find a way around it. Two law enforcement cars in succession pulled up next to us, each emblazoned with "City of St. Louis Police Dept." on the doors. The passenger window of the first car rolled down.

"Y'all know where you are?" asked the officer leaning over from the driver's seat.

"Yeah... At least I think we do," I answered. The officer raised an eyebrow. I could not figure out how he could drive perfectly while continuing to talk to us out the window.

"Well you fellas happen to find y'selves on the north side. This ain't the nicest part of town. Where y'all headed?"

"Across the Mississippi." At this the officer snickered the kind of snicker that said, *I'm laughing because I don't know how else to make light of what you are getting into. And if you knew what you were getting into...*

"East St. Louis—even better. Good luck," he said, rolled up the window, and sped away. The second car pulled up even with us and rolled down their passenger window. This time an officer in the passenger seat stuck his head out the window.

"You guys got any guns on you? You may need them," he said.

"No, we don't," I answered a nonchalant tone. "Can we have yours?" The officer laughed outright, but did not say anything more. He rolled up the window and the car drove away.

"I guess I didn't realize what we were getting into," Oliver said after the cop cars were gone.

"Yeah, you think they were serious? I mean, that cop asked if we're packing heat?!" I replied.

"I was almost gonna ask him if these guns counted." Oliver was sitting up with hands off the handlebars and arms cocked.

"Something tells me flexed biceps don't count as 'guns,' but I could be wrong…"

The officers' comments put an eerie spin on the mood. It was almost midday and the sun shone brilliantly. The streets were lined with brick apartments that were old but not dilapidated. Not a soul was outside on the sidewalks. At first everything just seemed quiet but now it was too quiet. I imagined gangsters watching us out of every window and behind every door, waiting to take to the street in unison and surround us. My heart beat faster and faster as we continued through the north side.

Dear Google Maps, please add an "avoid ghetto" option, I thought.

"Welcome to Illinois!" Oliver said as we crossed the bridge spanning the Mississippi. This was the first state I was not excited to see, because of what the officers and my friends told me about East St. Louis. The buildings were now legitimately run-down. The streets were deserted and every storefront window boarded shut. I cannot say why, but things felt more and more tense the deeper we rode into the city.

"Hey, I think we may have taken a wrong turn," I mused.

"I guess we should pull over and check things out. There's the post office." The last thing I wanted to do was stop moving, but it unavoidable. The post office was closed during the lunch hour but fortunately a nice woman, one of the few people outside I had seen in a half hour, pointed us in the right direction.

"I don't like this. I don't like this one bit," I said to Oliver when we resumed pedaling, now in the right direction.

"Yeah man, let's get out of here."

I believe the officers and reports that say we rode through dangerous territory and I do not doubt that when the sun goes down another world awakens. But even gangsters have to sleep sometime. The seeds of fear were sown in my mind and it totally changed my perception of where I was and what was happening. I would not be caught dead riding through East St. Louis after sundown, but I also doubt any loaded guns were leveled at us through broken windows.

The city of St. Louis received honors in 2010 for being the most dangerous city in the United States. It overtook such crime powerhouses as New Orleans and Camden, the respective winners in 2008 and 2009. A study from CQ Press reports that in 2010 there were about 2,070 violent crimes in St. Louis per 100,000 people. The national average is around 430 crimes per 100,000. The city even made its way onto a "Top 10 Most Dangerous Cities in the World" list. In the *world*.

What is the situation across the Mississippi in East St. Louis? Its crime index on city-data.com was over twice that of St. Louis proper in 2007 and six times as large as the national average. Its murder rate was 101.9 per 100,000. In the same year, the murder rate in St. Louis was a seemingly modest 39.6 per 100,000. The only reason I can imagine East St. Louis not topping the list of "Most Dangerous Cities" is that it has a relatively tiny and decreasing population of fewer than 30,000. The decline in the last half century follows the archetype of a Rust Belt city struggling to cope with lost industrial and railroad jobs. In 1950 the population of East St. Louis was over three times what it is now; maybe that is why it felt so empty.

Looking over these crime statistics I feel uncomfortable. On paper it sounds like we barely escaped a war zone, but in person the area just felt deserted.

Whether or not we were lucky to escape with our lives, we cleared the city and were promptly surrounded by fields of corn and sod. It was a long day of riding in the heat, but around a quarter to eight we pulled into a city called Murphysboro. As usual we knew nothing of where to go or what to do. Opportunity presented itself in a street populated by three churches. We tried the United Methodist establishment, but nobody was around. Similar luck was had investigating the Baptist grounds. The last church on the block, a Free Christian Church, was dark and empty. However, the house next-door situated on church property looked occupied.

I walked up to the door I could hear a TV inside and noticed a hanging decoration that proudly said "Welcome to our home. The Spangler's." Donning an Amateur Sleuth cap I walked back out to the church's reader board. Sure enough, underneath the name and service times I found the title "Pastor Ron Spangler." *The pastor's house. How very convenient,* I thought, beaming on the inside.

Returning to the doorstep of the house I did not even have time to ring the door bell before a high-pitched barking erupted behind the door. I knocked anyway, but nobody answered. I knocked again, but still nothing. What I assumed was a small dog continued to fill the house with its rancor. I walked halfway around the side of the house.

"Is anybody home?!" I asked.

"Come again?" a voice responded from the back yard.

"Hello! We were knocking on your front door but nobody was coming." A woman of medium stature and short hair poked her head over the fence. The faint wrinkles around her eyes told me she had spent a good part of her life smiling.

"Just a second. Gotta make sure the Duke is secure." She disappeared for half a minute and emerged from the front door, approached, and extended her hand. "Name's Lori Spangler. Who the heck are you?" I liked her already. And it was time to start the program.

"Well, my name is Scott and this is my friend Oliver. We are riding our bikes across the country and happened upon the fine establishment of Murphysboro this evening…" As I continued to explain our situation I watched her facial expression change from 'I am curious' to 'I am amused' to 'holy cow! That is amazing.' *She is hooked like a salmon; just reel her in.* "…so our question for you: what is our best plan for food and a place to crash tonight?"

"Hmm, let me think... I know! This couple Vivian and Hugh, I bet they would put you up. They have been part of the church for longer than we've been around. Come on around to the backyard and I'll get you something to drink while I give them a call." *You've gone done it again, Scott, you little devil.*

Oliver and I sat in the backyard drinking Gatorade while Lori made the call. The Duke, who I assumed was the wiener dog that had been barking incessantly since we arrived, must have been let loose by Lisa because he came running outside to be even more obnoxious to our faces.

"Your dog doesn't seem to let up," Oliver said when Lori came out the backdoor.

"Yeah, he can be a bit of a handful at first. But he will love you in about..." she appeared to be doing some quick addition in her head, "...twelve minutes. I talked to Vivian and she said you are more than welcome to stay with them tonight. They have a basement and an extra bed which should suit you perfectly. Hugh is going to come down here to show you the way to their house. In the meantime, you two have gotta be hungry. Can I interest you in some dinner? We went to the Barbeque Kitchen downtown on Saturday and have a ton of leftovers. Wow—" Oliver was scratching the Duke's ears, "you and the Duke are eleven minutes ahead of schedule."

Hugh came by as we were eating and talked with us while we finished up. He was good-natured, very interested in our adventure, and finished every other sentence with "that an' e'rything." He looked to be at least in his seventies.

"We've been here in Murphysboro for longer'n I can remember. Started here raisin' our kids and just stuck around after all that an' e'rything."

"What brought you here in the first place?"

"Well, I grew up on the family farm only 'bout seven miles outside of town. But when my dad passed away we sold it and moved into town. But the people around here are really nice an' I couldn't imagine living any other place. Got a good job workin' in the mine and a cute girl and it was all too good to think about leavin'. We always had strong roots an' e'rything here."

Pretty soon I wanted to add "that an' e'rything" to the end of everything I said as well. Once I actually did by accident, but Hugh did not notice. When it was time to go we bid Lisa and the Duke farewell and Hugh led us to his house in the dark. By the time we made it to their house and got settled it was ten o'clock and high time to go to bed. In the process of setting my alarm I realized the previous day it had been set for 6:30pm instead of 6:30am. *So that's why we did not wake up on time.*

We did not miss our alarm the next morning. Getting out of bed was not difficult because appetizing smells of a delicious breakfast were wafting my direction. I felt like a cartoon character mesmerized by the visible tendrils of an odor cloud that find their way into his nose. If I were Scooby Doo or Wile E. Coyote I would have walked right into the pot of boiling stew, but the real Scott retained control of his nervous system.

"Good morning!" Vivian said when I walked up the stairs. I was still a bit groggy. "Biscuits and gravy are on the menu. You like eggs and bacon? Hope you are hungry!" I would never have problems getting out of bed if mornings were like this every day.

Over breakfast we had the opportunity to learn more about our hosts and to share about ourselves. Hugh and Vivian were incredibly kind and had personalities that balanced each other beautifully. Vivian was the talker; Hugh liked to get his hands dirty.

"...And I told him, 'Hugh, I don't want you retiling that bathroom. You're gettin' too old and we can't afford you takin' a fall.' And so he said, 'alright honey, I'll go on into town, talk to Fred Johnson an' see how much it cost us.' But do you have any idea who I found standing in that bathtub takin' out tiles when I got home the next day?! *Him.*" Vivian pointed at Hugh and both smiled.

"But I did what I says I was goin' to do," Hugh defended

himself sheepishly. "Went on down to Fred and asked him exactly what I said I would. But it was fixin' to be a rather large sum and I didn't want to pay that much on a bathroom. All we was doing there was taking shits anyways. Figured since I ain't workin' no more my time is better spent doin' the thing myself and then take my wife out on a date with the money we save." Vivian could not argue. She explained,

"I just get worried every once in a while. But what is a worrisome one like me supposed to do?"

"We just keep on refusin' to get old. Know what I mean? You're only as old as you feel, that type of stuff an' e'rything."

"But we're gettin' old. Been a full fifty-one years since we met. Can you believe it, Hugh?" She turned towards us. "I shoulda known I was signin' up to be with a stubborn fella who would retile our bathroom at age seventy-four. I was working as a car hop at the Dairy King and this good-looking boy about your age pulled up in a car with his friend. Said they'd been in the fields makin' hay all day and were real thirsty. Ended up ordering three quarts of iced tea."

"Because I wanted more time to get to know her," Hugh interjected, "I couldn't let the nicest girl I seen all year just run away!"

"So he asked me on a date—"

"She said no."

"—I said no, I hardly knew him yet—"

"That's why I bought all the iced teas."

"—but after a year went by I finally said yes—"

"Finally."

"—and we have been happily married nearly fifty years since."

"Now the secret," Hugh said to us in a hushed voice, "is persistence. I kept givin' her my telephone number and talkin' to her whenever I saw her, until she finally tired of saying 'no.' That's when you know you got 'er—"

"And then you end up with a 'persistent' man hanging around for fifty years, and a retiled bathroom to boot." We all laughed.

"All I can say is if I *ever* retile my own bathroom—I don't care how old I am—I'll be very pleased with myself," I said.

"Now y'all started in Seattle, but where are you headed to?" Vivian asked.

"We're shooting for the Atlantic. Thinking that means Yorktown in Virginia. And from there we are going to continue on up to Washington, D.C., because neither of us has ever been there." When Oliver finished a pensive expression came over Vivian's face. She mused,

"Ah, that is great. We have gone there before…"

"Two times," Hugh added.

"…yes, twice we have been there. You two alright with a little bit of touchy-feely for the next minute?" Oliver and I nodded. "Well you see, I had a brother who was killed in Vietnam. Seventh of July, nineteen sixty-seven. Army. And like Hugh said, we have been there twice but haven't been able to see the Memorial. Once it was closed and the other time we were passing through and couldn't stop to see it. We've been so close, but I have never seen my brother's name on the wall."

Her words hung in the air for a few long seconds. I could sense the scars of pain and heartache now. Over forty years had gone by but reality does not change, even in the past. We had just acquired a new cause for our trip, albeit a small one:

"Vivian, we will go see his name for you. It will be like you are looking through our eyes." Her previously pensive expression softened.

"Bless your hearts," she said. "That would mean the world to me."

Breakfast ended up being a very long ordeal—which was not a bad thing—because the weather outside was dismal. Five minutes before we were going to leave the gates of heaven opened and let loose a fierce barrage of rain and wind and lightning. Hugh went downstairs to check the weather forecast and came out to talk with us in the garage, where we were readying our bicycles and putting on our rain jackets.

"Fellas, it ain't lookin' too good for ya today. Checked on the computer an' it says we're due for showers all day. I reckon you'll be getting' all soggy an' e'rything."

"Here you go you two," Vivian poked her head around the corner, oblivious to our plight. She handed Oliver and I each peanut butter and jelly sandwiches, apples, and granola bars. I looked inside the lunch bag and found a note saying "Good luck, travelers! We will be thinking and praying for you." Being adopted by surrogate mothers is one of the best things.

"Y'know," I said when we started riding away from Hugh and Vivian's house, "this could get miserable."

"Yeah," Oliver nodded in understanding. The rain had settled down to a steady drizzle, but black clouds ahead gave the future an ominous tint.

"Gonna be wet."

"But what's a little water?"

"Gonna be stormy."

"Could be struck by lightning, too."

"You ready for *that an' e'rything*?"

"I'm ready for that."

"An' e'rything?"

"An' e'rything."

A little rain never hurt anybody, right? I thought.

Chapter THIRTEEN

Murphysboro, IL to Marion, KY

H*EY ZEUS! DO YOU THINK you can get your act together and clear up this cruddy weather? It's about time you got over all of that lightning jazz. We aren't scared of your little-god syndrome; I know the odds that one of your sparks gets me. And oh, by the way—people stopped believing in you two thousand years ago.*

Zeus ignored our plea. The rain returned with such ferocity as I had never before experienced. Our clothing was soaked beyond hope within two minutes. My shoes were full of water and began to squish. If there is one thing I despise, it is squishy feet. I worried that an inattentive driver would flatten us because it was impossible to see more than ten feet through the falling sheets of water. Lightning sparked and thunder crashed instantaneously overhead. We were smack dab in the middle of nowhere, yet found ourselves at the center of everything. It got so dark that it felt like dusk. Water running down my face picked up dried sweat as it passed through my helmet and stung my eyes like the dickens. The downpour would not stop.

In that moment, middling a thunderstorm and barely able to keep my eyes open, I felt small. Completely powerless before forces larger than I could comprehend. I pulled up even with Oliver.

"You think it could possibly rain any harder?!" I yelled.

"I don't know man. But on the bright side, it doesn't look like we're gonna need showers tonight. Then again, it doesn't seem like this will be our last in-flight shower today." When the rain abated half an hour later, I was a shivering mess. It was not cold outside, but the combination of wind and wet left me miserable. Oliver, who did not put on his jacket at all during the storm, seemed to be doing just fine. One of us was making Bear Grylls, of *Man vs. Wild* fame, proud and it was not me.

"Oliver, this doesn't feel right," I said as we came to a stop sign at a junction.

"Yeah man, me too. My butt has been aching like a Saber-toothed Tiger with a cavity. Haven't been able to sit straight for the past twenty-four hours."

"No, no. I mean I think we should look at the map."

"Ah, the map! Why didn't you say so?"

"I was getting there."

Random aside: Saber-toothed Tigers are not actually tigers at all, being about as closely related to modern house cats as to tigers in evolutionary terms. The most well-known saber-toothed cat goes by the scientific name *Smilodon*. Ironic, because I would not be caught dead saying to one of them, "smile!"

We pulled out the map and I traced the thirty or so miles we had logged since Murphysboro. Unfortunately my finger following the red line marking our road went straight off the edge of the page. It was like Christopher Columbus sailing to the edge of the world.

Luckily there was a small general store at the intersection, so we parked our bicycles and walked inside.

"You said you was lookin' to get to Goreville?" the man behind the counter said.

"Yeah, that's the one."

"Well I be almost certain you take a right at this here stop sign an' that'll take you straight there. Been a while since I been that way, though…" A customer overheard our conversation and detained us momentarily.

"Where y'all headed to?" he asked.

"Tonight we're hoping to make it to Marion, Kentucky. But ultimately we're shooting for the coast in Virginia."

"Virginia?! Gee darn! That is a long ways away. Say," he said while his mouth stretched into a grin, "how you folks gettin' back? You gonna… *ride* home, too?" His elbow extended towards me such that I would laugh along with his jest. I laughed along, uneasily.

"No, we're not gonna ride. One way is good enough for us."

It started to rain again. The store clerk's directions were correct and led us straight to Goreville. With the name of the town, bleak weather, and aged buildings, it could have passed for the setting of a horror movie. Oliver and I wandered into the grocery store and immediately found the frozen pizza aisle. With smiles and halos illuminated above our heads, we approached the old lady at the checkout counter to ask if we could borrow a microwave. She assented, directing us to the employee's lounge area.

In order to reach the microwave we had to pass through the butcher's room. We walked in as a gruff-looking man was about to make a chop on a leg of ham. His right arm was raised, butcher's blade in hand, ready to bring it down with force. I cleared my throat.

"Um, excuse me. Do you mind if we pass through to the microwave?"

"Oh yeah, sure. Just head on through. You gotta jiggle the dial every once in a while if it doesn't start. Kind of an old piece of junk, you know."

"Thanks for the heads up," Oliver replied. We continued through to the next room. I jumped into the doorframe when I heard a loud *Chop!* behind me. I looked down and made sure that I still had all appendages and digits attached.

In the employee room we proceeded to devour frozen pizza after dollar-fifty frozen pizza. A good-looking young woman appeared in the doorframe. I choked on my cheese. She sat down and started talking to us like we belonged in the place.

"You know, that guy choppin' out there is the store owner. Well I didn't wanna come back this summer but he said he needed help, so here I am. Been workin' here for the past five summers. Can't wait to get back to college."

"Where do you go?"

"Southern Illinois, in Carbondale. You heard of it?"

"Yeah, we actually rode past it yesterday morning. We got lost."

"Oh… Well, where y'all going to?"

"Virginia."

"No way! That is crazy!"

"Maybe. Started out in Seattle and we're trying to make it across the country."

"That is so crazy! …Did you notice that it's a rainin' outside?"

"Actually we did. Whenever it rains, we get wet."

"Wow, crazy."

"Where d'you sleep?"

"Wherever, really. Churches, yards, parks, fire stations…"

"You guys are crazy…" She sat staring at us like we were aliens from Mars. It was uncomfortable. Something told me people in Goreville do not often interact with outsiders. I did not want to encourage her to continue speaking, though, because hearing her say "crazy" one more time would drive me *loco* myself. After passing a few more minutes in thick awkwardness we got up to leave.

"Well, it was nice to meet you. Good luck at college this year."

"Thanks and good luck with your journey, too. I'll be praying for you... You guys are *crazy!*" Our backs were already turned to her when she said this and I winced. In the next room, Mr. Meatman-Owner was making another chop. I jumped again. A chicken leg fell to the floor.

"You're not gonna tell anyone you saw that drop on the ground, will ya?" Mr. Meatman asked, tapping the blunt end of his butcher blade in the palm of his left hand.

"Of course not, sir," I said.

"Wouldn't even think of it," Oliver echoed.

"Good. I knew I could count on you two. Hate to have to *cut* you loose." He started laughing a deep and menacing laugh. I did not look back until we were clear of the store.

"When he said 'cut,' did he really—well, you know?"

"I do not care to find out."

The afternoon took a turn for the brighter and the weather lightened up. I was grateful, because my feet had been squishing for six hours. We came to Cave-in-Rock, a quaint town of about four hundred. It is named after, quite literally, a cave fifty-five feet wide etched out of sheer rock located close to the town. The town is located on the banks of the Ohio River, and a ferry shuttles cars and passengers across to Kentucky.

A ferry has been operating at the site for two hundred years. At the turn of the 19th century it was known as Ford's Ferry after its owner, Jim Ford. In this early era, the lands later incorporated as the southern part of Illinois were rife with bandits, highwaymen, and criminals of every kind. The Cave itself was a frequent crime scene, and robberies often culminated in murder.

Jim Ford was a shady character himself; together with his ferry operator and a man who went by the name of Potts, he made a business of taking the possessions of ferry-goers. Legend has it any passerby who took objection to Ford's "modern" way of doing business, they would simply disappear. After all, Ford reasoned, these objectors would have no place amongst the fine residents of Hardin

County. An intricate network of spies determined the wealth of ferry passengers and persuaded the moneyed ones to stop off at Potts' Inn to the north. Potts, jovial on the outside but with nefarious intentions, would then free his new customer of their worldly possessions and set their soul free of its worldly bounds if necessary.

Potts had a son who grew into the family business. As diabolical as his father, he quickly jumped ranks and was committing murders of his own. One such occasion was particularly gruesome and attracted negative publicity, causing him to flee the area. He spent twenty years pirating the Ohio River territory, thieving and pillaging, until pangs of homesickness urged him homeward. Knowing of his father's scheme, and wanting experience it firsthand so as to learn something for his own enterprises, he disguised himself as a weary traveler. At the ferry he flaunted his coin and identified the spy who urged him to stay at Potts Inn. Playing along, the younger Potts consented and arrived home.

Upon arriving at the inn, the younger Potts was cheerily greeted by the older Potts. However, the father did not recognize his son in disguise, believing him to be simply another passerby. In a stunning exhibit of *hubris* the younger Potts allowed his father to lead him out to the spring behind the inn to get water. Before he had a chance to see what hit him, the younger Potts was sent packing across the river, although it was the river Styx instead of the Ohio.

Rumor spread through the town that the old man Potts had murdered his own son. The merciless killer was so itched by these comments that he decided to dig up the body of his most recent victim in order to prove he had not done away with a member of his own family. His wife, nearby filling a bucket of water from the spring, took little time in positively identifying the remains as belonging to their son. The giveaways were a birthmark and scar from a hot iron poker that had been used to "correct" their son in his days of wayward youth.

To this day no one has been able to prove this piece of local folklore untrue. The inn building persisted until the early 20th century.

Remarked one traveler about the building in a diary entry dating to 1854: "[the inn] looks like a place for deeds dark and dreadful. The hills and rocks around have a wild and fearful look about and seem to be a fit place for the ghosts of the murdered dead, to howl in."

Oliver and I did not spend the night at Cave-in-Rock but instead continued on to the town of Marion, Kentucky. Who knows what would have become of our souls and meager possessions?

By the time we arrived in Marion it was dark and restaurants were quickly closing. The only one remaining open was a sandwich shop. The familiar aromas of freshly baked bread, deli meat, and spices filled my nostrils. We walked out the door with submarines that would make our Scottish friend Peter MacDonough proud and proceeded on to the city park, where we were told we could camp for free.

When I finally sat down on the park bench with my sandwich, Oliver had already finished half of his. I peeled back the wrapper to mine and was staring a turkey sandwich in the face. Either my sandwich had spontaneously changed form, or something else was amok.

"You wouldn't happen to be eating a buffalo chicken sandwich, would you?" I asked. Oliver stopped chewing.

"Oh, shoot! Sorry man," he said through a mouth full of chicken. "I guess I was too hungry to think about it."

"Don't worry about it. But I am going to take half of yours if you don't mind."

"Not at all."

About this time a pickup truck pulled into the parking lot. Two young guys hopped out.

"Whoa! John, check it out. There are people over there." They approached us.

"What're you folks doin' here? Ah, look, they got bags on their bikes."

"Yeah, we are staying here for the night…" I explained

"Here?! In Marion? What in the world brought you two here? The rodeo an' fair ain't for another month."

And so we explained our story, as briefly as possible. I was more interested to hear about this fellow named John and his friend Kyle. I asked them how old they were and what they were up to.

"Well, we both twenty years old. I been workin' in the mines with my Pop for 'bout three months now. Its hard work. But it pays good, you know." After John said this I looked down at my hands. Despite the residual bicycle grease, all of a sudden they did not seem so dirty.

"An' I may be going back to jail."

"Back to jail?"

"Yeah, I found myself in a bad situation with some guys who made some bad choices. We was over there behind that dumpster, see. The cops pulled up 'cause they was chasin' us. I didn't know it before, but one of the guys I was with was carryin' a gun, an' he started shootin' at the cops. I knew what we was doin' before was wrong, but I never wanted nothin' to do with any shootin' or nothin'. They may be puttin' me back in for a good while now 'cause I was already on probation an' shit."

John and Kyle were both twenty years old. Although two years older, I felt a lifetime younger in spirit. One of them was talking about going to jail for the better part of a decade. The other was looking forward to working in the coal mines for the rest of his life. Riding a bicycle across the country seemed juvenile compared to the "real life" they were experiencing. In this case I did not mind feeling like a kid.

Western Kentucky is charming, with field after field of golden grain and brick homesteads surrounded by trees cresting each hilltop. Goldenrod patches lined the roads we navigated. It was such an idyllic and pastoral scene that I briefly considered becoming a Kentucky farmer. If only there were real mountains and the ocean nearby. Sorry, Kentucky.

The peaceful silence was suddenly broken by frantic barking. Out of nowhere a large canine came barreling out of a roadside driveway. The dog's eyes were rabid and fixed on Oliver's right shoe.

"Hey! Back off mutt! Go home!" But our yelling only excited the dog further and it sped up to nip at Oliver's heels. Oliver looked mortified, torn between defending himself from the dog and making sure to not crash his bicycle. In a few seconds we reached the invisible threshold where the dog would chase no further. It slowed, barking reduced to a frustrated growl. My heart was pounding out of my chest; I never would have guessed being chased by a dog would beget such an adrenaline rush.

As per usual it was boiling hot outside by noon. We pulled off at a small general store craving Gatorade. Two other cyclists with the same idea were sitting outside on a bench eating sandwiches and sipping sports drinks. Oliver went inside to the air conditioning but I hung around outside for a minute to chat. I presented our dog incident of the previous hour.

"Yeah, the dogs out here're crazy. Gotta be real careful, especially when there's traffic 'cause you never know when one of 'em is gonna come runnin' atcha. Would hate to get hit by a truck gettin' outta a dogs way."

"So manic dogs around here aren't an uncommon occurrence?"

"Oh, no. Not at all. There're dogs all the way across the state. Don't know why the owners don't chain 'em up."

"If I had a gun I would've blown its head off." In the heat of the moment it was the truth. Seeing one hundred-and-fifty pounds of angry dog wanting to dine on human flesh puts one into survival mode. If it was me or the dog who had to go, it was going to be the dog. Apologies to the dog-lovers out there. Next time, please leash your Lassie.

"Me and my wife have been packin' for quite some time for the same reason."

"Packing?"

"Yeah, like packin' heat. Carrying a gun. Check it out: we got our holsters right there under the handlebars." I looked and sure enough, there were the black pouches concealing the weapons. I could not believe it.

"...So you really carry guns when you go out for a ride?"

"All the time. Never know what's gonna be out there, y'know."

"And the dogs?" I was picturing canine brains sprayed all over the road. Maybe blowing the dog's head off was not such a good idea...

"Well so far a shot up in the air has been enough to scare 'em away." *So far?* "But you never know, like I said. You never know."

Carrying a loaded gun on a bicycle seemed dangerous. What if he were to crash it accidentally discharged? I am not opposed to responsibly bearing arms, but this just seemed like a really bad idea.

We were about to get back on the road when a young cyclist pulled up to the store. Culture on the bicycle touring circuit suggests people present a trail-worn and salty image, which he fit perfectly: his bicycle was loaded with weather-faded front and rear panniers, and he wore ratty cargo shorts and a soiled button-down shirt with sleeves rolled up. Personally, I had no desire to spend any amount of time cycling in grimy casual clothes. Thanks for offering, but I will take the comfort of my synthetic shirt and padded spandex shorts. My butt will be happier sans saddle sore, too.

The young cyclist cleared his throat and addressed us,

"My name's David. Where'd you start from?"

"Seattle," I responded. "You?"

"Yorktown. How long you been at it?"

"About thirty-five days."

"Wow. You guys are really going for it," he said with surprise.

"I guess so."

"Only carrying rear panniers, huh?"

"Yeah, what you see is what we got."

"Well, I have been a huge fan of my Ortilebs. Best panniers ever."

"Yep."

"Ah, you're riding a Surly Cross-check. Heard good things about that model. My Surly Long-haul Trucker has been holding up great."

"Yep." Oliver's bike, so it was his turn to respond.

"Hmm…" David paused in thought. Now it was back to the panniers: "yeah, I sometimes wish I only had rear panniers. Been asking myself what I was thinking when I threw the vice grips and socket wrench in there right before I left my house. Gotta weigh five pounds between the two of 'em"

I did not care much for gear talk, but wanted to see if David had much to say about his adventure.

"So David, how has your trip been? I mean, has it lived up to what you thought it would be?"

"Aww, man. You don't even know…" *Actually I think I do. We have been riding for over a month, after all.* He took a deep breath, as if preparing to give birth to a profound revelation that was going to rock the very foundations of my world.

"Been the greatest thing to happen to me," he started. "Just so great. Quit my job because I hated it and needed to go out here and *do* something. Just been… great. I mean, everything… Yeah, great."

"Wow. That sounds… great," I replied, unable to think of anything else to say.

"Hey!" he suddenly resurfaced from a deep sea of thought, although for David that meant sitting up in the kiddie pool. "I stayed last night with this couple a coupla miles off the route. Great people. They gave me this business card to hand to someone on the trail. Told me they've been putting up cyclists for a long time. They're running a regular *inn* for us touring cyclists. Whelp, I gotta run. Flapping gabs don't make any miles, you know."

David quickly placed a plain-looking business card in my hand. Without further ado he saddled his bicycle and pushed off. The bicycle wobbled precariously under the many pounds of extra weight. Vice grips? And a *socket wrench*?

I stood there contemplating the business card, which read

"Doug and Gretchen Fredrickson, farmers extraordinaire." Once again, it all seemed too good to be true. Could this be a modern-day retelling of the Potts Inn fable? Was David part of a vicious spy network trying to get us to take the bait? Descendents of Potts family live on today, and everyone in Kentucky did seem to carry a gun. The headline *"Two bicyclists go missing, last seen yesterday in western Kentucky"* is something I would not want my parents to hear.

On the other hand, David could have just presented us with helpful information; a house and all of its amenities would be a tremendous boon.

If Joe were around, he would say simply,

"Scott, just follow the signs."

Joe believes the correct course of action is delineated by signs that surface at one point in time or another. At times those signs can be subtle. The questing individual would do well to keep their eyes peeled and head on a swivel—lest they miss a critical fork in their metaphysical road. The trick to following signs is to be in tune with your inner voice, so that when a sign decides to broadcast itself you will know how to respond.

Already on the trip we had been presented with many signs to follow. An example would be the Katy Trail; it was a motorcyclist in Colorado who first informed of the trail's existence. It felt like signs were pointing us towards the Katy, so we followed them. If we had not followed signs towards the Katy Trail, a critical portion of the journey would have been missing. We would not have met Shawn or Sister Erma, my tire would not have gotten chewed up by the gravel, and we would have missed the character-defining march into St. Louis to slay Joe's final boss.

The business card was a sign. It was either telling us we should follow the trail to this mysterious couple or steer as far clear as possible. Sometimes you know you have a sign, but do not know exactly what it is saying.

Chapter FOURTEEN

Marion, KY to Yeaman, KY

NOT LONG AFTER LEAVING THE general store, feeling refreshed in a way that only Gatorade can accomplish on a sweaty day, a loud Chevy Suburban towing a large camper passed by and honked at us. At the junction of our next turn, we found the same camper parked off to the side of the road. A sign big enough to cover the majority of the rear of the camper read "Bike Across America: Helping Haiti's Hospital Sacre Coeur." There was a man leaning on the side of the Suburban who flagged us down as we rode by.

"Hey! You guys riding the Trans-Am?" he shouted. We slowed and pulled off into the gravel.

"Yeah, we sure are," Oliver replied as he unbuckled his helmet.

Without the cooling breeze brought on by riding, we were both drenched in sweat instantly.

"Can I give you anything, then? Need a granola bar? Water? I got two guys coming who should be here any minute to take a break. Sure is hot outside today."

"You're telling me," I said. "And you must be the designated driver, I assume?"

"Yep, you got it. Name's Evan. Been driving this old sag-wagon since San Francisco."

In another minute two cyclists pulled up alongside. They wore matching jerseys of a similar design as the sign on the camper that read "Bike Across America." I also noticed with a tinge of jealousy that their bicycles were not laden with any panniers or other gear.

"Hey Jerry! Tim! These two young guys are riding across the country just like you."

"Oh, yeah? Way to be. Name's Tim," the taller of the two said and stretched out his hand. Oliver shook it after me. "And that over there is Jerry."

Jerry had gone around to the other side of the Suburban and came back with a bottle of water and granola bar. He raised his left hand in a half-wave while he gulped down half the bottle. After eyeing our bicycles he said,

"You two riding unsupported?"

"Yessir. What you see is what we've got." Jerry nodded in approval.

"Good for you."

"Yeah, that is really great you guys," Tim added. "If we weren't in our sixties with old knees and tired backs we would be right there with you."

"You forgot the gray hair, Tim," Evan said with a smirk.

"Who asked you, Evan?" But then Tim turned to us and said, "He is right; we are just a couple old gray-hairs plodding along."

Tim and Jerry "hired" a friend of theirs (Evan) to drive the camper across the states as they pedaled their bicycles. Doing a trip this way is called "supported," because the vehicle is always alongside them to carry food, water, bicycle parts, and everything else that could possibly come in handy on the road. Fermented beverages in a cooler come to mind. Each night they would find a campground and sleep on comfortable mattresses with pillows. It seemed like a life of luxury.

On the one hand, doing a supported ride across the country seems far less complex. There was no need for panniers and no extra thirty-five pounds to slow you down. No making a pile of stinky clothes for a pillow. But the best thing by far is that all you have to do is hop in the camper for instant shelter from the rain, wind, heat, or sun.

However, things are not always so simple on a supported bicycle tour. For starters it costs a whole lot more. When you throw another personality into the mix for two months, there is that much more of a chance for tempers to flare and personalities to clash. I heard firsthand the sad story of a man who had to abandon his cross-country journey because he ran out of money to pay his sag-wagon driver and preferred to ride in the early morning compared to the driver's desire to sleep in. He was well past the halfway mark when he had to call it quits.

Tim, Jerry, and Evan seemed to be doing just fine with the arrangement. Some elitists scoff at the idea of riding supported, but I say "to each his or her own." In my sixties I will be happy if I can sit on a bicycle seat for fifty days straight—panniers or no panniers. The greatest part about their story was their fundraiser to benefit the Sacre Coeur Hospital in Haiti. Tim, an ophthalmologist, spent time volunteering there and decided to use his trip as a means to raise money.

We spent the better part of the afternoon riding with them, trying to keep up with their unencumbered pace. I noticed that they climbed hills with relative ease. Descending, the difference between loaded and unloaded bicycles was less pronounced.

By the time the next town came around, Oliver and I were ragged and informed Tim and Jerry we were going to take a break. They wanted to continue onward so we bid them farewell. I was starving, and quickly unpacked a squished, half-eaten loaf of Oats & Nuts bread and jar of crunchy peanut butter. A bruised, warm banana completed the spread.

I plunged a dirty Spork into the jar of peanut butter and withdrew it loaded with golden cargo twinkling in the afternoon sun. In another second the peanut butter slopped onto the heel and another slice of bread. I could already sense the appetizing aroma wafting into my nasal cavities. Then it was time for the warm banana. As if giving birth to a creature from the womb, I drew back the protective layers of peel and extracted the ripened plant ovary. Parts of it were mushy because of trauma endured riding on the back of my bicycle, but I was undeterred. I broke the banana in half and carefully laid the split bundle of sugar and potassium onto one slice of peanut-buttered bread. The heel came crashing down, capping the completed masterpiece. My jaw dropped in sheer wonder and excitement and I thought *that was convenient; I guess I'll just keep my jaw down so I can take a bite.*

My teeth sunk in to the creation and electrifying approval instantly shot from the taste receptors in my tongue into the central nervous system and up to my brain. Peanut butter and banana: the perfect blend of carb and crunch, sweet but satisfying, and always, always sure to delight.

"Scott... Scott... SCOTT!"

"Yeah?"

"You okay? I called your name three times."

"Oh, sorry... I must've gotten into this sandwich a bit more than I realized."

"Well I can hardly fault you. Peanut butter and banana, you know. But I think we better get a move on because those clouds over there look real angry." I turned my gaze to the west, where Oliver was pointing. Sure enough, it looked like our minutes of blue sky and sunshine would be limited. A gray abyss was quickly devouring what remained of clear skies.

"Time to bounce like a beer gut."

Resistance was futile. Much like the storm outside of Murphysboro, this one came fast. One minute the sun was beating comfortably on my back and sixty seconds later the sky was dark and we were drenched. I did not bother to don my jacket because the temperature was still pushing eighty degrees. It was a choice between getting wet from the rain or soaking myself with sweat from the inside of a stuffy jacket.

Twenty minutes later the rain abated. The sun re-emerged and all returned to normal. The only sign of the storm was lingering puddles on the road, but even those were gone in an hour. My feet were not so happy because they squished all afternoon. Instead of letting the rest of me become angry, I sang an adaptation of a childhood song: "the feet on the Scott go 'squish, squish, squish,' all the way home." It is hard to take things serious enough to be angry when singing like this.

"Well look who we have here!" it was Evan again, yelling at us from the side of the road, again. "You fellas are *soaked!*" *Evan, bless your heart, tell me something I don't know.* "You see Jerry and Tim out there on the road?"

"No, we must've just missed them."

A couple minutes later our two AARP friends rolled up.

"Long time, no see!" Jerry said.

"Wow! You fellas are *soaked!*" Tim added.

"That's what I said," replied Evan.

"Some storm, huh?" Tim continued, directing his attention towards us.

"Yeah, I guess that was something, wasn't it?" Oliver responded. I was preoccupied with my sopping-wet feet and how they squished when I shifted my weight.

"We got caught in it hot an' heavy," Jerry mused.

"Didn't even have time to dive into the camper because Evan was a mile in front of us," Tim said while shaking his head wistfully.

I noticed neither Jerry nor Tim were wearing their "Bike Across America" jerseys. Tim had changed into a solid green top and Jerry was wearing a jersey from a microbrewery that I did not recognize.

"Well it's too bad you got all wet," Oliver said. *Oliver you are either really good at faking sincerity or you really were meant to be a priest.* I did not feel sorry for Jerry and Tim in the least bit. Misery loves company, right?

It was getting to be time to think about where we were going hole up for the night. Jerry must have been thinking the same thing too, because after a moment's pause he asked,

"You two have anywhere you are planning on crashing tonight? Tim and I are thinking about a campsite ten miles up the road. Our map says they've got some sort of store, although I am not sure what else." Oliver and I had already talked about the situation, figuring Tim and Jerry would offer to shelter us beside their camper or split a campsite with us. Bikers have got to stick together and survive, of course.

But for some reason both of us were intrigued by the mystery couple whose business card we received earlier in the day from David. We turned down Tim and Jerry's generous offer and ventured onto roads not charted on our maps.

After a few miles we came to a church whose parking lot was loaded with cars. It was a weeknight, so this was slightly surprising. A young mother was grabbing her infant out of the back seat of her car. We asked her if she had heard of anyone in the area who makes a habit of housing cyclists.

"Hmmm, let me think…" She looked at the business card and a light turned on in her head. "I reckon you mean Doug and Gretchen Fredrickson. They are up this road 'bout two or three mile. Look for the big stable to your right, and it'll be the first driveway on your left.

Y'all got courage, y'know—that hill ain't no slouch."

I looked to the right and saw what she meant. A narrow road shot up at an alarming grade, twisting quickly out of sight. We had already logged one hundred and twelve miles on the day and I was past exhausted. It had been a long time since food and my water was running low.

The "hill" to which our kind acquaintance referred was actually a series of brutal ascents and quick descents along steep, rolling terrain. I was close to getting off my bicycle to walk, but I did not know if that was going to be any easier. The two mile mark came and went, but there was no sign of the stable or driveway. After three miles there still was no sign of them. Doubt began to creep in, and I began to wonder if we overshot the driveway. To make matters worse, it felt like a garden gnome was riding on my arched back ramming a jackhammer into my skull. Besides a splitting headache, my legs were weak to the point of collapse.

A downhill bend in the road disguised the worst incline yet. I had to torque my neck just to see the top. It felt like hours before my overgeared bicycle made it to the crest of the incline. Somehow Oliver was doing fine, but I was a weak-kneed, angry mess.

"What the hell were we thinking coming this way?" I spat, frustrated and downtrodden. "We have no idea where we are. Who knows if we overshot the driveway. Even if we are headed the right way, they may not help us at all..."

"We don't even know if they exist," Oliver added, although unemotionally.

"We don't even know if they exist. Damn it. I'm sorry, but I am feeling like an idiot right now. We should've taken Jerry and Tim up on their offer. At least we'd be done riding by now."

"Doesn't really help us too much at the moment, though, does it?" Oliver was right and we both knew it.

"No, it doesn't."

"Tell you what," my riding mate said in a freshly upbeat tone, "We have ridden about five miles since the church. Let's go another two and see what there is to see—and if nothing comes up, we'll just figure something else out."

"You realize we have gone twice as far as they said to?"

My cynical and agitated self could not comprehend how Oliver could still be positive. We started riding again, losing the elevation we worked so hard to attain, only to gain it painfully back again. Exactly two miles further were the stable and driveway, just as the neighbor at church had described.

"This it?" Oliver questioned, looking at the nondescript gravel driveway dropping rapidly into a stand of trees. From the road it looked like it went straight into a dense forest, and no sign of residence could be seen. The properties to the left and right seemed to have greedily pinched off this unfortunate property, leaving room only for an access road.

"She did say it was the first driveway on the left," I said, trying unconvincingly to convince myself.

"If we go down this hill, there is no way we are turning back tonight," Oliver said with face stoically expressionless. My stomach sank along with the setting sun. Our situation seemed truly hopeless.

"Alright. Let's do it."

The steep gravel slope passed through the trees and seeing much of anything was difficult. The going was rough and the road was at least half a mile long. About halfway down we had to get off our bikes and step across a runoff stream created by the recent rain storms. Oliver was right in saying we would not return to the road that evening. I was questioning whether we would *ever* return to the road.

Miraculously, the trees opened up to a large clearing populated by two houses and a shed. A tractor was parked ten yards from the shed, standing watch over a field that sloped down and away from the houses. The larger house came alive with the frantic barking of multiple dogs. *No need to ring the doorbell, I guess.* But there really was no need to ring; nobody was home, and after the dogs calmed down an eerie silence descended upon the clearing.

After munching on a few Oreos and drinking my last sips of water, I was feeling somewhat better and could see our situation with more perspective. It was amusing.

"Next time we are suckers enough to listen to a crazy who tells us to ride ten miles off the route, without any idea where we are going, up and down those goddamn hills, and down that godforsaken driveway, only to find that *nobody is home*, please punch me in the face."

It felt like we got conned into buying a Sham-Wow.

"That guy who used to be on TV selling stuff has got to be laughing at us from his grave. I think his name was Billy Mays." Oliver must have been thinking the same thing, because he did not miss a beat in saying,

"…but call within the next ten minutes and we'll *double* your offer! That means you get *two* recent college graduates sitting on your doorstep without your knowing for the price of *one*. And that's not all. Be one of the first twenty callers and we'll make them extra-special smelly absolutely *free!*"

"Oliver I know you are being funny, but let's just think for a second. What happens if they come home tonight?"

"Good question. I hadn't thought about it."

Right on cue we heard the distant rumbling of a car coming down the driveway. It stopped for a moment and then proceeded at a markedly more agitated pace down to the houses. The driver's door swung open and, even before the masculine figure emerged, a string of profanity that could peel back paint belched out of the car's interior.

"… and I've had enough of this shit. We just got that driveway redone three days ago and now all this goddamned rain is already washing everything out and—look at the hay! Little fuckers're all bent over because it is so goddamn wet. Damn it all to hell!"

In the meantime the passenger door opened as well, begetting a woman of a drastically different disposition than her partner. She was a bit on the short side with short-ish blonde-ish hair and an inviting smile. Oliver and Scott, meet Gretchen and Doug Fredrickson.

"Well this is a little bit of a surprise," Gretchen said and extended her hand in greeting. "Name's Gretchen and over there that's my husband, Doug."

Doug, wearing a hat obscuring the rage in his eyes, intended to walk over to the closest stand of not-standing hay but got caught in a deep puddle hidden under the grass. He let out an angry cry and hopped around trying to shake the water out of his shoes. This only caused more water to splash in. *I hate squishy shoes too, Doug. I feel for you.*

"And who might you be?" Gretchen asked, and my attention snapped back to the kindly figure in front of me.

"Oh, sorry. My name is Scott."

"And I'm Oliver. So is he—well, gonna be alright?"

"Yeah, he will be fine. Just give it a few minutes." She looked at Doug, who had started to kick the shin-deep puddles in frustration. "But I would definitely give it a few minutes."

"We're really sorry to just kind of show up here without any notice," I said, changing the subject. "We tried to call earlier today but just got the answering machine. Then when we got here and nobody was around..."

"Don't worry about it," Gretchen replied with a nod of understanding. "But you do need to tell me how the hell you found us."

"Earlier today we bumped into this guy named David who gave us your business card. He said you were worth a bit of a detour."

"Ah, yes. David was a nice boy. Interesting—but nice. Looked us up on WarmShowers.com. You heard of that?"

At this point in the trip we had heard about the Warm Showers website multiple times. It is a networking site that pairs cyclists looking for a place to stay with willing hosts in cities across the nation. User profiles ensure neither hosts nor cyclists recently escaped from an insane asylum (although embarking on a bicycle tour brings into question one's sanity). And voilà, matches made in heaven on a regular basis. In theory it is possible to arrange every night's stay of a bicycle tour via Warm Showers.

I never looked at the site, not even once. For other people it works great, but for me the thrill of the journey came from the uncertainty. The twin goddesses Spontaneity and Randomness provided us with so many warm showers in their great benevolence that it seemed silly to use technology in order to acquire what was already ours.

"...although maybe we should've used it so you would have had some forewarning."

"I am serious. No inconvenience at all. Let me show you two the guest house. And I will apologize beforehand because the inside is a mess. This room is where you can sleep. If you need water or anything else, the kitchen is all yours. Go ahead and get cleaned up and come on over to the other house and we'll feed you some dinner."

It did not seem like these kind people would be the type to operate a robbery/murder operation out of their guest house *a lá* Potts Inn. But at this point I could only guess Doug was kind, because my only experience was seeing him angrily stomp around in a puddle. After cleaning up, we walked over to the main house. I was instantly assaulted by the delicious aroma of dinner and Doug shaking my hand graciously.

"I'm really sorry about that out there. Been a frustrating week to say the least, and it just got the best of me."

"No worries Doug, none at all. Although I will say that for a second I was ready to run for it because I thought you were mad at us."

The composed gentleman conversing with us was a far cry from the other Doug. Coming in at a hair under six feet, he was not the intimidating figure I had previously assumed. Similarly, the goatee that originally said to me "be afraid, be *very* afraid," now said, "I am too lazy to keep shaving, so what you see is what you get." His goatee and hair were graying.

Oliver and I gave Gretchen and Doug the short version of this story up until… now. The two of them were engaged and interested in what we had to say, and the conversation wandered among such topics as life aspirations and where we grew up. They found our observations about Kentucky (there seemed to be more churches than people and the accent is outrageous) amusing.

It was time to be done talking about us. I noticed as early as Doug's profanity string that they were not originally from Kentucky because they did not reveal even a trace of the tell-tale Kentucky accent.

"Alright, I can tell that you two are not from here," I shifted gears, "but I have no clue where you're from. So where are you from and why did you end up here?"

"That could be a long story," said Gretchen, "and I would hate to bore you. But here it goes. We are originally from Jersey. That's where we raised our kids and such. I worked in the insurance field and Doug was a teacher. Things were good and fine, but we'd always dreamed about working a farm. We looked around the state for a while, but land in Jersey is expensive and hard to come by. Then I realized I'm at a place in my career where I can do most of my work wirelessly. Only have to fly back maybe two or three times a year to meet with clients. It was time for Doug to move on from his job, so we came down here and were able to get sixty acres very affordably about four years ago."

"And what has the experience been like?" Gretchen deferred to Doug for this question.

"Hell," he said jokingly. "But seriously, it has been a work in progress. We had no clue what to do at the beginning. And there is a lot of knowledge, a lot of intricacies to farming you just never will know until you try and do it yourself. When it came time to harvest what little hay we had grown after our first year it was an ordeal just to get the plow hooked up to the tractor. There are so many different tools and tractor attachments and factors to consider…" He paused to look outside. "…and then there's the rain."

"At least it seems like the Kentucky people are kind and helpful. We are accosted at every gas station by a posse of locals who just want to talk."

"Yeah, the people are talkative around here," Gretchen said. "But it is more complicated that you'd think. Some of the old farming families that have been here for ages don't take too kindly to foreigners like us who come from other places."

"We call ourselves ex-pats," Doug added.

"Us and some other neighbors in the community who came from the 'outside' all call ourselves that. There are times when we really do feel like foreigners here. Especially when Sunday morning rolls around and we aren't in church. But there are always two sides to the coin. Lots of people—native Kentuckians and ex-pats alike—have been very supportive and helpful as we learn the ropes. There is a strong sense of community around here that I didn't always feel in Jersey."

"Something like a 'we're all in this together' attitude."

"Just so long as your skin is pale."

"But that's another story in and of itself. The bottom line is there are some people here living in the nineteenth century and others who have moved on to the twenty-first. For us it was the right thing to do. We really needed a change and this was it."

"What do you find to be the most rewarding part of life here?"

At this, Doug's brow furrowed in thought. I was expecting an answer such as "wiping the sweat off my brow after a hard day's work in the field," or "reaping the harvest after investing so much time and energy." His response had nothing to do with sweat, work, or the harvest.

"It has reinvigorated our marriage. We had to reinvent ourselves in translating our entire lives here and in the process I have grown much closer to Gretchen and vice versa."

Wow. Gretchen was nodding in agreement. There I was thinking Doug was a tough guy with a bone to pick with Mother Nature, totally equivocated. The authenticity of his answer surprised me so much that I did not have any follow up question prepared. It looked like Oliver was experiencing a similar reaction. For a few moments everything was silent, until Doug continued,

"When you are pushed so far out of your element you just have to rely on each other. We had to rely on each other. There have been some times when things have been really challenging—today was nothing in comparison. In those times it is simple: you support them and they support you, or else you don't make it. Depend on each other, or else you don't succeed. And to me, the fact that we are still here talking to you now after multiple years—hay or no hay—is a success. We will probably never get it perfect but we followed the path to where we were supposed to be and we are doing what we are supposed to do. Sometimes it ain't easy, to follow through with your dream and deal with the consequences of your dream coming true." He paused, pensively scratching his goatee, then exhaled slowly and repeated,

"Sometimes it ain't easy."

Before me were two people doing with their entire lives what I was doing for two months: going on an adventure. The tremendous courage and faith in each other needed to survive, let alone make such a move in the first place, impressed me greatly. So many people—myself included—have wild dreams just like Gretchen and Doug, but so few respect their wildest dreams enough to see them realized. It all goes back to following the signs. Gretchen and Doug followed their signs straight to Kentucky and were rewarded with the unshakeable knowledge that they are doing *exactly* what they are meant to be doing.

In my mind there is no greater success.

Getting the business card was a chance to follow the signs. We had every opportunity to talk ourselves out of it, and could have easily settled to follow Jerry and Tim or done something completely different. But then I always would have wondered who those people were on the card given to us by a complete stranger.

Following the signs is not always a cakewalk. Sometimes storms come and decimate a harvest. Sometimes one must venture off the map and into the unknown. Sometimes the hills will hurt without any assurance of security on the other side. In the end, though, I was glad to have followed the signs to Gretchen and Doug. I actually would not have it any other way, and understand now why most people who endure extreme hardship in their life say "I wouldn't go back and change a thing." Following the signs has less to do the arrival at a certain destination and more to do with everything that happens in the meantime. It is a state of being. A person who follows the signs is being what they are meant to be.

Sometimes it ain't easy.

Chapter FIFTEEN

Yeaman, KY to Buckhorn, KY

"JUST REMEMBER TO LOOK UP every once in a while and appreciate where you are," Doug said as we unloaded our bicycles from the bed of his pickup truck the next morning. We were at the top of their driveway, lucky he offered to drive us back to the road. His comment reminded me of the plaque on Renee's wall in Kansas that said "Enjoy the Journey."

"Thanks again for everything," Oliver said.

"I would seriously consider taking your blueberry French toast to market somewhere. It could be big," I added, referred to the superb breakfast we just enjoyed.

"I think I'll keep it a secret for people like you who just end up on our front porch," our host replied with a smile. "Take care and be safe, now."

I was worried we would have to backtrack in the morning to get back on route. However, it turned out taking the leap of faith to find Gretchen and Doug's house actually was going to save us time and effort in the long run. Looking in the rear-view mirror it seemed comical that I was so concerned about the "wasted" effort; following the signs can be fickle like that.

One hobby Gretchen picked up in Kentucky is quilting, in a non-traditional sense. She paints quilt square patterns on eight by eight foot sheets of aluminum. If that sounds strange, it did to us as well. The interior of their guesthouse was full of the metal sheets, both painted and unpainted, leaning against the walls.

What does one do with a sixty-four square foot quilt square? One hangs it on the side of their building, of course. Call it a central Kentucky fashion statement, a "barn bling-bling" of sorts. As we rode through the beautiful Kentucky countryside, many barns were adorned with at least one of these decorations. To be honest, it grew on me in a quirky-cool sort of way.

We stopped for lunch at Dairy Queen in a place called Elizabethtown. I rolled up to the drive-thru and stuck my head into the window.

"I'll have a large, fudge-dipped cone please," I implored.

The drive-thru attendant blinked twice and looked at me funny as she ran up my order on the till. She maintained a raised eyebrow when we walked into the store and sat down at a table to eat our lunch.

A few hours later we arrived in the city of Bardstown. Central Kentucky is famous for producing Bourbon, and Bardstown is the Bourbon capital of the world. I mentioned this to a friend of mine who is well-versed in the language of spirits.

"Scott, you *have* to go on a Bourbon tour. This is an once-in-a-lifetime opportunity! But seriously, if you don't go, well, I just don't know…"

And so we set off looking for a Bourbon tour. The only problem is most tours close at 3:00pm and it was already fifteen past the hour. That eliminated every option but one. I dialed the Heaven Hill distillery, and a cordial feminine voice answered on the other end of the call.

"Yeah, we were wondering when your last tour this afternoon is?" I hung up the phone and said to Oliver, "alright, we've got a half hour to find this place. Let's make it happen."

On the way there was a car that had to slow down momentarily before passing. They yelled something nasty as their tires screeched and peeled out around us. They must have really wanted to get to a distillery tour on time, too.

The average person on a Bourbon tour has already been receiving the senior discount at the local bowling alley for quite some time. The unofficial dress code was exclusively Ralph Lauren polo shirts tucked into crisply ironed khakis that screamed, "my 401k is much, much bigger than yours." It was a hot afternoon and we were sweaty. Dressed in spandex, we did not comply with the dress code. We walked up to an attractive young woman operating the front desk and asked for a spot on the next tour. She also stood out in the crowd, but for reasons other than sweaty spandex.

"Of course!" she said with a smile. "You two are in the green group. Just pay attention and we will call out when we are ready."

"Thanks much," I said and smiled back. *Look, I know I haven't even gotten started on my 401k, but I've got other things going for me…*

Like most skeptical tourists, I ended up being pleasantly surprised with the experience. Our tour guide was knowledgeable. I learned Bourbon belongs to the whiskey family but for it to be classified as "Bourbon" it has to be aged in new charred oak barrels and cannot go through any extra filtering process. That is why brands such as Jack Daniels, which pass through a filter adding maple flavor, are called "Tennessee Whiskey" and not "Bourbon." Distilling Bourbon is a delicate process, influenced by even the minutest of details such as whether the barrel sat close to a window or the ceiling in the aging sheds.

Heaven Hill distillery alone produces ten labels of Bourbon that go from twenty to hundreds of dollars a bottle. The reason some are so expensive is that they come from individual barrels distilled in a "good year" and aged for a long time. One we saw was aged twenty-seven years, meaning it started sitting in a charred oak barrel five years before I was born. It retailed for a modest $350. At the end of the tour our guide was adamant we try pouring a few drops of water into our bourbon sample.

"You'll notice that it smoothes things out and liberates the aromas. A much more pleasing experience. And let me also say you should never ever shoot Bourbon like this. It is just too good. Find some other cheap garbage if you just want to get tipsy."

We left Heaven Hill Distillery with another smile from the young woman at the front desk and the knowledge that if I ever spend a bunch of money on a bottle of Bourbon I will be sure to add a couple drops of water whenever I drink it.

The region known as Appalachia stretches from the northern portions of Mississippi, Alabama, and Georgia all the way to the Southern Tier of Upstate New York. The centerpiece of the region is, not surprisingly, the Appalachian Mountains. At one point in time the Appalachians may have been the tallest mountain range in the world. They were formed 350 million years ago during an event known as the Alleghenian orogeny. "Orogeny" is a term used by smart folks with pocket protectors meaning a collision between two tectonic plates. The deformations resulting from such monumental collisions become the mountains that we love to climb up, ski down, and photograph today. The orogeny which birthed the Appalachians happened when the North America part of the continent Euramerica bumped into the Africa part of the continent Gondwana to form Pangaea. Over time the elements have worn the range down to the modest elevations observed today.

The Appalachians have seen dinosaurs and a broad sampling of the Animal Kingdom in their millions of years of existence. Today, large mammals such as the White-tailed Deer, Moose, Elk, and Coyote exist in significant populations. The Black Bear, infamous among the hiking community for its attraction to human food and comfort around humans, also makes residence in the mountain range. Small mammals such as squirrels, skunk, raccoons, and rabbits roam the canopy and forest floor. The Beaver is making a comeback from the point of near extinction in the region, surprising because of the popularity of its pelt in the times of Daniel Boone. Birds include the Wild Turkey, hawks, owls, and songbirds. Luckily we never saw any of the Timber Rattlers or Copperhead snakes that inhabit the region. Amphibians such as the Wood Frog round out the terrestrial fauna.

What animal has the distinction of being the heaviest in Appalachian forests? Salamanders. No, salamanders are not bigger than Black Bears—although it would make for a great sequel to Jurassic Park. But as a measure of total biomass per unit area in the forest, salamanders collectively weigh more than any other vertebrate species.

The people inhabiting the region are often stereotyped as country bumpkins, colloquially "hillbillies." This view has existed for hundreds of years; as the lowland areas of the Eastern United States filled up, arriving immigrants were forced further and further inland. Daniel Boone is the most widely known of these frontierspeople characterized by fierce independence and "backcountry" lifestyle. Access to the region remained difficult for decades and its residents largely existed as subsistence-level farmers through the better part of the 1800's. As the nineteenth century turned, many farmers in the region sunk into deep poverty due to difficulties with mechanizing their labor.

The first half of the twentieth century saw booms in industries such as coal mining and logging, but those jobs were lost as labor gradually became mechanized. Cynical accounts lament the fact that this region so rich in natural resources has kept little of the resulting wealth. What will remain for a very long time are the scarred mountaintops blown to smithereens from the damaging practice called mountaintop removal, in which surface layers of ground are removed to access coal deposits underneath.

Missionaries came to areas such as Eastern Kentucky around the turn of the twentieth century to open schools and educate the population. They were surprised to find many residents could not read or write. Because of poor literacy and oppressive poverty, the region has been likened to a third world country. In the 1960's Appalachia garnered national attention and in the ensuing decades much work has been done to alleviate poverty and modernize infrastructure. Of the 420 counties in the region, the number classified "economically distressed" has decreased from 223 in 1965 to 82 in 2011. The most significant grouping of those counties still in distress is spread across all of Eastern Kentucky.

The Appalachian Mountains—and even their foothills—are hellish to ride. They are more painful and mentally exhausting than the Rocky Mountains. Even though we never reached altitudes exceeding a few thousand feet, those Appalachians do not know when to quit. The terrain is incessantly hilly, and steep. As soon as we crested one hill it was time to descend quickly and start the process all over again. It was as if we were a modern-day Sisyphus, toiling up the same slope over and over again without respite.

I do not recall the Eastern Kentucky segment in terms of a linear daily progression like I do for the majority of the journey. It is as if we had entered into a cage fight on a spinning merry-go-round and were let off two and a half days later, beaten, bruised, and dizzy from the fight with the foothills. The rapidly oscillating topography, hyperactive weather patterns, and a culture unlike any other made me feel like a foreigner in the foothills. We might as well have been part of C.S. Lewis's Space Trilogy or traveling on Mars.

From this ethereal experience images emerge that are seared into my memory bank, but I cannot pin to a specific time or city.

"Say, where you folks from?" I was asked at a gas station. The man who posed the question had gotten out of the back seat of a beater car filling up with gas. He had trouble focusing his eyes and his chin was covered in sloppy stubble desperately needing a shave. The t-shirt he wore was full of holes and his jeans were stained. While he was talking to us his friends argued about who forgot to bring the hunting knife along.

"Hey don' worry y'all. I got it right here!" he said back to them, pointing at his waist. He then turned back to us but almost lost his balance in the process.

"Well, this morning we started from Buckhorn but originally we started riding from Seattle."

"You come all the ways 'cross the country?! On them bikes?!" he looked at the Pocket Rocket and the Motorboat. Judging by his dropped jaw and incredulous look, I am not sure he believed us.

"Yep, been riding since the beginning of May."

"Then how you's a gettin' home? Fixin' to ride back too?" He started laughing and I laughed along.

"Probably not," I then replied.

"Well, uh, y'all have a safe trip then. Uh, d'you say where you was headed?"

"Washington, D.C."

"Wowee! Ah, yeah, well have a safe trip!" With that he turned and jumped into the beater of a car just before it sped away. Just then Oliver came up and said,

"I was talking to that old guy sitting on the milk box over there. Asked him what he was doing and he said he comes down here just to watch things happen."

"Watch things happen?"

"Yeah, you know, like see the cars go by and the people fill up with gas."

"Huh. I'll be darned."

Later in the day we were in a grocery store loading up on pastries and chocolate milk.

"Where you comin' from?" a man said, materializing out of an aisle.

"Seattle."

"Shit! Thassa long ways!"

That was all he said. Looked at us for another second, and continued on with his business.

I will forever remember the shirtless man driving a sit-down lawn mower over his grass. He was driving parallel to the road in the opposite direction as us. The vehicle he was operating was much too small for his obscenely bulbous belly. In order to fit in the seat and manipulate the steering wheel, he had to splay his legs at a ninety-degree angle. The ground was rough and sent the lawn mower bouncing up and down, even though it did not go very fast. The man's breasts and belly experienced successive bouts of weightlessness and gravity force in tandem with the bouncing mower. Up and down they went in hypnotic rhythm as the man's facial expression remained stoic. Did I mention his chest was extremely hairy? Just thinking about those splayed legs and jiggling globes of adipose was enough to send me rolling on the floor in laughter for the next week.

Then there was the woman we passed who was weed-whacking around an old, rusty pickup truck the middle of their yard. It looked like it had not moved in decades, with plants growing in the bed of the truck and insides a mess of rusty metal and torn seat cushions. Instead of getting rid of junk, it often becomes part of the landscape. The narrow, grassless yards nestled into the sides of the hills along the road were full of tires, swimming pools, jungle gyms, rotting fences, caged dogs, dilapidated sheds, and broken cars. After being there for a certain amount of time the junk takes on the same faded, amber hue of rust and fallen leaves.

It came time one morning to get off the bike and take a bathroom break. However, for a couple miles there was nothing and by the time a small convenience store appeared I was barely able to pedal and maintain my composure. We pulled into the "parking lot," leaned our bikes against the wall, and went inside.

"You have a restroom?" I asked frantically.

"Aww, no man, we don't got no toilet 'n here…" said the man behind the counter. He wore a checkered flannel jacket and, like every other eastern Kentucky man I had seen, gravely needed a shave.

I gave him a desperate look.

"Oh! Well just go 'round back and piss on th'wall if you gotta."

I was in too dire of straights to respond verbally, but did give a thumbs up and walked out the door and around to the back of the brick building. I felt a bit awkward, because nobody had ever told me to urinate on their store before.

As I was allowing my bladder pressure to decrease behind the store, a cock came out of nowhere and walked right past me. A hen followed, then another. It was the strangest thing. After I finished up I quickly ran back around to the front of the store to tell Oliver that there were chickens on the loose. But the chickens had already beaten me to the worm and were nonchalantly walking circles around him.

"I see Kentucky fried walking around on two legs," he remarked.

"I don't think I would bother with those." The chickens were rail-thin, giving the impression they were on their own to find food.

Later we passed a gang of kids hanging out on the side of the road. They were either gauntly skinny or excessively rotund, but nowhere in between. A few of them were riding an ATV up and down the road. When the kid driving the ATV saw us he turned around and caught up. I thought he was going to start messing with us, but instead he simply yelled the question,

"Where're you from?!"

"Seattle, Washington!"

"Great Falls, Montana!"

With that he slowed down, turned around again, and returned to the others. I could hear him repeat our answers and then the rest started cheering. The only reason I can imagine they would be cheering was for us. That got me thinking; how small is their world, that they would feel the need to cheer for transient cyclists from the other side of the country whenever they pass by? Growing up, I saw enough different places and kinds of people to not be amazed when I met someone from the other side of the country. I got the impression that the foothills were the only thing those kids had known. And maybe will ever know.

"How much do you want to bet that they are all related?" I asked, although I regret saying such a thing now. Oliver shook his head.

"I don't know man, I don't know."

That night we found out the answer to my question made in jest.

"Almost everyone around here belongs to four or five different families," explained our new friend Henry Barnes. He was pastor of the Presbyterian Church in the city of Buckhorn, and was also kind enough to let us lay out our sleeping bags on the church's community room floor.

"You'll notice they won't ask you questions like 'what do you do?'" he continued. "Instead they will ask 'who is your kin?' because there is a strong sense of family and community. By asking about your 'kin' they are trying to find some way that they are connected to you. And like I said, it often doesn't take much more than an aunt and uncle here, cousin there, and another marriage before all of these people belong to each other. It is much different than the way some of us 'modern' folk approach things. My friend Ken, whose house you passed earlier today, couldn't care less about where you may work or how much money you make or your social status. He cares about making a connection to you. He could teach a lot of people a lot of things about how to live in community. And people around here, they really look out for one another."

Maybe we really were foreigners in the foothills. But contrary to my previously held notions, it was us "modern folk" who would do well to learn a thing or two. Not only us, but many individuals living in white-collar alienation. And so the next day Oliver and I belted John Denver's tune about Appalachia with newfound respect for our hillbilly counterparts: "Country road, take me home, to the place I belong. West Virginia, mountain mama…"

Chapter SIXTEEN

Buckhorn, KY to Rice, VA

JUST LIKE MR. DENVER'S SONG, country roads led us straight to West Virginia. The state holds distinction as the only state to have seceded from a Confederate state, doing so from Virginia in 1863. It also happens to be the childhood home of the "Rocket Boys" featured in the movie *October Sky*. Their story is an inspirational one; protagonist Homer Hickam and three of his friends defy the status quo of entering the West Virginia coal mines after high school, instead entering and winning a science fair competition whose prize is a full ride scholarship to attend college. Their winning project were homemade rockets, and of course Homer ends up working for NASA. The Homer Hickam of in real life is quite the author, having published the memoir Rocket Boys—upon which *October Sky* is based—and a host of historical and fiction novels.

Oliver and I did not rocket through West Virginia in quite the same fashion as the Rocket Boys. The hills of McDowell County, known as the Cumberland Mountains, got steeper and more claustrophobic than their counterparts in Eastern Kentucky.

Inclement weather did not help matters. I donned a cotton flannel shirt out of solidarity with a friend from the state who always wears flannel. Within ten minutes it was soaked by the fourth rainstorm to hit us in a span of six days.

The southern region of the state is very green. In that sense it reminded me of my home in Western Washington. However, the canyons through which we rode were so steep and the vegetation so thick that I got claustrophobic. All I wanted to do was break free of the trees and hills to see a valley or a mountain. I would have even settled for a corn field from Kansas. Maybe all the Rocket Boys really wanted by making rockets was to get some perspective afforded by higher altitude, because riding through the canyons was pushing me towards insanity.

We were only in West Virginia for a matter of hours. A few miles before our quick jaunt through the state came to a close, we passed through the town of War. That is right, a town really named "War." I can only imagine the conversations on airplanes.

"Where are you from?" the aisle neighbor to the left asks, uncomfortable with silence.

"War."

"Oh… Hmm… ha… ha…" as they uncomfortably insert headphones into their ears.

"So where are you from?" the neighbor to the right asks, returning from the restroom.

"War."

"Which one?"

Our war with West Virginia was short-lived. We reached the state line and crossed into Old Virginia. Almost simultaneously the rain abated, clouds cleared, and terrain opened.

Coinciding with the change of statehood was a change in mountain topography. The sporadic, dense nature of the Cumberland Mountains gave way to what is known as "Ridge-and Valley Appalachians." As the name implies, this topography is characterized by long, linear valleys partitioned by equally straight, uniform ridges.

The ridge-and-valley topography has given nightmares to railroad planners searching for an east-west passage to the West for almost two centuries. It was a welcome change for us. All we had to do was conquer one ridge, and then could enjoy miles of cruising on a gradual downhill through an expansive valley filled with idyllic scenery. The going was so good and pleasurable that we made twenty miles in just over an hour—the fastest average speed over a large distance I can recall from the entire trip.

Our target was a small community called Rocky Gap. When we showed up at Rocky Gap, Oliver and I were discouraged to find almost nothing; no restaurants, no gas stations, no water refills, and no lodging accommodations that readily presented themselves. Despite having ridden almost a hundred miles already, we had no option but to carry on.

We were getting hungry, though, and also a little concerned because the sun was fixing to dive behind the ridge to the west at any second. Off to the side of the road there were two cars parked and two people conversing. One was a short elderly woman with white hair and the other was a burly man who could have been her son. We approached them looking for any kind of information about what was ahead.

"Hmm, let me see," the son mused. "Well, I know there is a general store up there past Holly Brook. But you're looking at another seven or ten mile before you get there. And I don' know when they close, but it's gettin' kinda late."

"You think we have a shot at making it?" Oliver asked.

"I don' know how fast you ride," he replied.

"But you're sure there is a store up there?" I inquired.

"Yep. I'd go to the grave with it."

"Alright that is great. Thanks for the help."

"Say, where you boys comin' from?" the elderly woman piped in, now that she had a chance to speak. Off we went reciting our story, worried the five minutes we spent with her meant going hungry that night. She was impressed, but also very concerned because it was already six o'clock in the evening and we still did not know where we would be sleeping.

The words which then poured from this well-intentioned lady's mouth were the most ironic of the entire journey.

"Y'all be extra careful now. And remember: don't talk to *strangers*." The last word had an evil-sounding hiss to it, like when Voldemort speaks Parseltongue to snakes in Harry Potter. What this old woman incredibly failed to realize was that a mere five minutes ago she herself was a stranger to us. Following her advice we would have never spoken to her, nor would we have found out about the general store from her son. Thankfully we did not have an aversion to strangers.

"Hello, my friend and I are riding bikes and are wondering how late you are open tonight. We would like to order a pizza—no, we *need* to order a pizza."

"We're open 'til seven-thirty this evening." It was a kindly feminine voice on the other end of the line.

"Have something like a meat combo?"

"Yep, sure do. We'll get one of those in the oven for ya."

"Why don't you make that two."

We arrived just as the store was closing. I quickly paid for the pizza and rounded up some iced tea and supplementary food.

"Here's your pizza," a kindly young woman said as she brought out our pizza boxes. "Where y'all from?"

"I'm from Seattle and Oliver here is from Montana."

"I thought you were from the West Coast. You talk real fast."

We scarfed that cheesy, meaty discs of taste bud tantalization faster than a Randy Johnson fastball, but the day was not done. In the twilight, with 124 miles on the books, we followed instructions to the town of Mechanicsburg, Virginia. However, I believe "hamlet" may be a more accurate representation. There was nothing more than a street with about ten houses and two churches, one at either end. The name does not show up on Google Maps, even on the most zoomed-in setting.

It was almost completely dark by the time we arrived. The silhouette of a figure was walking down the middle of the road. *Maybe they'll be able to help us out*, I thought.

"Hey, do you know which way the Methodist church is?"

"Huh?" *There I go, talking too fast again.*

"Sorry. We are looking for the Methodist church. Do you know how to get there?" In the quarter-light I could finally evaluate the silhouette. He was tall and lanky, sporting jeans and a faded army fatigue jacket. Then the bottom dropped out of my stomach. *Is that a rifle he's got slung over his shoulder?!* It was. I had not noticed at first. The benign strap around his shoulder was not so benign after all, because it supported a jet black barrel and stock that were almost invisible in the darkness. This time he understood the question. He stood there for a second looking at us. *This is bad. Now he knows exactly where we are going to be for the night. And that we are clueless and have no way of defending ourselves.*

"Yeah, I do… Just go down the end of this 'ere road and take a left. Church'll be right 'round the corner on yer right."

"Thank you, sir," I mumbled and quickly mounted my bike. Oliver, also having noticed the gun, was in a similar hurry. We wasted no time pedaling down to the end of the street and out of sight. We found the church, a small building covered in white siding. There was a basement and through a window I could see someone had left a light on, but it seemed nobody was home.

We planned to pitch our tent behind the building in one of the nooks out of sight from the road. I did not like the idea of camping without permission, especially because Mr. Man-with-Rifle had to know we were staying at the church overnight. But there was nothing else to do. I walked up the steps onto the front porch to look at the main door. In the dim light I could see the U and dial portions of the padlock were rotated apart. I tried the doorknob and it creaked open.

Just then the sounds of a car could be heard coming around the corner. I scurried down the steps and out of sight behind the building just as the headlights illuminated the front porch like searchlights in a prison. Listening carefully for engine noises, I crept back up to the porch and slid the padlock off. The church was open. I found Oliver on the back side of the building, about to unpack the tent.

"You won't be needing that tonight," I said.

"Huh?" he was confused.

"Church is open."

"Oh it is, is it?"

"Yup. I say we crash inside."

"Boom boom," he said. I had no idea what that meant.

"Boom boom?"

"Boom boom. Let's make it happen."

The inside of the church was spooky in the dark, with the pews and windows taking on a Gothic feel. I kept looking over my shoulder expecting to see a floating ghoul or necromancer preparing to banish me to the underworld. Turning on any light would have been ill-advised, because it would make our presence obvious to any passerby.

I also did not have the slightest clue what we would say if someone showed up at the church early the next morning and discovered us spread across the floor. But that actually seemed like a minor complication compared to the specter of Mr. Man-with-Rifle showing up unannounced at some odd hour of the night. Each time the windows were illuminated with the lights of a passing car we would cover our headlamps, hoping to be unnoticed.

At night I dreamed about being discovered. When I woke up it took me five minutes to realize nothing had actually happened.

Our ride to Mechanicsburg marked the seventh consecutive day that we rode over a hundred miles. At 128 miles, it was also the highest single day mile total of the journey. Nobody bothered us at the Methodist church that night and when we left the next morning we signed the guest book,

"Scott and Oliver, June 19th, thanks for letting us crash!"

Going a hundred miles per day, every day, eventually takes its toll. And so it was with us the next day. Riding across the Blue Ridge Mountains and into the heart of Virginia, I felt flat and unenthused about riding. All indications would have suggested otherwise: the terrain was beautiful, the weather perfect, the roads were fine, and we took a good long break at the library to type up an email update and clarify our route for the next few days. It bothered me that my mood dipped without explanation. Sometimes over the course of two months it happens; indifference stemming from habituation can make even the extraordinary seem unpleasantly ordinary.

Early in the morning we came to a fork in the road unmarked on our makeshift map and directions. We guessed to turn left and flagged down the first car passing in the opposite direction.

"Excuse me; do you know if Dublin is this way?" (That is Dublin, Virginia—not Ireland).

"Umm, yeah I am pretty sure it is up ahead. But I have been away for a few years at college so I'm not one hundred percent sure..." The driver and passenger were both attractive, the kind of femme fatales in college who always seemed to leave me pulling out my hair and screaming *they are so impossible!*

"Very good. Thanks for the help," Oliver responded. "I think we'll just keep on going then and see what happens."

"You do know Dublin is... kind of a long ways away, don't you?"

"Actually we didn't. That's why we got in your way on the road."

"Oh, right... So I think it is more than ten miles away. Like, eleven miles from here."

"We'll keep that in mind."

"Okay, well good luck!"

"Oliver, I have seen that face before," I said once the car pulled away.

"Really?"

"No, not her specifically. But she looked exactly like a girl from college who drove me nuts. I took her on a date. She said she had a great time. Asked her on another by writing her a song on guitar and playing it for her. She said 'yes,' but bailed out right before, saying 'Sorry, I am going to go with a group of friends.' Then, two days later, I saw her holding hands with a third guy. Wanted to ask her what mind-altering substance she was taking, but I thought the better of it. Then I was going to ask her how many guys had ever written her a song, but also thought the better of that. It just makes you think that by saying one thing they mean the exact opposite."

"You wanna turn around then?" he asked.

"No, I think I trust this one."

"Hmm…" was all Oliver said in response.

Although our streak of one-hundred mile days was broken (we only completed ninety miles), we started a new streak by staying in a United Methodist Church for the second night in a row. This one, in the city of Stewartsville, was currently in use. Looking through a basement window it appeared to be some sort of meeting. Riding a bike for ten hours a day had cured me long ago of any sense of shame or concern for socially appropriate behavior. I opened the door and walked through the entryway.

"How are you all doing this evening?" I began. All eyes turned in my direction and about three quarters of the eyebrows were raised. Given my appearance I could hardly blame them. But I continued anyway, unfazed. "This is going to be just a bit random, but my friend Oliver and I are riding our bikes across the country…"

Reciting our Speech had become as natural as unpacking a pannier or setting up the tent. I watched as one by one the eyebrows in the audience lowered and were replaced by nods and smiles. *One, two, three... eight, ten, twelve...* I felt like a magician. *My first trick will be to change your facial expression from incredulousness to awe. Zap!* "...so we totally understand if you'd rather us leave on the double, but would really appreciate a bit of help."

"Why don't you stick around for a while until the meetin' is over? Then we can talk some more. But feel free to help yourself to the food in the meantime. Hope you are alright with buffet-type casseroles and such."

It was a Lions Club meeting upon which we stumbled. The buffet was delightful. *And for my next trick, I will make all of this food disappear!* I had never before seen the Lions in action, or really had a clue what they do. They are a community service organization dedicated to such projects putting eyeglasses and hearing aids in the hands of those who cannot afford them.

Mandatory protocol during meetings is to refer to other members as "Lion so-and-so." If you forget and simply address another member as "so-and-so," it will cost you a quarter. That gets expensive really fast.

This meeting covered the inauguration for newly elected officers. One of the senior members from the region, Lion Tanner, had come to preside over the ceremony. Before taking the new officers through their vows he gave a keynote address in which he praised virtues of the organization and admonished the members of this Stewartsburg chapter to increase membership.

"I really believe that Lions is the best-kept secret in this country. I think about my life before I started attending and look at where I am at right now, and it is a night-and-day difference. Think about how much light this group has brought to your life. Look around you. It is obvious you're small in number right now. But that doesn't mean it always has to be this way. We need to bring in the younger generation, because we're only getting older. Young people are just too busy these days to give up time. It's a hard battle, but you've gotta convince them to consider switching around their kids' soccer practice and piano lesson schedules so they can come for meetings."

It sounded a lot like the discourse at my church back home. And it got me thinking: is the spirit of volunteerism that has characterized this country for decades on the decline? I cannot say. After Lion Tanner's words I realized the attendees were exclusively officers and their spouses. The room began seeming a lot emptier.

The next morning was dreadfully bleak. We woke up at six, hoping to get an early start. Dense cloud cover and rain muted the advancing light, making the scene outside very ominous. Rain is bad enough when it starts in the middle of a ride and you have no choice but to continue. Saddling a bicycle in rain pouring from the start is another beast entirely. It is like standing in the shower before turning on the water and being pelted with the initially freezing-cold stream.

Visibility was terrible through the morning twilight and rain. Riding at this time was probably not the safest thing we had done.

The rain intensified to such a level that I could not see more than five feet ahead, so we pulled off at a gas station to wait out the worst of it. Fifteen minutes later we were about to start again. Still in the gas station parking lot, less than ten feet away from the highway, the brake cable on my Pocket Rocket snapped. I was rendered brakeless and about to enter a steady stream of fast-moving traffic. Captain Punishment was about to be punished.

I leaned hard anticipating the sharp turn; either I would change course and avoid the traffic, or fall down in the process and hopefully skid to a stop before the highway. Luckily I was able to avoid both traffic and falling to the pavement.

Returning to Oliver, I cursed under my breath both poor luck and my own stupidity. Poor luck, because this was the first and only brake cable I have ever snapped in eight years of cycling. Stupidity, because I had only one functioning brake to begin with; the front brake jammed two weeks earlier and I had yet to fix it.

The miracle is that the brake cable snapped when I tapped it lightly at the gas station. Minutes before it snapped, I squeezed it hard trying to slow down on a steep and slippery hill. If the cable decided to snap then, or a few minutes after pulling out of the gas station, the consequences could have been dire.

We had to hitch a ride in a pickup truck fifteen miles backwards to Roanoke. Backtracking was deflating, and I felt like an old helium balloon that just cannot seem to stay afloat any longer. It was only eight o'clock in the morning and most bike shops do not open until ten or eleven. The one we found opened at ten, so we sat outside in the poor weather for two hours until the early shift came in to open the store.

We were within mere days of reaching the Atlantic Coast. Getting repairs in Roanoke cost half a day's worth of time and distance. My insides ached for the moment of arrival. Starting fifteen miles behind and in the midday heat brought out my impatient side. I was in a sour mood, but Oliver did not seem fazed in the slightest. *Of course Mr. Perfect-Priest would be amiable at a time like this.* I was embarrassed at my own tendencies but grateful he was around to keep me company and lift my spirits.

By eleven o'clock both brake cables had been replaced and we were again ready to ride—or so I thought. In the frustration of the morning's events I left my helmet at the gas station, so I walked out of the Cardinal Bicycle Shop in Roanoke cash-poor but with brand-spanking new brake cables and Styrofoam life insurance policy (helmet).

Fifteen minutes after pushing off from the bike shop, a bike-laden minivan swerved sharply to the side of the road and slammed on its breaks in front of us. A medium-old, medium-gray man got out of the vehicle and waved us down.

"Hey! You guys on the TransAm?" he yelled, even though we stood only ten feet away.

"Yeah, we are."

"Wow! That's great. I haven't seen anyone in a long, long time. See, I started in Astoria at the beginning of May and..." He explained how he started a TransAm ride with a film producer as his driver. They were making a documentary hoping to get other medium-old, medium-gray people to go outside and be active. The man spoke loud and fast like a rocket ship. The jet propulsion fueling his discourse radiated from veins and tendons bulging on all sides of his neck, standing out vividly on his anemic frame. He looked like a stripped-down Star Wars robot with a tight skin covering.

"People my age are scared to *move*. They sit at home, indoors, with plummeting self-esteem and no happiness. They lead disempowered lives. What they really need is to get moving and active, get the endorphins rushing. Oh by the way, name's Frank." I shook his hand, amused by the way every sinew and vessel stood out in contraction.

We talked to Frank for an unconventionally long time by side-of-the-road conversation standards. Frank went on to explain, voice still booming, that his filmmaker left because funds dried up. He wanted to sleep in a motel every night while Frank wanted to camp, which put the two at odds. Apparently it did not end up very well. But Frank, impressively undeterred, continued on with the journey. He would drive the van a ways up the road during the day, park it, sleep, wake up early (2:00 a.m.) to beat the heat, and ride a round-trip route on his bicycle that brought him back to the van. Then he would drive some more, park, and repeat the routine. Although he did not ride a continuous route across the country in such a manner, he did get to see and ride all the parts of the country that one riding a continuous journey would have seen.

The whole time we listened to Frank I was eyeing the bike rack on his van. I wanted badly for him to offer us a ride. We briefly mentioned our unfortunate morning, but without even asking him he said,

"I wish I could take you two, but the back of my van is just loaded with too much stuff."

Bidding Frank farewell, we continued on our way. An hour later we reached a gas station and wanted to refill water bottles. I walked inside to use the restroom, and when I came back out Oliver was sitting on a bench chatting with—you guessed it—Frank. How and why he ran into us again is beyond me. But this time I was a bit more forward with him. I looked in the back of his van and realized two bikes could easily fit inside.

Ten minutes later, Oliver and I were hitchhiking with Frank. Was it immoral to spend one hour out of the 1,320 on the journey hitchhiking in the belly of a fossil-fuel-burning, four-wheeled giant made of steel? My conscience was not speaking up in protest. And Frank was a riot, so even a little guilt would have been worth it.

He dropped us off in Appomattox, but stuck around to tour the courthouse where General Robert E. Lee surrendered the Confederate Army to General Ulysses S. Grant's Union forces to end the Civil War.

"I am really proud of what you two are doing," he said just before parting ways. "If I had kids, I would want them to be like you. But I never had kids—at least that I am aware of." Oliver and I resumed our journey with Frank's resonating belly laugh ringing in our ears.

The end of daylight was fast approaching when we reached the small town of Rice, Virginia. All was quiet until we turned a corner and saw upwards of seventy cars lined up in a Baptist Church's parking lot.

"I think we should check this out," I said to Oliver.

"Like we were the librarian and this was a book," I commented. What I actually was thinking was "...check this out like we were Adam and this was Eve after the Fall." *Now I can add lust and false testimony to my growing list of Sins Against the Priest*, I thought.

"That's exactly what I was thinking, too," Oliver replied.

I noticed a middle-aged woman walking to her car in the parking lot. "Hey! This is going to sound random, but you see my friend Oliver and I here are riding our bicycles across the country..."

"Let me go get Pastor Everett and see what he has to say." She went inside and the pastor came out a minute later. He was a good-looking man of about sixty, dressed in a full suit. I would have been very intimidated if not for his tie, which featured the Tasmanian Devil character from Looney Tunes.

"Howdy, y'all. Name's Everett, but you can call me Ev," he said while extending his hand. We explained our situation to him. He looked back and forth at Oliver and me, as if sizing us up for a fight. His eyes narrowed.

"So how do I know you won't rob us dry, or break all the windows in the church? We aren't made of money here in Rice, you know. What if you eat all the food in the pantry?" As he continued, a grin spread across his face. "Or forget to flush the toilet? Now I'm just messin' with y'all. You're more than welcome to stay. Right now we got a once-every-two-month Baptist Convention but c'mon down and we'll get y'all fed. You're hungry, right? Just come downstairs through that door over there in back. We're back-door people 'round here, y'know. Ain't no reason to ever keep it locked."

"I like that," I said to Oliver when Ev had gone back inside. "'back-door people' is a good way of saying trusting, friendly, and informal."

When Ev said he would get us fed I had no idea just how "fed" we would be. Within seconds of walking downstairs—through the back door—we were accosted by a half dozen grandmothers trying to sell us on their contribution to the potluck.

"Here is my green bean casserole! Been a family recipe for seventy-five years."

"Over here, boys. You *need* to have some of my homemade potato salad."

"Did I mention my speckled lemonade is world famous?!"

"Leave some space on your plate for my ham and biscuits!"

"And don't forget the baked beans!"

"What about some chicken casserole?"

"Or some potato casserole?"

"Don't forget my cheese casserole!"

"You better go back for seconds!"

I had to pinch myself to make sure I was not dreaming. We went back for seconds, thirds, and two desserts. A boa constrictor that makes a killing such as this would not have to eat for a year. After buffets on two consecutive nights in Virginia, I understand why people in the South are at an elevated risk for obesity. And if there is a heaven, it will be full of casseroles and grandmothers.

Chapter SEVENTEEN

Rice, VA to Williamsburg, VA

"Check this out! They left us ham sandwiches and cookies all wrapped up for the road!" There was no better way to wake up. I looked outside the window suspicious we were living a dream. But no, we had not ascended into the clouds; grass and trees and cars remained firmly planted in the ground of Rice, Virginia.

We were very close to the end. However, over a period of one and a half months it is difficult to maintain perspective. It was not difficult for my parents, who each had a map of the United States hung on their wall at work and would track each day's progress. If I did not tell them where we ended up on any given night, I would wake up to a text message the next morning that said,

"Are you okay? Just updating my map and wondering where you are. Everyone in the office has been stopping by and I don't have anything new to tell them."

Progress must have been easy to see on a map, but it felt like we were pedaling in place on a hamster wheel, scenery changing on a slowly advancing background. We could have been a sequel to *The Truman Show* and it all would have felt the same. When you ride a bicycle every day for forty-two days it seems the end will never come. Whether we truly grasped it or not, there remained only 125 miles between us and the ocean. Only a few of the string of dominoes, stacked in a train across the country, remained standing.

An eastward journey across the United States is a journey back in time. Oliver and I had almost rewound the tape to the start—but who knows anything about rewinding tapes anymore in this DVD world?

The tidewater region of Virginia is part of the Atlantic Coastal Plain. It stretches inland about one hundred miles from the coast, to the start of the Piedmont region in the Appalachian foothills. This demarcation is where early navigation expeditions were halted, because they could not contend with the Piedmont's waterfalls and rapids. The tidewater area is where the British chapter of the country's history began.

What did this have to do with us? For starters, riding across the coastal plain was easier than ascending mountains. Alternating corn fields and stands of hemlock made for a pleasant riding experience. That is, until we had to pass through the outskirts of the greater Richmond metropolitan area. Increased population density inevitably leads to higher stress levels. In the city of Hopewell we entered a gas station looking for directions.

"Do you know if the bridge to cross over the James to Highway Five is up this way?" I asked. The cashier raised his eyebrows.

"Why y'all want ta cross that bridge? Ain't no shoulder. I wouldn't do it if I had ta choose 'tween that and eatin' a squirrel off a roastin' spit." I kept looking at him, silently, until he answered the question. Maybe I looked desperate. "But yeah, it is. Jus' keep on up this road another mile an' you'll see signs ta take a left."

Riding the bridge across the James River was a white-knuckle experience, but traffic was much nicer on the other side. We found ourselves on the piece of land cradled between the James and York Rivers. Many of the first permanent English settlements were laid down here, beginning with Jamestown in 1607. However, Jamestown was not the first English attempt at throwing down roots in the New World.

That distinction belongs to the attempts of Sir Walter Raleigh and Sir Francis Drake to colonize Roanoke Island, a small tract of eighteen square miles off the coast of present-day North Carolina. In 1585, Raleigh, an English aristocrat and explorer, sent an expedition led by the military captain Ralph Lane to establish a settlement there. The expedition arrived too late in the year to plant crops and spent the winter subsisting on limited supplies. When Sir Francis Drake stopped by in 1586 for a visit, the colonists had had enough and decided to ride with Drake back to England. This was probably the prudent choice, considering the fact that Lane had murdered the local Native American tribe's chief over a stolen cup.

A year later, in 1587, Raleigh sent another expedition to Roanoke Island. This one was led by John White, an artist who is thought to have built expeditionary rapport while on a ship searching for the Northern Passage a few years prior. Relations with the tribe inhabiting the island were strained, due to Lane's misguided murder of the tribe's chief. The colonists were leery about resettling there and hoped to establish themselves on the mainland. However, their hired Portuguese pilot was itching to go chase Spanish ships and refused to ferry the colonists to the mainland.

After only two months ashore as the expedition's leader, White returned to England for more supplies. He left behind his daughter and newborn granddaughter (named Virginia Dare, the first English child born in the New World). *Some leader indeed,* would be my thought if I were one of the colonists remaining on the island. Upon returning to England, White got caught up in the naval confrontation with the Spanish Armada for two years. It was not until 1590 that he could return to his family and the Roanoke colony. He was horrified by what he found.

The colony was abandoned. Not only that, but it seemed to have been plundered. The only clue to be found was the word "Croatoan" carved on a nearby tree, the name of a native tribe on a nearby island. An inclement hurricane forced White to return to England without further investigation. He would never again be able to make another trip to discover what happened to his family and the other colonists.

Theories abound as to the colony's fate. Between 1937 and 1940, stone fragments with an encrypted message were found that some thought contained a message from Eleanor Dare to her father John White. However, the stones turned out to be a hoax. In the 1880's, a man named Hamilton MacMillan happened upon the Pembroke tribe in Southeastern North Carolina and was surprised when they claimed to descend from "Roanoke in Virginia," the same way that Sir Walter Raleigh referred to Roanoke Island. The tribe spoke perfect English, carried many of the last names of the original colonists, and had Anglo-Saxon elements in their bone structure. But after 300 years it is difficult to prove anything besides that the Pembroke tribe assimilated and interbred with Europeans and descending white Americans.

When settlers landed at Jamestown twenty years later, natives told them stories about light-skinned people coming to the Chesapeake Bay and settling. Unfortunately, as Jamestown leader John Smith would discover, the conglomeration of tribes in the Chesapeake region was ruled by Chief Powhatan, known for hostility to incoming settlers. Any unlucky colonist arriving to the area was most likely exterminated upon arrival. What is there to make of the message that White found on the island? The going hypothesis is that the Roanoke band split up. Some travelled north to their untimely fate in Virginia, while others traveled south and assimilated into the friendly Croatoan tribe. No conclusive evidence has ever been unearthed to resolve the mystery, and with the passing years the brave effort at Roanoke will be forever known as the "Lost Colony."

The new settlers at Jamestown would not have an easy go of thriving—let alone surviving—in the Chesapeake area. Unlike the Disney-fied version of the story told in *Pocahontas*, the first years were filled with fear, bloodshed, famine, and disease. In the first few months, over fifty of the five hundred settlers were dead. Fast-forward to 1610, after worsening relations with the Powhatan Confederacy and a year of famine, and just over sixty were still alive. I would have been looking for some clause in the fine print that would give grounds to sue Her Highness in England. *You never said it was going to end up like this. I want out of here on the next plane, err, ship!*

I felt the need to make a detour and see the Jamestown settlement myself, even though almost nothing of the original colony remains. The National Park Service has done a good job of recreating elements of the fort and a sprawling, modern building welcomes visitors. Adjacent to the visitor center is a parking lot large enough to accommodate every charter bus in the state of Virginia.

The problem was Jamestown closed a mere fifteen minutes before we arrived, at five o'clock in the afternoon. Undeterred, Oliver and I subtly slipped through the closing "exit" gate when the rangers were not paying attention.

Maybe sweaty spandex gave us special invisibility powers. Earlier in the day we slipped onto the grounds of the Berkeley Plantation, site of the first Thanksgiving and the place where taps was first played, without paying an entrance fee. Something about not taking a shower across the entire state of Virginia was giving us a sense of moral superiority: *I have forgone the creature comforts afforded civilized society, therefore I am exempt from any requirements or restrictions society may impose.* At the time it sounded logical. A portly woman dressed in an antiquated bonnet and dress looked at us blankly as we meandered through the estate gardens.

"The history video is about to start in the cellar," she said.

"Thanks, but we're just taking a walk around," Oliver replied. She paused for a second and blinked, like an old Macintosh computer overwhelmed with a multiple kilobit task. Finally, she nodded robotically and walked down to what must have been the cellar. I am convinced that working at historical sites in costume robs people of their very souls.

Jamestown Island itself is underwhelming. This is actually one of the main reasons it was chosen as a site suitable for a colony; at the time of arrival in 1607 it was unoccupied because the tribes in the area deemed it unsuitable for habitation. The island is swampy, filled with bugs and disease, and did not have easy access to potable water. However, it was easily defended and had a good port.

As we toured the recreated settlement a surreal "this-is-where-it-all-began" sensation came over me—even though contemporary training in political correctness reminds me that "it" really began twelve thousand years ago with the arrival of the first Americans via the land bridge between Russia and Alaska. Jamestown ushered in the era giving rise to the country across which I rode. It started with humble beginnings on a single island little more than three miles wide, but now spans thousands of miles and (for better or worse) has greatly altered the course of human history. That is a lot of falling dominoes.

I tried to consider all of the prerequisites necessary for my journey to be possible. National borders that stretch from sea to sea, a continuous network of paved roads across the entire country, a reliable dollar—and enough of them—to make it economically feasible would be naming just a few. All of these prerequisites have intricate and intertwined histories, and trying to grasp their combined significance leaves me overwhelmed and confused. The more I learn, the more I realize how little I actually know.

My uncle and few friends from college have degrees that say "History." The oft-repeated defense of that rearview-mirror subject is that by understanding the past we can make better decisions in the present.

Retracing the trail of fallen dominoes to a point of origin illuminates the way things are in the present. From the realm of infinite possibility, only certain outcomes emerge. Those outcomes truly come alive only when their origins are appreciated. Ninety-nine people out of one hundred in line to see the Mona Lisa walk away underwhelmed by its small size and bland colors because they fail to appreciate the incredible domino train of history stretching into the painting's past. Similarly, Jamestown is just a small, swampy marsh. But it was *the* swampy marsh where an impressive string of dominos had its beginning.

There is a difference between living simply to be entertained and living with the purpose of understanding. The people who live simply for entertainment walk away from the Mona Lisa disappointed. They are also the ones who ride their bicycles across the country just to snap a picture of the Atlantic Ocean to prove they could do it. On the other hand, those who pursue understanding find the Mona Lisa's mysterious facial expression and historical implications fascinating. Those who pursue understanding grasp the significance of crossing the country by bicycle under their own power, and emerge with a greater understanding of themselves and the world around them. Living-to-understand is more meaningful, enlightening, and fulfilling. The thing is, it usually ends up being more entertaining as well.

Millions of people see the Atlantic Ocean every day, and some even ride their bicycles next to it. Seeing the Atlantic would be different for Oliver and me because of the long domino train stretching back to a rear wheel dunked into the Pacific Ocean, where the cross-country journey began. I could see the last dominoes falling.

Chapter EIGHTEEN

Williamsburg, VA to Yorktown, VA

THE SUN WAS SETTING ON Day Forty-Two. After touring Jamestown that afternoon, Oliver and I found ourselves in Williamsburg. All I could think was that we were only thirteen miles away from completing the TransAm. *Thirteen miles*. However, those thirteen miles would have to wait because of pending darkness.

The normal routine of getting food and finding a place to sleep seemed trivial so close to the "end," but we could not spend the night on the street—I doubt the police would be too thrilled and it would be hard to finish our bike ride from the confines of a jail cell. We asked a startled passerby where food still comes in "Super-Size" and they pointed us to a neighborhood bar and grill filled with students from the nearby William and Mary College.

Outside the door to the restaurant we found ourselves in a conversation with a tall, greasy-haired man. He had the look of a computer geek in his late twenties, observations which later proved accurate. Eventually we got around to explaining what we were doing with spandex and bikes laden with gear.

"...I mean, you look like you belong in the circus," he said good-naturedly. "By the way, the name's Rover. Don't ask—been called that my whole life."

Rover's stream of consciousness seemed oblivious to the social conventions that make interactions with other humans pleasant and natural. Luckily for us, he was as generous as he was awkward. Within seconds of explaining our situation he offered up his office for the night.

"It's nothing special, but it has a floor..." *good* "...and a roof," *also good*. "Really easy to find, right across from Busch Gardens in the Busch Industrial Park. Only thing is, we're gonna be busy until later tonight. So I'll give you my phone number and we'll be in touch. Man, you guys are cool."

It seemed like a good situation, so we swapped phone numbers and agreed to track him down in a few hours after we ate some food.

The hostess inside the restaurant sat us down at a table sharing a backrest with another booth. There were four students sitting down, two girls across from two guys. It had the looks of a double date.

"I am so fed up with summer classes *already*," complained the girl sitting on the outside end of the booth. "I haven't been able to go to any of the Delta Phi parties yet because I'm always doing Dr. Bond's chemistry."

"I know," echoed the girl sitting on the inside. "And I heard last night they had a free keg and dancing on the roof."

"That is, until the fuzz came and broke things up," replied the first girl.

"I heard my friend Jeremy was singing Spice Girls on top of a table," piped in the guy on the outside end of the booth.

"Really? Jeremy Sanders? Wasn't he the quiet one in chemistry class last fall?"

"Yeah I think he was…"

As the conversation was developing, I could not help but feel far-removed from college already. We ordered burgers and a hefeweizen apiece and sat back to enjoy booth seats with padding. The boy on the inside of the booth had been silent during the entire conversation about the fraternity party. His head was covered in curly red hair and freckles, and he wore an athletic watch on his right arm.

The pair sitting on the outside ends of the booth got up simultaneously to "use the restroom." It was obvious they wanted to leave the curly ginger with the girl sitting across from him. And it was equally obvious that he of the burning, bushy mop top was nervous. The girl was pleasing to the eye, which did not help calm his nerves.

"So…when you go to… err… parties, well, umm, do you like them?" he mumbled.

"You mean the parties?"

"Yeah."

"Well, I guess they are alright every once in a while. I talk to my friends and sometimes meet new people. Fairly benign, I guess."

"Cool."

"I guess."

"So… what don't you like about chemistry?"

"It's not that I don't like chemistry, I just get fed up when it's all I'm doing twenty-four seven."

"Oh." Then there were a few painful seconds of pause. The girl smiled weakly out of pity. I wanted to help him, but there was nothing to do besides listen to him silently languish in a self-inflicted vacuum of awkwardness. *Carrot-top,* I thought, *you need to ride your bicycle across the country. Then even if you're awkward like me, you'll have something to talk about.*

I called and sent multiple messages to the phone number Rover gave, but got no reply for over two hours. I started to doubt whether I entered the number correctly in my phone. Oliver thought we should start looking for other places to stay. We did, but found only dead ends.

Finally, Rover sent a message back with his address. I tried calling but he did not pick up. We asked everyone how to find the Busch Industrial Park, but nobody had a clue. We found a gas station with a road map and spent ten minutes scouring until we found his street. It was two miles in the wrong direction, but at this hour we had no other choice.

When we got to his street, it was impossible to find his small office. This last night before triumph was turning into a nightmare. Salvation came in the form of another text message: "sorry for not answering my phone. We're on the way and will be there soon."

Another half hour passed and I nearly lost my patience with Rover. This was ironic, because he was generously offering to accommodate Oliver and me in a time of need. When his car did finally pull into the industrial park, I was about to scream. Those emotions dissipated instantly when he got out of the car.

"Sorry man, we got carried away. You know what happens when you open up one too many bottles of wine. Come on in and check out my digs. I've been running my own website out of here for over three years. The office upstairs is unoccupied right now and the door's open so I think its fine that you guys crash up there."

It was eleven o'clock at night and we were ready to go to sleep. Rover was not. We spent another hour humoring his questions and talking about life. It was uncommon the level of personal disclosure he provided us within hours of meeting him. And he seemed to care about us, too.

"I know you probably get this a lot," he said, "but can you put me on your email list?" I was about to say, *You're goddamn right I will put you on the email list! Why? Because believe it or not, hardly anyone is interested enough to ask us that. You may think you are common, but dear Rover, your genuine interest in the lives of others sets you apart.*

"Of course you will be on the email list."

"So what is your plan for tomorrow morning?"

"We're thinking about getting up really early and riding over to Yorktown to catch sunrise on the beach."

"You fellas are ending at *Yorktown?* That is hardly a beach. Listen, you need to go to Virginia Beach. Tomorrow I will take you over there. That one is really worth seeing."

"Thanks Rover, but I think this is just something we have to do."

"You sure?"

"Yeah, positive."

"Well I'm not going to twist your arm. But if you change your mind, I'm happy to show you what real Virginia beaches are all about."

When things were finally wrapping up and we were saying goodbye, Rover surprised me yet again.

"Alright fellas, bring it in for 'real friend' hugs now."

Before I knew what hit me, I was wrapped in his lanky arms with nothing else to do besides squeeze back. My face came up to his armpit and I caught a whiff of ripened body odor. An amount of time unconventionally long passed before he released. Oliver, a couple inches shorter than me, was completely swallowed up. Five seconds later we both emerged gasping for breath.

Rover was a paradox. His inconsistent communication sent Oliver and I traipsing across Williamsburg in the darkness for hours trying to find his office. It was frustrating and unnerving to spend so long at night feeling homeless. He did not feed us dinner or offer breakfast the next morning. By these criteria, he was far superseded by many kind and generous hosts throughout the trip.

Yet there was something unique about Rover. He was authentically and enthusiastically interested in us, even though we were complete strangers. That somehow won a special place in my heart.

In my mind Rover stands out compared to someone like Sister Erma, the nun in Missouri who let us sleep in her church's basement and cooked us breakfast. To Erma, spending time with us was nothing more than a good deed, an opportunity to check off "welcoming the stranger" from the holiness list and cash in fifty more heaven points on the day of Reckoning. She cared little for our story and was much more comfortable talking about herself. Rover, on the other hand, made every attempt to accompany us on our journey. Not physically, but in the sense that he tried to see the experience through our eyes and wanted to stay connected for the rest of the time we bicycled.

Given the choice between Rover and Sister Erma, I would choose Rover in a heartbeat. Even if that meant we were a little hungry the next morning around breakfast time. Even still if I had to catch another whiff of his armpit during a "real friend" hug. I prefer to spend time with people who value my individual experience, rather than with people who view me as an act of charity.

The hard part was turning down Rover's offer to take us to Virginia Beach the next day. It sounded great, but I had been drawn to the idea of catching sunrise on the Atlantic. Ignoring the signs so late in the journey seemed foolish. It was past midnight when I finally laid my head down on the pile of clothes to catch a few precious hours of sleep. Sometimes following the signs is exhausting.

At 4:00 a.m. I was ripped away from a dream and thudded painfully onto the ground in the land of the awake. My alarm was going off on my phone and I wanted desperately to throw it through the window. I stood up and almost lost my balance. My head was foggy. I shook Oliver awake and went about packing up my things in a half-sleeping stupor. I bit down into a cold, oatmeal-raisin Clif bar but my teeth only made it halfway through.

What the heck am I doing? I thought. Getting up early seemed ridiculous.

It took a superhuman effort to get the Clif bar down. We turned on headlamps and flashing tail lights and took to the road. Three minutes later, a car passed dangerously close to handlebars, almost sending me to the ground or worse. In daylight this would be unpleasant, but in the darkness it was absolutely terrifying. We were well inside the shoulder and there was no reason for a vehicle to come so near. Could drivers not see our flashing tail lights? All of a sudden I felt naked and defenseless: who knows what would happen if the driver of the next car was falling asleep at the wheel?

What the heck am I doing?

Twilight was slowly advancing as the miles ticked by. From the Colonial Parkway, a scenic thoroughfare linking Williamsburg and Yorktown, we caught sight of the tidewaters between the York River and Chesapeake Bay. Lights from the Coast Guard base and Coleman Memorial Bridge twinkled a few miles ahead. The sky was transitioning from navy blue in the east to the faintest hint of red and orange in the west. I was giddy.

The last mile of the Colonial Parkway veers away from the waterfront, bypassing Yorktown proper. Unable to see the water, my anticipation increased. Scenes from the previous weeks flashed through my mind like a montage on fast-forward. We took a left on Zweybrucken Road and continued past the monument commemorating the surrender of General Cornwallis to end the Revolutionary War. At this point the monument was the last thing on my mind. A right hand turn swung us around the monument and down the beachside cliffs on a tree-lined road terminating at the beachfront.

There it was: the Atlantic Ocean. Some would later point out to me that it technically was not the Atlantic, but rather the York River two miles before it empties into the Chesapeake Bay. I did not care. After forty-two days on the road and an Adventure Cycling map telling me this was mile zero, Yorktown was good enough for me.

Water gently lapped up against a border of white sand. To the left was a fishing dock extending thirty yards out into the water. To the right stood a rocky bulwark providing shelter for the small cove. I kicked off my cycling shoes and sunk my toes into the cool sand. They pressed against some shells and small pebbles, causing an almost painful sensation. The smell of salt was in the air. This was a beach. This was *the* beach.

Our timing could not have been better. A fiery sunrise on the eastern horizon was slowly growing larger and larger. Incident light played off the high purple clouds running diagonally across the sky and crimson streaks marked the clouds' borders. The scene in the heavens silently exploded across the calm seawater, iridescent shimmerings that danced on gentle waves. All the while the blaze on the horizon kept spreading and developing more colors.

Oliver and I took turns wheeling our bikes down the gentle, sandy slope to complete the second half of the ritual that started with the back tires of the Motorboat and Pocket Rocket submerged in the Puget Sound. That was the Pacific, now for the Atlantic. I plunged the front tire into the water and paused. This was it; I made it. The realization was strange. After so much time anticipating and struggling and surviving, the present moment was focused on the place of completion. It caught me off guard, like a news reporter going "live" who forgot their lines.

I looked for the right thing to say or do or think. Then I took a deep breath and stopped trying to explain the significance to myself.

This is what the heck I am doing, I thought, standing there transfixed by the glory of the morning. I could not ask for a better scene if I had every artist and graphic designer in the world at my beck and call. This sunrise was special in the way Tom Hanks delivering the package at the end of *Castaway* is special. It was forty-three days and 3,628 miles special. And it was special for me like it could be special for no one else. It was not just about the brief minutes of sunrise, but about the countless hours spent pedaling through the rain, sun, wind, and everything in between.

I heard Joe's voice clear as day in my head. *How do you eat an elephant, Skip? One… Bite… At… A… Time!* A feeling of elation welled up in my chest. I raised my fist in the air and started screaming. Oliver began yelling too.

I screamed and screamed until my voice was hoarse.

It had to be a strange sight, two people making a racket at six o'clock in the morning with their bicycle tires in the ocean. But I did not care. I had not cared for a month and a half, so why start now?

Chapter NINETEEN

Yorktown, VA to Washington, D.C.

MARYLAND HAS ALWAYS CONFUSED ME. What flavor of mind-altering substance was Lord Baltimore taking when he shaped his state like a Super Soaker?

After reaching the water at Yorktown, Oliver and I turned north towards the nation's capital. But in order to enter the District of Columbia, we had to leave Virginia and enter Maryland first. Maryland gives the capital a 270° bear hug, right around where the trigger to the squirt gun would be.

With about five miles remaining before the border with the District of Columbia, we happened upon a minivan pulled off to the shoulder of the highway. The vehicle's driver, a heavyset woman named Tanya, appeared flustered as she talked on the phone.

"Can we help you?" Oliver asked. She shuddered, not expecting anyone to address her on the side of the road.

"Oh! Uh, you'd do that?! I've got a flat tire and I have no idea how to fix it. That would be a *huge* help. Thank you so much!"

Oliver grabbed the jack and wrench and went to work unbolting the flat tire. Tanya's trunk was filled with cardboard boxes that had to be consolidated and removed in order to access the spare tire. They were full of old vinyl records, faded clothes, and I could only guess what else. Moving them was a precarious endeavor because the edges and corners of the boxes were all ripping. One misplaced application of force and the box would break. I did not want to see records running every which way down the road.

"Sorry 'bout all that," she said. "I been meanin' to take it down to the pawn shop to get some cash but haven't got around to it yet."

"No problem—I just need to get them out so we can get to your spare tire."

Most of the boxes came out easily. But then I felt under the only box left in the trunk. *Oh, God*, I thought; it was damp with unidentified moisture. When I shifted it to get my hands underneath, sticky fluid leaked onto my forearms. My face contorted in disgust, and I did not want to know what the box contained. Miraculously, the bottom of the damp cardboard did not break open when I moved the box.

Oliver changed the tire, I put all the boxes back in the trunk, and Tanya was ready to get back on the road. The picture I snapped of her and Oliver became one of my favorites from the trip. Oliver has the tire wrench and Tanya is holding up the gate to her trunk, because it would not stay up by itself. In the process her shirt lifted and exposed a generous portion of her large midriff.

As she began to thank us a tear precipitated out of her right eye.

"Thank you boys so much. I gotta go pick up my three-year-old from day care an' I don' know how I woulda made it on time without you."

We crossed into the District of Columbia and I was expecting to be immediately assaulted by the glamour and pomp that would befit the capital city of the most powerful nation in the world. We were greeted by a completely opposite reality. As politicians lament the expanding gap between the rich and poor, the District itself offers one of the most pronounced case studies nationwide. It has both the highest per capita income and a poverty rate only exceeded by the state of Mississippi. Illiteracy is high, but so too is the proportion of individuals with college degrees. The HIV/AIDS infection rate tops three percent—well above the one percent required to be classified as a severe epidemic by the Centers for Disease Control. Some have noted that this infection rate puts the District on par with many developing countries in Africa and Southeast Asia. At the same time, about 93 percent of the District's residents have health insurance, one of the highest proportions in the country.

The dichotomies observed are largely split along racial and socioeconomic lines.

The District's footprint was originally a square oriented such that its corners point to each compass direction. Retrocession of land originally belonging to Virginia south of the Potomac River in 1846 has left the square looking like someone took a bite out of the southwestern portion.

Our point of entry was along the southeastern border, east of the Anacostia River. Neighborhoods on the eastern side of town are known for being very rough. I had to stop to refill our water supply and use the restroom. Walking into a Shell gas station, I was immediately spooked by the bulletproof glass and rotating doors through which cashiers would exchange money and goods. Even the packs of gum were behind the glass. The cashier would not refill my water bottles and there were no public restrooms.

Outside on the street everyone eyed us suspiciously. It felt like we were riding on pins and needles—not a good situation for bicycle tires—while getting honked at by passing cars. Even though I had to urinate like a steam engine we did not stop until the bridge across the

Anacostia.

"For some reason I feel lucky that we made it through there alive," said Oliver.

The dynamics changed instantaneously across the river. We were transported to a tourist's Promised Land in a matter of minutes. It was crossing the River Jordan.

We pointed out a large, pomp building to a passerby, only to discover it was the Capitol Building. We took pictures at the base of the Washington Monument and wandered down to the other end of the mall to see the Lincoln Memorial. I was disappointed to discover the reflection pool at the base of Lincoln's step was drained for repairs. There would be no Jennies running into the pool yelling "Forest!" today.

Riding towards the Washington Monument along the Mall, we stopped at a red light next to another cyclist. He was decked out in a full racing uniform advertising Trek and Clif Bar as sponsors. His bicycle made me drool. It was a Cervélo brand racing machine, paper-thin and feather-light, with elegant contours balanced by an aggressive red and black color scheme. I would not be surprised if it cost $2,500.

The only thing that did not jive with the image was the man's protruding belly.

"Where are you two riding today?" he asked.

"Oh, just up to Georgia Street."

"Then what's all that for?" he inquired while pointing at my panniers.

"Well, we started in Seattle and rode across the country."

"Wait—you're telling me you rode across the country on *that?*" the man sneered, casting a haughty glance down at the dusty and tired-looking Pocket Rocket. I was beside myself and ready to get into a fight. I guess after spending a month and a half with the Rocket, the bicycle had become close to my soul.

"Actually yes, I did," I replied.

The sport of cycling tends to be image-driven, but this prick took that to a level I had never experienced. It took every ounce of restraint to refrain from pointing at his bulging belly and shouting:

"And you ride around D.C. with *that?!* How do you manage with all the extra weight? Imagine how fast you could ride if you just lay of the doughnuts and un-fat yourself. Then maybe—just *maybe*—you would do that cute little bicycle of yours an ounce of justice. But right now you are unworthy, my friend, unworthy. And as for the Pocket Rocket: we could beat your ass up and down this mall even with gear loaded."

I did hold my tongue, and when the light turned green we peacefully pedaled away from Mr. Beef-Belly.

A friend of mine from college named Jessie was living on the north end of Washington as she completed a year of service work with the Jesuit Volunteer Corps. When I called her three days prior to tell her we would be coming into town she was not sure what I meant.

"…You did what?! And now you're here?! Well of course I would love to see you! Oh, and don't worry about being homeless: we've got two couches for you and your friend. Actually its only one couch, but in the shape of an 'L.' I hope that is okay for you."

Finding Jessie's house was a breeze thanks to the D.C. "grid." Roads running north/south are numbered consecutively, while roads with an east/west orientation are lettered A through Z. After Z it starts over again with A, but with two-syllable words. After two syllables, words with three syllables are used. There is even a convention for diagonal roads, which are named after states.

Jessie's house was on Georgia Street and, although we had never been there, we had some idea of where it was. Grids are nifty. When we showed up at her house at about five o'clock in the afternoon she was sitting on the porch, reading a book.

"Well look who it is! Hey, Jessie!"

"Welcome, welcome," she said, descending from the porch to

open the small gate at the street. I gave her a real-friend hug that would make Rover proud. She started choking on the dreadful smell of my underarm.

"You guys sure are smelling like roses today," she joked.

"Oh man. Right. Sorry about that; we haven't showered since Kentucky…"

"That was six nights ago!" Oliver added.

Jessie was unfazed. Being able to get up-close-and-personal with a ripe armpit—and still keep her cool—will take her very far in life. It would come as no surprise that she is currently enrolled in law school after being a finalist for one of the most prestigious law scholarships in the country.

"Six nights, huh? I am impressed. Really something to be proud of," she jested. "And I mean I want to honor your streak and everything, but we do have a shower if you wanted to clean up."

The first shower in nearly a week was delightful, as was the rest of the time spent in Washington. I met up with friends living on the East Coast I had not seen in over a year. We took tours inside of the Capitol Building and the Library of Congress. Although my eyes had been seasoned by many an ornate cathedral during European travels, I was impressed by the architecture and history woven into those buildings and the city in general.

One such place that caught my attention was the Old Senate Chamber in the Capitol Building, where the Unites States Senate met from 1819 until 1859. That semicircular floor was the stage on which issues such as the Missouri Compromise were forged. It is topped with a half-dome, giving the space strange echo properties. The tour guide told us about how one senator overheard two other senators gossiping about him from the other side of the room. I feared the juvenile comment I made about funny-looking man standing with his back to us would be heard from a hundred feet away.

It is mind-boggling just how many important entities are located within the small area of the D.C. We would be walking on a random city block and stumble upon important-looking structures emblazoned with titles such as "Department of Homeland Security" and "Internal Revenue Service."

Seeing the city from a volunteer's perspective was interesting and different from that of the typical visitor sporting expensive Canon camera equipment and large fold-out maps. The neighborhood where Jessie lived was far from "safe." During our stay in town, there was a shooting only a couple of blocks away.

"But I find things to be much more interesting up here than down by the monuments," she explained. "If you've seen the monuments once, you've seen them a thousand times. Life in this neighborhood is more vibrant and real. There is culture up here. This is the real D.C. And I am sick of tourists and the way they flaunt their money."

Oliver, Jessie, and I were seated on the "L" couch in the living room of the volunteer house. Just as she finished the bit about money, one of the other volunteers living in the house poked their head around the corner and said excitedly,

"Hey, who splurged on getting name brand butter at the store? Land-o-Lakes meet fried bean patty goodness tonight. It is gonna get r-e-a-l!"

Jesuit Volunteers are housed in groups of four and seven. They are paid a minimal stipend for living expenses, rent, and utilities. After bills are paid, the house is typically left with about sixty-five dollars monthly per resident to spend on food pooled into a communal budget. What some in the District may spend in a night, these volunteers spend over the course of a month. I doubt many government and corporate bigwigs are concerned about whether their butter happens to be name-brand.

The conversation shifted to Jessie's place of work. She had spent the past year working in a nursing home, comforting and entertaining those who are about to die.

"It kinda makes you cut out the bullshit. I used to care so much about material things, status, and getting ahead in life. But to these people who are dying none of that matters one iota. You can't cure them. You can't alter their fate or give them anything tangible that will last. All you can do is love them. All you can do is be with them physically and in spirit. I know now what really is important. And it has nothing to do with filling up a house too big for me in the first place with stuff I don't need. It is not about winning an argument about some policy on Capitol Hill or even being the best at something. Important is way bigger than that."

For a brief couple of minutes the next day, I felt like I was doing something very important.

The Vietnam Veterans Memorial is tucked away in a quiet corner of the National Mall. A subtle homage to the 58,272 servicewomen and men who lost their lives in the Vietnam War, the Wall was completed in 1982 with $9 million of exclusively private contributions.

When the Wall is approached from behind, it blends perfectly with the hill into which it is built. I was expecting to find a much larger, attention-grabbing structure and was surprised to almost step off the top of it. The list is actually ordered chronologically, beginning with the first individuals who lost their life in 1959. Luckily, a directory assists visitors looking for specific names.

With the help of the directory, I located "David C. Qualls" from Murphysboro, Illinois on the Wall. I reached for my camera, ready to fulfill the promise Oliver and I made two weeks prior to find Vivian's brother on the Vietnam Memorial. My finger was millimeters away from the camera button that would capture the image of Vivian's brother forever, but something terrible happened.

The lens retracted and screen went blank, save for the simple message "Please Charge Battery."

My heart sunk. The irony was too severe to appreciate and my inner Self shook his head in disgust.

You came thousands of miles, over mountains and through storms, only to forget to charge the camera? Scott, you are a mess. A real mess.

I stood staring at the wall, languishing in a cesspool of frustration and cynicism. Suddenly a light bulb flicked on in my head: *use your memory card in someone else's camera.*

"Excuse me," I said to the closest passerby. Around his neck was a fancy Nikon D-SLR camera with a lens as expensive as my entire trip. "Do you mind if I borrow your camera for a second?"

He gave me a suspicious look. I realized a bit more explanation was appropriate.

"Sorry—the battery for my camera ran out and I was wondering if I could put it into your camera to take a couple of quick pictures."

"Err, I guess that would be okay," he replied, reluctantly handing me the camera. I swapped the memory cards, took the picture of Vivian's brother, and returned the camera to its owner. The man's shoulders, which were creeping farther up his neck every second the camera was out of his grasp, instantly relaxed as he let out a tension-cleansing sigh.

"Thank you so much," I said. He was too busy stroking his electronic child to notice.

In another couple of hours I had to say goodbye to my second riding mate. Oliver and I were standing outside a metro station in the Columbia Heights neighborhood, having just finished packing and shipping the Motorboat back to Joe at a UPS store.

"Y'know, this moment came around really fast."

"Yeah, I know."

"You gonna be alright flying solo for a bit?"

"It doesn't seem like I have much of a choice," I responded with a grin. "But I think I will do just fine. And who knows? Now that you're gone, maybe I'll stand a chance if a cute girl comes my way."

"Just keep your chin up and chest out."

"So that's your secret?"

"Man, forget the girls. I mean on the road. And remember the elephant thing?" Oliver had the look of introspection.

"Yeah—why?" I asked.

"I think all that's left to eat are the tusks and the ears."

"You make it sound so appetizing."

"Seriously, this could be the hardest thing you've done yet. Tusks. And you'll have plenty of time to yourself; use it to listen. Ears."

"Ever thought about being a used car salesman? That sounded almost believable."

"Yeah, it was really hard to choose between that and the priesthood…"

"I guess they both give you keys. Anyway, thanks for coming out to ride these two weeks."

"My pleasure. It was a blast."

"Yeah, it was."

I watched Oliver disappear underground. Although I had spent a mere eighteen days with him, it felt like bidding farewell to a friend of many years.

Thirty seconds after he vanished from view, it hit me: I was alone. Not just thinking about being alone. Not just talking about being alone. I was purely and simply alone.

That evening Joe called me, almost prophetically, voicing similar loneliness:

"Skip, I haven't been sleeping very well so far in Denver. I don't know if it is the altitude getting to me. Or the dry air. Maybe I'm just more stressed out about the job than I am letting on. But I keep waking up in the middle of the night not knowing where I am. And here's the weirdest part: every time I wake up I *swear* you are somewhere in my apartment."

Companionship was something I took for granted. At every step of the way there was Joe or Oliver to share the experience with me. In times of frustration, they were there to make a joke. In times of elation, they were there to echo my shouts of joy. They offered a stabilizing perspective and encouraged me. The same was true from me to them.

Without companionship, there would have been no Pocket

Rocket and Motorboat, no Gingerbread Man and Captain Punishment, and no divinely inspired guidance from a priest. And no one to turn to when I was asking myself "is this really happening?!"

A sunny, warm morning accompanied me northbound leaving the District of Columbia and returning to the state of Maryland. Right at the state line there was a drive-thru liquor store. That is right—a drive-thru liquor store. I cannot think of anything that makes less sense. Take the number one cause of motor-skill impairment (alcohol) and put it freely in driver's cars at the highest of concentrations available. The sight of empty beer cans on the side of the highway was disconcerting, but a bottle of Jack Daniels would have been terrifying.

"You look like you're in it for the long haul," a voice said into my left ear, startling me. I turned and saw that it was another cyclist who had pulled up to wait for the same red light as me. He looked very young.

"Yeah, you guessed it. Started in Seattle at the beginning of May and here I am."

"Wow! That is wicked," he said.

"Wicked?"

"Y'know, wicked awesome?"

"Oh. Right."

"Anyway, name's Bryan. Nice to meet you."

Our handshake was cut short by the light turning green. We started off and I quickly discovered keeping up with him would be difficult. After a few minutes I was huffing and puffing.

"So I grew up just across the border in Pennsylvania. But went to college in Baltimore and now I got this job doing the books for this company up in Adelphi. My wife and I live just across the state line in D.C."

"Wait...you said... you had a... wife?"

"Yeah, I do. Been married four years, and I'm twenty-eight. I know what you're thinking—this guy looks to be about eighteen years old. Don't worry, I get that a lot."

Honestly, Bryan did not look even a year out of high school. I empathize with him, because I also get asked what year of high school I am in quite frequently.

"Hey, why don't I give my parents a call and see what they're up to this evening? They live about twenty miles away from Gettysburg, and that is where you said you were going next."

"That would be great!" I replied. At the next red light, Bryan tried giving them a call but nobody answered the phone.

"Tell you what: give me your phone number and I will let you know what my pops tells me. They would love to have a visitor."

Once again it sounded like things were too good to be true. The universe was conspiring in my favor, and all that I had to do was follow the signs to the next great evening filled with generous people and rejuvenation. My mind happily floated along as my legs pedaled, imagination traversing peaceful meadows and idyllic countryside on the way to the house of Bryan's parents.

The shoulder of the road was somewhat narrow and forced me to follow Bryan instead of riding side-by-side. I did not think anything of it because my mind was in such a peaceful state of Nirvana. Traffic on the road was steadily increasing and now a solid line of cars formed a wall to my left.

Suddenly and without warning Bryan swerved to the right. When he cleared my forward view, I realized a long line of concrete curbs lay dead ahead. They created a barrier between the car lane and the shoulder. With a wall of cars to my left and curbs to my right, I was trapped with nowhere to go. My vision started playing back in slow motion and I made a split-second calculation of options presented. The only hope was to weave through a small gap between the first two curbs. The gap was less than a foot wide.

I gripped the brakes but hardly had time to slow down. With Zen-like focus I waited until the last possible moment to turn the front wheel of the Pocket Rocket, hoping to pass through the gap with the largest angle of incidence possible. When the time came, I leaned and angled the wheel hard. It passed cleanly through the gap. I started to correct to the left so as to avoid the ditch on the side of the road.

For a split second it seemed the maneuver was successful. The front wheel was two feet through the gap and I was about to raise my fist in triumph. Then my saddle shot upward as though a spring were released directly underneath. Just like a semi truck that cuts a turn to sharp, the rear of the bicycle caught the curb. It launched vertically while the front stayed on the ground. I soared through the air head-over-handlebars. A midflight freeze-frame allowed me the opportunity to appreciate the falling action and anticipate the agony to come.

This was not what I had in mind for the first day alone in the saddle. Suspended in air, I did not know what would happen to my body upon returning to the ground. Nor was the future of the Pocket Rocket sure. Its wheels were old, so old that a collision such as this could very well put my beloved bicycle permanently out of commission.

Falling action is a literary phase. It is not meant to be taken literally.

Chapter TWENTY

Washington, D.C. to Reisterstown, MD

THE PROFOUND MOMENT OF CLARITY I experienced while flying through the air was abruptly shattered when my shoulder thudded and skidded against the road. The elbow was next to hit ground, along with my lower leg. The ensuing tuck and roll catalyzed a disorienting eruption of pain spreading across my body. Somehow my bicycle cleats came unclipped, thankfully. It would have been a shame to tuck and roll with bicycle still attached.

Before my mind could catch up, I was hobbling around trying to walk off pain that would not go away. I could not think about anything else. I could not even scream.

Minutes later, the pain subsided to a manageable threshold. A survey of damage revealed formidable scrapes to my elbow and outer leg already dripping blood. The wounds stung badly, but worse still was the invisible throbbing of my shoulder and hip joint. At least my head did not hurt. *Thank you, brand-new bicycle helmet.*

I gingerly limped back to the Pocket Rocket. It was much further away than I would have guessed. The panniers somehow remained attached throughout the incident. Both wheels were still there, but the back one was terribly bent out of shape. In bicycle-speak this is a "taco-ed" wheel, after the shape of a gently folded taco. When I tried spinning it, the rim successively hit the brake pads on both sides of the frame.

At this point Bryan realized I was no longer riding behind him. He turned and came back to the crash scene. I wished he would have just continued along his merry way, because I was not happy with him—and that is stating it lightly. It is difficult to see around another bicycle, and Bryan failed to signal the concrete curbs. As a result I was left with the unfortunate choice between a concrete curb and solid wall of traffic.

"Oh my gosh man! I am so so so sorry."

"Don't worry about it. It's fine," I said. On the inside I was thinking, *are you out of your f***ing mind?! Why the hell didn't you signal? Did anyone teach you how to not kill your following rider?*

"You alright?"

"Yeah, I said I'm fine."

"Man, that really sucks."

"Yep. It kinda did."

"I am so sorry. You sure you're alright?"

"Yeah."

"That sucks."

"I know."

"I feel bad."

"Don't."

It was silent for a couple of seconds. Then Bryan started talking again.

"Err, well, you gonna be alright flying solo?" It sounded like the question Oliver asked me twenty-four hours ago.

"I think I'll do just fine," echoing my response from the day before. Although this time I was not so sure of myself. The mood on Bryan's face changed from somber to bubbly in less than a second.

"Well then I gotta run. Accounting work doesn't take care of itself, you know. Good luck!"

As Bryan rode away I imagined what I would do if I had a voodoo doll of him and his bicycle. I would start by popping his tires. Then I would wait for him to fix them, and pop them again. I would poke holes in his water bottles. And I would tickle his armpits whenever he approached concrete curbs.

I am becoming more and more like my parents as the years go by. I feared this was true of Bryan, too, so I did not bother to call his parents.

That the Pocket Rocket was able to be ridden was a small miracle, even if it needed repairs desperately. Appreciating this small miracle was difficult with aching hips and bleeding joints. If a one-way plane ticket to Seattle floated down from the sky and landed in my lap, I would have cashed it in and headed home a heartbeat. I did not know if the bicycle was ultimately fixable. I was completely alone. And I had to make it to New York City to catch a train home in a matter of days.

I felt sullen, desolate, and weary—like a Furby left to wander the Gobi Desert. *U-nye-boh-doo?* (Furbish, a language that someone actually cared to invent, for "how are you?"). I would have a hard time answering the question because there are no Furbish words to express "God-awful."

The closest city with a bicycle repair shop was miles away and off the route. In other words, not the way I wanted to go. To make matters worse, the city was a sprawling one. Not large; just sprawling. I found myself riding in the far-right lane of a seven-lane speedway, complete with cars entering and leaving the thoroughfare at every possible angle and opportunity. After a couple close calls and angry honks, I was about ready to swerve left into oncoming traffic (if I were to even make it that far) and end things for good. Luckily, the bicycle repair shop came into view before the Pearly Gates.

It was still early, no later than eight-thirty. Like the shop in Roanoke, this one did not open until late morning. I spent two hours pacing in front of the store, munching on a Clif bar and anxiously contemplating potential outcomes.

Outcome one: the Rocket's rear wheel is fixable. The folks at the shop give it a quick tune-up and I am back on the road an hour and some twenty dollars later. I continue to ride for the better part of the day and the crash becomes a distant memory brought up when I need to tell a good story over a round of alcoholic beverages.

Outcome two: the Rocket needs a new rear wheel. This would also be a relatively quick fix, but exponentially more expensive. $150, maybe? Ouch.

Outcome three: the Rocket's wheel is neither fixable nor replaceable. Going against the bicycle repairman's advice to desist, I would decide to risk continuing to ride it in poor condition. The back rim would fracture thirty miles away from the nearest sign of humanity and I am left with a useless piece of scrap metal. I stick out my thumb to hitchhike and hop in the passenger seat of an old, rusty Ford pickup headed north to New York. I find out the pickup is not actually bound for New York as the spooky orchestra music begins to play. And so begins the next Hollywood horror production.

I really hoped either of the first two options would happen.

When the shop finally did open its doors I was the first customer in line at the repair counter. I explained my situation to the young man standing behind the counter and he came around to look at the wheel. His arms were covered in tattoos and ears were gauged to at least zero.

"Where'd you get this bike? It is a beauty—really should be hanging up somewhere on display."

"Yeah, you're probably right." He may have been right, but

neither I nor the Pocket Rocket were in the mood for a lecture. "What does it look like?"

"Hmm... What I can say is that the components are old-school Campy and all we have in the shop here are Shimano and SRAM derailleurs and cogs. That means throwing a new back wheel on is impossible because the brands are incompatible with each other. Leaves two options: straighten the wheel, or give the existing wheel a rebuild with new spokes and rim..." He paused for a second and rubbed the edges of a thick but well-trimmed goatee. "...But we are fresh out of thirty-two spoke rims. And I doubt you can hang around for a wheel while we custom-order parts for you. Which means you're left with one option: see if the wheel will true up enough to make it rideable."

Minor wheel imperfections can be corrected by tightening some spokes and loosening others, but sometimes the damage is beyond repair.

"I've never straightened a wheel this bad before, but I guess there's only one way to find out if it will work."

The repairman worked on the wheel for what seemed like hours. My watch told me it was no more than thirty minutes. He cranked violently on the housings of more than half the spokes. Over-tightened spokes break easier than normal ones, so making adjustments is a fine balance between adding sustainable pressure and too much pressure. After tightening the spokes, the repairman resorted to a more archaic approach: banging the wheel on the ground. He looked like a frustrated ape. He straightened and wiped a bead of sweat off his forehead.

"I've never straightened a wheel by doing that, either. That's the best I can do. I don't think the rim'll be hitting any part of the bike frame any more. Be careful though, because I had to ream down on some of those spokes. It'll be ten bucks, they can ring you up at the front counter."

"You think the wheel has another three hundred miles in it?" I asked.

"Can't say. I would really hate to give you the wrong answer."

"Yeah, I understand. Well thanks anyway."

"Of course. Good luck."

Over the next forty miles I looked down at the wobbly rear wheel at least a thousand times. Every bump and crack in the road sent waves of paranoia cascading through my body.

The wheel held up just fine for the rest of the day. I was about five miles away from Reisterstown, Maryland, my anticipated stop for lunch on the way to Gettysburg. Out of nowhere came the depressing, all-too-familiar sound.

"Pop! Hiss…"

The rear tire was flat once again. I let out a choice expletive much louder than necessary. Later I was grateful that I rested the Rocket against a tree instead of throwing it on the ground.

For ten minutes I could not summon resolve to change the flat. I sat on the side of the road with my arms hugging my knees, rocking back and forth in the fetal position. I really felt like crying. Reflecting on the experience, I wanted to tell the Scott sitting there *C'mon man, get over yourself. Remember what Oliver said? Chin up and chest out.*

The pump on my bicycle could barely inflate the new tube. I wished I would have taken the pump off Joe's Motorboat. After ten minutes of pumping there was barely enough pressure in the tire to continue riding. I stumbled into Reisterstown in the afternoon heat having bitterly abandoned my goal of reaching Gettysburg.

Adversity welds deep bonds between those who endure it together. But when you have to face it alone, adversity is rotten.

Misery loves company. But when company cannot be found, alternatives such as apple pie and sweetened dairy products suffice. Reisterstown is large enough to support a grocery store called the "Food Lion." Paying for these items at the checkout line I came up a dime short. When it rains, it pours. The cashier looked at me helplessly shaking my wallet and checking pockets for a dime. She shook her head and sympathetically shooed me through the line.

I walked out of the store with my head down in frustration, almost bumping into two bodies standing directly in front of me. Automatically saying "sorry," I sidestepped out of their way. My mind was barely tethered to the physical world and I failed to notice each pair of feet wore matching cycling shoes. My gaze slowly rose past clean-shaved legs, feminine curves, and matching white cycling jerseys. It stopped to rest on two pairs of blue eyes and heads full of blonde hair. One being was taller than the other. The region above each of their heads may have cast circular shadows on the ground. It was as if two guardian angels had come to apologize for not protecting me earlier in the day.

"Hallo," the tall one began tentatively. "Ve vere passing by on our bicycles and noticed zat bicycle over zere. Does it belong to you?"

"Yeah, err, well yeah it does." *Why do I always stutter at times like this?*

"And are you riding ze bike across ze TransAmerica?"

"Yeah…"

Their questions were focused and accurate. The two young women looked at each other and began conversing excitedly in a language I did not understand. The tall one then looked at me and spoke again.

"Ve saw ze bicycle outside and vondered if its rider is on a tour like us. Zis is ze fifth day since ve started in New York and ve hope to make it to San Francisco."

"And now ve are hungry," piped in the shorter one for the first time. "Vat do you Americans eat? Zese huge markets are impossible!"

"Yeah, they can be intimidating if you don't know what you're looking for," I replied, still not exactly sure if these two were mortal or of the spirit world. If they really had to eat, that means they must belong on Earth. "I'll show you around for some good and cheap food to look for in this monstrosity—by the way, the name's Scott."

"Ah, yes, very good. I am Inge," said the tall one.

"And my name is Anna. Pleased to meet you," followed the shorter.

"Nice to meet you two as well. You need to tell me one thing: where are you from? It's got to be either Germany or somewhere in Scandinavia, but I've got no idea." Inge chuckled and said,

"Very intelligent you are. Ve are from Norvay."

"So you were speaking Norwegian."

"Well, yes…" Inge answered, sounding confused.

"Oh, sorry. I was thinking out loud." On the inside I was thinking *Scott, you should be ashamed of yourself; almost your entire family is Norwegian but you can't speak a lick of your homeland's language. It's time to start eating lutefisk and join the Sons of Norway.*

On the second pass through the store, with two attractive accented women in tow, I was in better mood. The first aisle I showed Anna and Inge was the peanut butter aisle. I grabbed a medium-sized jar of Skippy Super-Chunk.

"This," I said while pointing at the jar, "is what will save your life and your wallet all the way across the country."

I was waiting for looks of awe and wonderment, or at least a nod of understanding. The pair raised their left eyebrows in tandem.

"Zis peanuts butter, yes," Anna mused. "Vwe don't understand vy you Americans eat zis thing. It looks like poo smashed into ze jar."

There it was. True Norwegians must not eat peanut butter.

"Well have you ever tried it?" I asked.

"No," Inge replied.

"Do you want to?"

"Maybe," the two echoed.

"Okay, I tell you what. I've got a jar already, and later I'll let you try some. But I am warning you, your life won't be the same afterwards."

They walked out of the store with an apple and banana apiece. We sat together on the curb to eat our food and I could not help but feel a bit like a fat slob with my apple pie and ice cream. After finishing the apples, each of them pulled out a Clif bar and I almost gagged. I had eaten so many Clif bars I vowed never to eat another in my life.

"How do you spend tonight?" Anna asked with a mouthful of chocolate chip Clif bar.

"No idea yet."

"And how do you use a computer?"

"I've just been stopping at public libraries along the way. They usually have free internet you can use?"

"Really?! Can you take us zere?"

"Sure—as soon as I find out where it is."

I walked back into the store and got directions to the library. I had never seen two people of any age so excited as the three of us walked into the Reisterstown Public Library. Like kids in the candy store, Inge and Anna spent an hour and a half catching up on Facebook correspondence and their blog. It was fine by me, because it had been a good long while since I had sent out an update email myself. We walked together out of the library.

"I sink it would be good zat ve find somewhere to spend tonight togezher," Inge said.

"Yes, can ve follow you? Vere vill you go?" Anna asked.

"Ve have used campgrounds so far and zey have been very good," Inge added.

"Campgrounds are not a bad way to go," I responded. "But I think we can do better tonight. Follow me and we'll see what happens."

Inge and Anna looked puzzled. In addition to the library's whereabouts I had inquired about the location of the city's churches. We pulled out of the library parking lot to the left and started riding down a residential street. At the end of the block a large roadside readerboard announced the Reisterstown Episcopal Church. In addition to the church steeple itself, many auxiliary buildings were tucked behind trees in the extensive grounds. Most notable was a miniature lighthouse in the center of everything, reaching a height of about four stories. I slowed to a stop and dismounted.

"Vait—vat are ve doing?" Inge asked.

"I was going to see if anyone was around and ask them if they could help us out tonight."

"Vat do you mean exactly?"

"Well, people at churches as a whole are very generous and they have been a great help to my friends and I all the way across the country. Basically I'm going to go see if they mind that we pitch a tent somewhere on church property."

"Even zough you don't know zem?"

"Yeah."

"And even zough zey don't know you?"

"Yep."

"And zis is normal here in zis country?"

"I wouldn't say everyone does it. But it has been working for me quite well."

"And you sink it vill vwork zis night?"

"Only one way to find out."

I peeked through the glass door of the community room adjacent to the church and found three people sitting around a folding table placed in the room's center. Inge and Anna followed me through the open door. When the two middle-aged women and white-haired man noticed our presence I cleared my throat to speak. The two Norwegians stood behind me, noticeably uncomfortable with the situation.

"This is going to be slightly random, but do you have a minute? My name is Scott and these are my friends Inge and Anna from Norway. We bumped into each other this afternoon here in Reisterstown and are riding our bicycles in opposite directions across the country. Like I said, we ended up here for the evening and are wondering if there is any way you would be able to help us out. Or any member in the community who could. Or if you knew of any good restaurants in town..."

"Best wait for the pastor to get back," said the man with white hair. He looked at his watch. "I reckon fifteen minutes or so. But you say you're serious about riding across the country?"

The pastor returned while the six of us were still talking. He was tall and stocky, maybe fifty-five years old, and wore a Baltimore Orioles baseball cap.

"Name's Bud," he said, holding out a thick and gnarled hand to Inge, Anna, and finally me.

"Hey Bud, these folks are ridin' their bicycles across the country!" said one of the women.

"I'll be damned—err, darned," Bud said before putting his hand up to his mouth. The man with white hair laughed. "What can we do for you?"

"Well, at the moment we have no place to stay tonight. We completely understand if you are uncomfortable with strangers around church grounds, but do you think it would be alright if we pitched our tent in some far corner of the property?" Bud scratched his stubbly chin but did not have to think too long before answering.

"Don't see any reason why that would be a problem. C'mon outside and let's take a look at where you can pitch it." After traversing past the lighthouse and over to an outdoor basketball court, Bud stopped walking and stood scratching his chin thoughtfully. "This is the spot, no doubt. But I am thinking some of the neighborhood kids may stay after youth group tonight and play some basketball. Wouldn't want you to have to deal with that noise into the wee hours of the night. Do you mind sleeping on a floor inside? After the women's Bible study gets done tonight you can put up in the house across the way. No shower, but it's got a bathroom, kitchen, and running water."

The three of us gave the most heartfelt thanks we could. But there was one more very important question to ask.

"Where should we go to get some good grub in town?"

"Aunt Mary's, no question. Got sandwiches so big they will blow a hole in your stomach if you're not careful. Tell you what: you go get some food, then come back around nine tonight and I'll let you into the house."

The sandwiches at Aunt Mary's were as big as Bud said. Inge and Anna had no idea what any of the items on the menu were. After hearing my recommendations, one went with a Philly cheesesteak and the other ordered a burger with bacon and Swiss. If they were not going to eat peanut butter, the least I could do was inspire them to eat some good old-fashioned American beef. Halfway through the meal I got up to refill my soda at the fountain. The two foreigners looked at me funny when I sat back down.

"Is zis okay, to get a second drink?" Inge asked.

"Yes indeed. Fill and refill to your heart's content," I responded.

"You Americans are crazy," she said while shaking her head. "First you give zem internet free, zen you welcome complete strangers to come sleep in your house, zen you give zem free drinks at ze restaurant. Is everyzing free here?"

Later in the evening the three of us were sitting on the lighthouse steps waiting for the church meeting to adjourn. When it did, an old lady walking out the doors noticed us and came over to talk. We explained our cross-country bicycle excursions. Without a second thought she took out her wallet and put a $20 bill in Inge's hand.

"Y'all get some breakfast tomorrow, on me. I don't want to hear about three bicyclists starving to death in the morning paper."

Inge's gaze was transfixed on the portrait of Andrew Jackson in her palm. Anna watched the old lady slowly amble away into the darkness. Both of the Norwegians were silent for some time.

"I don't believe it," they said suddenly said in unison. I saw in their faces the same wonder that Joe and I experienced in Kansas when Len slapped the $50 bill down on the table. *Is this too good to be true?* Generosity such as this contradicts a transactional worldview defined by contracts, investments, and returns. There was no way Joe and I could repay Len. And no recompense Inge or Anna could offer the generous old lady. Why then would these people behave in such a benevolent manner?

The only reason I deserve this is because I am human and so are they.

Inge did not know what to do as the recipient of such generosity.

"Here, Scott. You take it. If it vasn't for you, ve never vould 'ave been here in ze first place."

"No way, Inge. She gave it to you. And I have already received plenty in the past seven weeks."

"But... I... vell... al-right..."

I believe Inge tried to give the money to me because it was the easier route to take. That is not to say generously offering the money to me was inappropriate. What I mean is that humbly receiving charity requires one to change in ways that are challenging and perspective-altering.

By simply passing on the gift to me, Inge would have come out break-even; the incoming good deed would be immediately counterbalanced by the outgoing. Conversely, keeping the money herself meant acknowledging a debt payable to humanity at large. As many people in the country are discovering these days, outstanding debt has a profound impact on one's course of action. An account payable to the human race will drastically alter one's way of living—if any attempt is made at repayment. Going into debt in this manner is a worthwhile and necessary component of the human experience. Saint Paul of Tarsus said it best:

"Let no debt remain outstanding, except the continuing debt to love one another."

Addressing love and charity may sound sappy. However, in the evolutionary past humans developed a sense of love, altruism, and general emotion. It had to serve some purpose, or else evolution would have stamped it out. The ability to relate to other humans is directly tied to our beings. Blinded by the egotistic independence of today's society, it is easy to forget that we depend on one another. Forgetting this is forgetting a basic element to our humanity.

If you never go into debt, you will never be blessed to see the world through another's eyes.

Two weeks after saying goodbye to Inge and Anna I got an email from them that started, "Spent the night in a brand-new Methodist church in Girard, KS. Sweet, huh?!" I was floored because they continued to experience and rely on the good will of others on their journey.

As my own journey neared the final stop, it was clear that it really was not my journey at all. Rather, it was a two-month testament to the generosity and benevolence of the human race. Retiring to the thin sleeping pad and pile of clothes acting as a pillow, I was reminded abruptly about my crash earlier in the day. Waves of pain shot up from my sore right side. A gasp escaped before I was able to choke it back.

"Are you okay?" asked Inge.

"Yeah. But I think I may be especially sore tomorrow."

Chapter TWENTY-ONE

Reisterstown, MD to New York, NY

I STARTED FROM REISTERSTOWN EARLY the next morning after saying goodbye to Inge and Anna. I hoped the day would be boring. Two hours later I crossed into Pennsylvania, the fifteenth state of the trip. Shortly thereafter I pedaled into the sleepy town of Gettysburg. Nearby fields were the stage of the most well-known battle in the Civil War—even though the battle at Antietam claimed more lives. Many define Gettysburg as the turning point for General Ulysses S. Grant and the Union Army. And it was in Gettysburg that Abraham Lincoln began an address with the famous words "Four score and seven years ago…"

Today the town is still relatively small and the battleground is peaceful. I looked out on a gently sloping field populated by golden wheat swaying softly in the wind and imagined Pickett's infantry charging Cemetery Ridge. From there I went to the spot where Lincoln is hypothesized to have given the Gettysburg Address. I shared the moment with a tour bus full of sixty AARP members in sunbonnets and slacks.

The undulating terrain east of Gettysburg in Lancaster County is home to an Amish population of 30,000. All told there are over 260,000 members of the Amish church in the United States, so the Lancaster Amish comprise a significant portion of the population. Roots of the Amish Church extend back to the Anabaptist movement in Europe around the time of the Reformation. The denomination's founder, Jakob Ammann, separated from other Anabaptists in 1693 when he adopted policies for his congregation such as twice-yearly communion (as opposed to once-yearly) and forbidding beard trimming. During the eighteenth and nineteenth centuries the Amish immigrated from France and Switzerland to North America, where they have remained ever since.

The lifestyle and appearance of the Amish lead many to stereotype them as backwards and primitive. In many ways, however, they have been ahead of the curve for many years. For example, they were among the first to put forth the idea centuries ago of the separation of church and state, which angered the Catholic and Protestant establishments in Europe. Now they find themselves exemplars of the "green" movement, rarely using electricity, fertilizer, or fossil fuels in their agricultural practices. Hardly any of the Amish are unemployed or live on government subsidies. They pay taxes just like everyone else (but opt out of paying/receiving social security), and somehow manage to survive and compete with Big Agriculture and its gargantuan army of machines.

It felt like the history of Lancaster County was alive and breathing. As I continued eastward, fewer and fewer of the farmhouses had electrical lines running to them. The road shoulders widened to the width of horse-drawn carriages, and I had to weave back and forth to avoid piles of horse dung.

Finally I saw what I had been anxious to see: a horse-drawn buggy. I was so excited that I turned around to snap a picture of the contraption and its rustically dressed operator. Later I realized how stupid of a thing it was to do; if I were Amish, I would get awfully sick of people pointing cameras at my homemade clothes and impressively thick beard. As far as I know the Amish don't believe having one's picture taken equates to soul robbery, but taking their picture with technology they choose to reject is nonetheless disrespectful.

The small Pennsylvania town where I chose to end the day's ride was named Intercourse. That is right, Intercourse, PA. Of all the lascivious places in the country where city names such as this would be celebrated, one would hardly expect to find "Intercourse" in Amish country. I was so amused that I went into a gift shop and bought a glass that said "I ♥ Intercourse."

My brief visit to Intercourse was a great one and I owe it all to a raspy-voiced female gas station clerk. She suggested I pay a visit to the volunteer fire department to look into overnight accommodations.

When I arrived at the station I had hardly dismounted my steely steed when three men came out to greet me. One was in his middle ages, with an impressive beard and equally impressive forearms. The other two looked to be in their early twenties. One had a miniature beard in the same style as the older man, the other was clean-shaven. All wore suspenders, simple brown britches, button-down shirts, and top hats.

"You don't look like you're from around here," the older man said inquisitively.

"You're right. I am definitely not."

"In that case the Intercourse Department of Volunteer Fires welcomes you."

"He meant volunteer fire*fighters*," one of the younger ones interjected.

"Exactly what I said," the elder continued. "Anyway, the name's Ned. And these two are Samuel and Jacob Allen."

"Nice to meet you all," I replied.

"Same to you. Now I don't mean to be nosy, but it *smells* like you have got a story to tell." Ned wiggled his nose.

"Been a while since I have taken a shower, I guess…"

"Me too. But I was going for the figurative evocation of the verb 'to smell,' as in 'to seem' or 'to suggest.' I used an inquisitive inflection pattern to construct a perceived reality for you to confirm, elaborate, or deny." Ned took a deep breath. I could barely follow his fast-flowing verbiage.

"So then, was my sense of 'smell' spot-on?"

"That would be in the eye of the beholder," I responded.

"Now we are talking about sight?" Ned countered. "Lest I remind you one's sense of smell is much more closely linked to memory formation and propagation than any other sense—sight included. I would much prefer to stick to the domain of odors." At this point Samuel and Jacob Allen were shaking their heads.

"Alright," I said, "odors it shall be; your sniffer sniffed sufficiently."

"I knew it did! So then what is your story?"

I told them about my trip. They were enthusiastic like few others I had encountered. Ned gave me a baseball cap that read "Intercourse Fire Dept." It quickly became my favorite hat. Jacob Allen offered his parents' guest house to me for the night. Generosity seemed to come as naturally to them as the seasons.

After twenty or so minutes Samuel looked at the clock on the wall and said to Jacob Allen,

"We pullin' rope today?"

"Yeah we are. People should be showin' up any minute." Jacob Allen then directed at me. "Why don't you go over to the grocery store and grab some supper. When you get back we'll either be down on the field yonder pullin' rope or at the baseball diamond watching the softball game."

"Sounds good to me. But one question: pullin' rope?" This question made both of them laugh.

"Oh, right. I mean like tug o' war. The Intercourse boys have been champs at the county fair three outta the past four years."

I found Samuel down at the baseball field after consuming copious quantities of baked beans and potato salad from the grocery store.

"You want to go for a ride in the buggy?" he asked out of the blue. He had to be reading my mind.

"That would be incredible!"

We hopped into the two-seater and landed on hard, wooden seats that somehow managed to be comfortable. I was surprised to find a dashboard populated by a considerable amount of buttons, levers, and gauges. Samuel pulled a lever that illuminated the dashboard and turned on headlights and taillights. Previously I did not consider that buggies have to be street-legal. The horse started trotting with a brief flip of the reigns. Samuel pushed another button, which triggered a blinking right turn signal and we turned onto the road's shoulder.

The sun was setting over the idyllic Pennsylvania countryside. Small lights twinkled in the windows of homesteads positioned at the base of sloping hills covered in rows upon rows of corn, plowed and planted without any mechanized vehicles whatsoever. There was hardly any traffic on the road, buggy or otherwise. I looked up at the stars just emerging from the darkening canvas of the sky. It was a very peaceful scene, and soon the rhythmic gait of the horse lulled me into a trance.

"You're going to need to excuse my ignorance, but I didn't know that electric lights were allowed in the Amish religion."

"Don't worry about feeling ignorant at all. We actually get that a lot from people who aren't familiar with us or how we live. The bottom line is if we want to take our carriages and buggies on the road, they must have lights or else we are breaking the law."

"So you are caught between a rock and a hard place, breaking a state law or religious law?"

"Kind of, but that's not completely it. It's more important that we have a means of transportation at night than to follow every single archaic rule to the 't.' There is a board of Amish members that spends a lot of time deciding exactly what should be permissible and what is frivolous and unnecessary. It's a matter of keeping the intent of the laws alive amidst changing times."

"You have any other examples?"

"Sure. I don't know if you noticed earlier today, but there are quite a few solar panels on many of the farmsteads. Many Amish families are using them to generate their own electricity. Again, the issue isn't whether electricity should be completely avoided. The real question is 'what does this mean to my life if I were to incorporate it?'"

"So that is why Jacob Allen has a smart phone?"

"Once again, you're almost there but don't have the whole story. Amish people do use phones on occasion. But there has to be a purpose for borrowing one, say to communicate the news of a funeral or to arrange a business accord. I am not going to just use a phone for the sake of using one. The same goes for things like riding in a car. If I have to commute sixty miles to work there is no way I could make it on this buggy. Old Sampson here would throw a fit—and probably never be able to walk again."

"If that's the case then doesn't a fancy smart phone still seem a bit unnecessary?"

"That is the second piece to the puzzle. Being a member of the Amish community is on a completely volunteer basis. I don't know if you had it in your mind that it is something forced upon us. I think maybe some outsiders portray us that way, and it may be true about some of our communities. Anyway, in our adolescent years before getting married there is a period called *rumspringa*, a word in Pennsylvania Dutch which basically translates to 'run-around.' It is a time when we're permitted to experiment with the English world, before we have to make the decision to join the church in full."

"'English world'?"

"That basically means everything besides Amish. Weird, I know."

"No, it makes sense: when the Amish came here it was only them speaking Dutch and the majority English-speaking society."

"See, you probably know more than me."

"Doubtful—I heard a little bit at a gas station today. Anyways, we were talking about Jacob Allen, I think."

"Ah yes. Jacob Allen is in his time of experimentation. I was there not too long ago myself."

"Was it difficult, the choice to become a full member of the church?"

"It was something I wrestled with for a long time. It isn't easy to live the way we Amish do. But I found myself drifting further and further away from the person that I had in my mind I wanted to be. And I will not lie, I fell into some of the vices the internet and modern technology make easily accessible. At that point I realized I am lucky to have the opportunity to choose to live what many would call a 'simpleton' life. Last year I made up my mind, asked my wife to marry me, cancelled my cell phone contract, and became a full member of the church. I know it's not for everyone. But it was for me."

"'Lucky' to not own a smart phone. This may sound crazy but I feel much the same way about the past seven weeks of riding my bike. In unplugging myself from many of the modern creature comforts I feel more plugged into the elemental aspects of… of…" I was frustrated at myself for not being able to find the right word. Samuel helped me out:

"…of life."

"Yeah. Exactly. And there I was trying to look for a fancy or impressive word when a simple one was the right one. So I guess I am not there yet."

Samuel laughed, and I joined with him.

When we pulled up to the field adjacent to the fire station it was pitch black outside. I had no idea how much time had passed on our buggy ride. We found Jacob Allen watching the evening's softball game. Although it was only an amateur sporting event, the crowd of spectators was impressive. The stands were an odd mix of baseball caps and homemade top hats. Nobody seemed to notice the dichotomy besides me.

After the game I followed Jacob Allen to his house. Bicycles fall into the category of "mechanized travel" and are not generally permitted among the Amish people. What they do permit, however, are two-wheeled scooters with handlebars and a platform on which to stand. Jacob Allen's looked like the fad Razor scooters of my childhood with larger wheels and a wooden makeover. He got that foot-powered contraption moving fast.

We talked on the way about his brutal work schedule. He had a full-time construction job and helped out on the family farm as well. Days normally started at four o'clock in the morning and ended at six o'clock in the evening, later during harvest times. My pedaling efforts paled in comparison. Actually, I felt like an outright sissy. It was already past eleven and I was worried about getting my eight hours of sleep, but Jacob Allen worked fourteen hour days six days a week only sleeping four.

I slept that night in the guest house of Jacob Allen's family. The electric lights and sink—which would have struck me as odd a few hours ago—did not seem so out of place now.

The Amish still did not make perfect sense, but thanks to Samuel and Jacob Allen I caught a glimpse of what they are really about. They do not maintain a life separated from mainstream society in the Puritan vein, driven by fear and aversion to change. Their lifestyle is a choice they freely make on a daily basis; a choice to remain true to their values, values that transcend hair-splitting questions such as whether turn signals should be allowed on their horse-drawn buggies.

To many, the Amish way is nothing more than comical. Look no further than Weird Al's song "Amish Paradise" or the TV series *Amish in the City*. Although humorous, they completely misrepresent the essence of Amish life.

People will get fed up with the shallow connectedness and abstract stresses of modern times. Answering emails from a chic, high-powered mobile phone will only be cool for so long. Facebook may indeed succeed in connecting every person to every other person in the world. But when hyper-connectedness loses its novelty, the disillusioned masses will knock on the Amish door for tips on how to lead a "simple" life. Samuel and Jacob Allen will be rolling on the floor laughing their suspenders off.

Within half a day of leaving Amish country, I found myself munching on a cheesesteak sandwich in a completely different world. I was in the middle of the City of Brotherly Love, Philadelphia. The restaurant did not feel the need to denote that it was a "Philly" cheesesteak.

Crossing the Delaware River on an overpriced passenger ferry, I struck up a conversation with a couple passengers.

"Do you know the best way to get through Camden on a bicycle?" I asked a gruff man sporting a trucker hat. He choked on his Coke.

"Hold on. You said you gonna *ride* through Camden? On that?"

"Well yeah. Not any other option at this point, as far as I can tell."

"Boy, you got some real courage there. Lemme see that map." I handed it to him. "Lessee, you best head on this one right here until it bumps into this bigger one. And I wouldn't stop 'til you clear the city by twenty mile."

Camden goes toe-to-toe on a yearly basis with St. Louis and New Orleans for the "most dangerous city" honors. I had a knack for finding myself in dangerous places. But, like St. Louis and every other "dangerous" place I had been during the daytime, nothing was astir and I passed through without a problem. That is not to say the scenery was aesthetically pleasing, though. Streets lined with abandoned factories and trash told stories of prosperity's past and a hope-starved present.

With Camden in the rear-view mirror, I made my way east through New Jersey on a busy, seven-lane thoroughfare. In some places the shoulder completely disappeared and I was hung out to dry in the right-most lane, fending off impatient Garden State drivers. After many close calls, honked horns, and middle fingers thrown my direction, the gray hair count on my head went from zero to at least two. I felt it. As for the frequent middle-fingered hand gestures flying my direction, I just pretended they were saying "Scott, you're Number One!"

When I had finally cleared the madness and was back on a quiet two-lane road, I passed by a pair of tween-aged boys walking alongside the road.

"Spandex Warrior!" one of them shouted. Having battled frantic traffic for hours on a busy street, they could not have said it any better.

The extra gray hairs I sprouted came in handy when I needed to blend into the over-fifty-five community where I found myself at night. I crossed paths with a retired nun out for an evening stroll who was kind enough to offer me a place to stay for the night.

"You're not going to kill me, are you?" she said jokingly.

"Wasn't planning on it," I replied.

"Bummer. I've been taking self defense classes and I was hoping to have a chance to practice…"

The pork roast she prepared for dinner was delicious, but I am convinced the mashed potatoes had mind-clouding properties—I do not remember anything else from the night and was asleep within minutes. My dreams featured ninja-nun superheroes practicing self-defense skills.

"What you're going to do," she said to me the next morning, "is head straight out of town on the main road out front. Then you take a left at Dover road. Follow that to Toms River, turn right on highway thirty-seven, and that will take you straight to the shore."

I was headed to the Jersey shore. One of my professors from college is from New Jersey. He explained it this way:

"The shore is special. It's a common point in the narrative of New Jerseyans young and old, rich and poor. The state often gets a bad rap for a number of reasons—especially from New Yorkers. Some say the state smells bad, which it does. Others point to some of the roughest places in the country like Camden and Newark. Others still ridicule the way they speak. Anyway, the shore is an escape for many who are trapped in the monotony of life. Everyone has a place on the shore, or knows someone who does. Fridays are a mass exodus to the east. If you ever see the shore, you will understand why; the beaches are perfect."

The only other exposure I had to the Jersey shore was the appropriately titled reality TV series *Jersey Shore*. Airing on MTV, it follows the lives of eight individuals who come to the shore to live together in a train-wreck of personality and sex. But they aren't just any eight individuals; cast member Vinny Guadagnino said a friend asked him to fill out an application looking for "the orangest, most muscley, spikey-haired people" around to be part of a TV show.

Unsurprisingly, the combination of clashing personalities, high-charged sexuality, and novel culture of the cast has attracted a large audience in the short two years of the show's existence. On the other hand, many Italian-Americans find the stereotypes perpetuated in the show to be demeaning. Others say the show is plain and simply terrible television.

Dr. Albert was right when he said the shore is perfect. Clean, sandy-white beaches stretch for miles upon miles. It was Saturday and they were chalk-full of beachgoers in all shapes and sizes. Some shapes and sizes were more visually appealing than others.

Regardless, it was hard to imagine lounging on a pristine beach with warm sun and mild water and feeling anything but content. That is, until I moved to test the beach for myself.

"Hey, you! Yeah, I'm talking to you over there in the tights!"

The woman confronting me wore pants hiked up past her belly button and had a very low voice. People from Jersey have a characteristic way of pronouncing the silent "L" in words like "talking." I think she was some sort of beach patrol, because she was dressed in uniform.

I gave her my attention.

"You can't go any further unless you have a beach badge. Eight bucks for a day on the beach. And the bike…" she paused to make an emphatic hand-waving gesture that I did not fully understand, "…is gonna have to get off this boardwalk in ten seconds starting *now!*"

She looked down at her watch and I could see her shiny boot tapping every second. I walked to the edge of the boardwalk and waited until nine seconds passed before taking the last step.

There are nice things to Jersey, but sometimes Jersey does not let you appreciate them. That was the first time I had ever seen a beach that charged for access. A friend from the East Coast told me I grew up spoiled by the free beaches on the West Coast.

For lunch I sat outside at a beachside café eating a muffin, utilizing the down time to people-watch. There were plenty of thick men in wife-beater T's and women basted bronze walking up and down the boardwalk. For all I knew they could be the *Jersey Shore* cast.

Across the street from the café an auto shop had its garage doors open, and mechanics had a few cars raised up for repairs. Despite the distance across the street I could hear a conversation between two of the mechanics as clear as day. They spoke in a nasally, high-pitched Jersey accent.

"'Ey Chuck, did I tell you what this dewsh bag said to me the othah day?"

SQUEAKY WHEELS

"No you didn't Jimmy. Enlighten me."

"Well I was a sittin' at the front countah sippin' on a soda and this asshole come up in a preppy orange collared shirt an' asks if we service Mercedes 'roun 'ere."

"But we don' do 'em Benzes, Jimmy!"

"Yeeah, you're right Chuck. So that's what ah told 'im, an' he went an' put a stick up 'is ass or somethin'. Goin' 'round the store makin' a scene."

"So whaddid you tell 'im?"

"I says to 'im, 'man, go outside an' read the sign that says we only do Japanese auto. I'd rather service your grandmother than that car.'"

"You really said that?"

"Sure did. An' this wisecrack looks like he got hit with a fastball from the Rocket 'imself. Straightens up his back, repositions the stick still up his rear, bottom lip all quiverin'. Opens 'is mouth coolly an' says 'I'll... be... back.' Son-uv-uh-bitch turns 'round and storms out the door. Ain' 'eard of 'im since."

"How long ago was that?"

"Week ago Tuesday."

"Jimmy! He's due to come back any second! An' you insulted his mother's mother?!"

"Aww, Chucky don' worry. I could tell he wasn't the type to..."

The conversation trailed off as the two colorful mechanics went inside to the counter to talk to a customer who had just walked in the front door.

I had long since finished eating and was sticking around for the pure enjoyment of listening to the conversation. There was really no hurry, because only fifteen miles remained between me and the ferry into Manhattan. Once again I saddled my bicycle and told my legs to resume the methodic, gyrating dance routine that had taken me all the way across the country. I heard Joe's voice echo in my head:

"Where were we?... Ah, yes. That's right: pedaling."

A passenger ferry shuttles foot traffic between the north Jersey shore and Manhattan Island. I wheeled my bicycled onto the boat.

"You're not from around here, are you?" one of the ferry attendants asked me.

"How did you guess?" I replied jokingly, as I had been accustomed. The ferry attendant ended up being very kind and explained to me the intricacies and topography of New York City. It is a much more complicated place than I originally imagined.

"See this bridge? It is the Verrazano Narrows Bridge connecting Staten Island and Brooklyn. Brooklyn is on the end of Long Island, which goes way out to the east. New York City is divided into five boroughs: Staten Island and Brooklyn that you see now, as well as Manhattan, Queens, and the Bronx... Now we're in the upper portion of the bay and you will see the Statue of Liberty in just a second..."

The Statue of Liberty?! He spoke nonchalantly, like he saw it every day.

"...And you can see the Brooklyn Bridge now, too. If you hadn't figured it out yet, all of the skyscrapers you see are part of downtown Manhattan. The biggest one, under construction, that's the Freedom Tower they're building at Ground Zero. The other two boroughs, Queens and the Bronx, you won't be able to see from this boat... We'll be dropping you right in the thick of things—think you can handle it?"

"We'll see, I guess." It was the same thing I had been saying for almost two months.

The ferry's trajectory mirrored that of the steamships bringing the newest crops of Americans from around the world a century ago, who would all have to pass through Ellis Island in New York Harbor to be naturalized as citizens. My journey was ending at the place of so many beginnings—and there was Lady Liberty, arm perpetually raised and torch ablaze, to welcome me just as she did to my ancestors many years before.

It was sunny and the wind whipped sharply off the eastern seaboard. The afternoon angle of the sun reflected off the waves crashing up against Liberty Island, sparkling brilliantly. I tried to put myself in the shoes of the immigrants looking at the statue for the first time, thinking about how they would have reacted to Lady Liberty and ideals for which she stands. I considered the hopes they might have hoped, the anxieties, and the fears they had to overcome. But above all I was drawn to the dreams their minds dreamt.

We the People of the United States are a mixed bag, but I think the oft-repeated "melting pot" characterization is insufficient. To suggest we are boiled down to a homogenous mixture discounts our great variety. In my opinion we are more like minestrone soup, incomplete without any one formative component. To suggest a coal-mining Appalachian, cattle-driving Montanan, and metropolitan New Yorker are of homogeneous consistency would be preposterous to each of them. Amidst this great diversity of experience and opinion it is easy to lose track of that which holds us all together—today more than ever before. News media and politicians are not helping.

We are painted in all colors and creeds. We are cut out in all shapes and sizes. We sing in all types of languages and accents. We are so different. And yet we all salute the same flag and we call this country home. That which draws us together is stronger than that which tears apart.

What exactly draws us together? We are a population of dreamers who still depend on one another to make our collective and individualistic dream of a better tomorrow become reality.

In order for my dream of riding across the country to be possible, I needed help at every pedal stroke from the Pacific to the Atlantic. And I got help in spades and from all angles. Atheists, agnostics, Mormons, Methodists, Presbyterians, Baptists, blue collars, white collars, conservatives, liberals, and fellow cyclists would be naming just a few who offered their assistance. That is what tells me we still want to help each other achieve our dreams.

In eras past it was easier to see that we depend on each other. We needed each other to make it through a harsh winter. We needed each other to win our freedom and defend it from tyrants and villains. We needed each other so as to be able to build, run, and define the nation. We were asked to make sacrifices for each other.

It is easy to lose the sense of mutual interdependence in the abstracted reality that characterizes modern life. Rarely venturing out of the home-garage-car-work-car-garage-home cocoon does little to remind us just how connected to each other we really are. Our nation has spent the better part of the past decade at war, but the majority of the population felt no major effect. In cheapening and quantifying our "connectedness" to people and networks of people, the social media have cheapened our real need to live in community with one another.

We all belong to one another, we are in a basic sense all in this together.

The ferry docked at Battery Park in lower Manhattan, mere blocks away from Wall Street and Ground Zero. The journey was essentially complete. I went out onto the busy streets, fending for myself and trying to not get clobbered by the manic New York cabbies. I had to find my way across the Brooklyn Bridge to a friend's apartment near Prospect Park. Along the way I passed thousands of people milling about, many of whom complemented my stark tan lines.

When I see a stranger walking down the street, I do not see black or white or red or blue. Instead I see is an individual with dreams and a story of their own. And I know that our dreams and stories are in some way all related. At the very least, because we are walking the same street. I hope others see past my bicycle spandex and come to similar realizations.

We the People are dreamers, because that is what we do best. It is the American experience to follow a dream. The question every one of us has the privilege to be able to ask: *what if?*

The answer just might turn into something marvelous.

EPILOGUE

MORE THAN A YEAR HAS passed since completing the journey. My metabolism has long since returned to a normal level. The tan lines etched into my skin after countless hours under a merciless sun faded quickly, and my pasty-whiteness returned with vengeance. For a little while my family and friends were interested in hearing about the trip, but life has largely settled into a new rhythm with only faint echoes of adventures now passed.

I continue to ride my bike grinning ear-to-ear. Shedding those thirty-five pounds of baggage makes me feel like a rocket—until getting passed by cars going 25 mph brings me back to earth. I have gained an appreciation for some of the basic creature comforts. Showers and carpet and tall glasses of cold milk come to mind.

It will come as no surprise that the trip changed me profoundly. The worldview I inherited from a religious upbringing says humans are basally flawed, even to the extent of being called "evil." News media devoting inordinate amounts of attention to sensational killings, trauma, and all other grisly details of the human experience are not helping.

That negative view of humanity is inconsistent with the multitude of blessings bestowed on me by people of so many non-faith and faith traditions. If the majority of strangers were anything but benevolent, how could we spend only *five dollars* apiece on lodging across the entire country? I have come to believe that humans elementally want to do good. They may wind up doing bad things, but their nature underneath desires good.

Until we start believing in our own goodness we will be stuck in the rut of history, acting horribly towards one another.

"There are bad people out there, Scott," my grandmother told me before I left, echoing the aforementioned sentiment. She feared I would become a news story—the victim of a freak homicide or kidnapping. Obviously there was a chance that something unfortunate would happen, whether at the hands of another person or an unintentional accident. I was in a constant state of evaluation so as to avoid suspect people and dicey situations. Joe, Oliver, and I are cautious people. The problem is that many people confuse caution with fear. Willie Weir, one of the most famous modern touring cyclists, has this to say:

"Caution keeps you aware. Fear keeps you away."

On the first day, questioning my sanity and what the unknown future had in store for us, I looked Fear in the face and said "no." We started riding. It was one of the best decisions I have ever made.

Long hours on the saddle gave me plenty of time to re-question that decision. The one-word answer to my questioning every time: patience. Patience is like a muscle that has to be exercised in order to grow and survive. I needed it to overcome wind, rain, poor vehicle drivers, hunger, and heat. Other times things were just plain *boring*. Looking down a perfectly straight road stretching miles ahead and knowing it will be another hour before the scene changes is a sensation I wish upon no one.

There have been a surprising number of people who, after hearing about my trip, respond by saying,

"There's no way I could ever do something like that."

After spending two months riding, I want to respond saying emphatically *Yes you can! All it takes is patience!* Patience, to believe that the present day can be connected to the following day, and the one after that, and so on, until an incredible result is reached. Doers of truly great things have learned to patiently string individual days into a coherent whole. It is the same concept as eating an elephant, which can only be consumed one bite at a time.

I still talk to Joe. The month we spent together eating moon pies and complaining about how bad our bottoms ached brought us very close together. A bond forged in the fires of such constant and excruciating pain is not easily broken. It does not cease to amaze me that we never got on each other's nerves. We still talk about Day One and riding through the rain and Butch and the Rocky Mountains and Kansas and what a shame it is that we cannot get away with eating donuts like the good ol' days. Joe still goes by the Gingerbread Man and I when we exchange letters I sign "Captain Punishment."

Oliver I am not so sure about. He really did join the priesthood and could be anywhere at this point. If I had to take a guess, he is somewhere remote in South America saving lives and making the world a better place. Although I have no idea where he is, one thing I do not doubt is Father "What-a-Waste" has continued to frustrate the intentions of smitten women young and old, near and far. Whenever I need to find him, I will follow the trail of broken hearts.

The characters in this story—whose names have obviously been changed—continue to occupy a warm place in my heart. I have stayed in contact with some, but not everyone. Joe, Oliver, and I formed infinitesimally small, twenty-four hour pieces of their realities. I have little to do with Butch in West Yellowstone or Renee in Kansas or Rover in Virginia. In the time immediately following the trip, this was troubling. Some of the people we met were incredible and I still miss them.

Some have commented on the occasional interactions we had along the way with individuals who were not thrilled to offer help to two struggling cyclist-strangers. What I've tried to do in this narrative is capture how we felt in the moment to experience rejection, knowing full well that not everyone would trust us when we said we meant no harm. Themes of generosity, interconnectedness, and adventure are central to this story. We missed an opportunity to connect with those individuals who were not comfortable with helping us. However, that is not to say that we felt entitled to barge into every person's narrative or that we in some way deserved the incredible generosity we received.

"Why go through all the trouble of meeting people, if all you're going to do is miss them in the end?" a rather cynical friend asked me. I think everyone needs to come up with an answer to that question, because it is about something much bigger than just a bicycling trip. The moments I shared with people along the way are in no way cheapened or diminished because they were ephemeral. The good and bad news about memories is that sometimes they stick with you for a long time.

Speaking of memories, the ones that most readily come to mind are the simple, silly, and stupid ones. Not having a clue how to get out of downtown Seattle on Day One. The incessant howl of wind in Eastern Washington and Wyoming. The way Joe said "upsy-daisy" every time we went up a hill or mountain. Putting three packets of mayo on a grilled cheese sandwich just to ingest additional calories. Conquering mountain passes and descending at 40 miles per hour. Keith's dirty jokes in Kansas. Fireflies and Gene's discussion of the

Rapture. The drone of mosquitoes when I had to change a flat tire on the banks of the Missouri River. Changing flat tires in the snow of Colorado and the mosquitoes along the banks of the Missouri River. Practicing my Kentucky accent with Oliver. The dogs that chased us and our dog pistols. The chocolate milk at the end of every hard day of riding. Watching shirtless people ride/jiggle on top of lawn mowers. Crashing outside of Washington, D.C. Talking my way out of a ticket for not paying my subway fare in New York City.

The fact that these simple, silly, and stupid things are what I end up remembering tells me just how important it is to appreciate the moments where memories are made. If I spent fifty days riding across the country and was miserable at every step of the way, it would have been a grand waste of time. Time is a precious thing, and there are only so many hours to each day to pedal your miles.

I hope that you have enjoyed this hodgepodge narrative of the journey that changed my life. Please think about your own wildest dream, and go do it. The world will thank you when you return from your adventure, transformed. When you see a bicyclist riding alongside the road laden with panniers, a front handle bar bag, and faded clothes, consider giving a polite and encouraging honk on your horn. They are recreating the story you just read.

And if you have not done so in a while, think about getting on a bicycle yourself. You never know where it may take you.

Scott
a.k.a. Captain Punishment

ABOUT THE AUTHOR

Scott Hippe is a medical student and long-time resident of Washington State. At the time of the publication he is 24 years old, up to his nostrils in medical school debt, and already looking forward to the next big adventure.

If you enjoyed this book, share the good news with a friend and help Scott pay for medical school. Purchase online at:

www.createspace.com/4106612

Made in the USA
San Bernardino, CA
18 February 2016